British Muslims

British Muslims

New Directions in Islamic Thought, Creativity and Activism

Philip Lewis and Sadek Hamid

EDINBURGH
University Press

Edinburgh University Press is one of the leading university presses in the UK. We publish academic books and journals in our selected subject areas across the humanities and social sciences, combining cutting-edge scholarship with high editorial and production values to produce academic works of lasting importance. For more information visit our website: edinburghuniversitypress.com

Edinburgh University Press Ltd
The Tun – Holyrood Road
12 (2f) Jackson's Entry
Edinburgh EH8 8PJ

Typeset in 11/13 Bembo by
IDSUK (DataConnection) Ltd, and
printed and bound in Great Britain

A CIP record for this book is available from the British Library

ISBN 978 1 4744 3275 7 (hardback)
ISBN 978 1 4744 3276 4 (paperback)
ISBN 978 1 4744 3277 1 (webready PDF)
ISBN 978 1 4744 3278 8 (epub)

Contents

Preface

This is a work of collaboration by two friends committed to under-standing and making sense of Islam, especially as lived within the many different Muslim communities in Britain today. Both of us have written on Islam in Britain.[1] One of us is an insider, the other an outsider. Philip has spent thirty years building bridges across the different religious and secular traditions, learning to share public and civic life in Bradford, as the Inter-faith Adviser to a series of Anglican bishops in that city. For fifteen years, he also lectured on 'Islam in the West' and 'Religions, conflict and peacemaking in a post-secular world' in the Peace Studies Department at Bradford University. Sadek has also engaged with different British Muslim communities for over three decades as an activist, youth and com-munity development professional and academic. He has taught Islamic Studies at the Universities of Chester and Liverpool Hope and is currently a Research Associate at the Oxford University Centre for Islamic Studies. He has written widely on issues relating to British Muslims, young people and religious identity formation.

We have sought to write a short and accessible book which aims to offer insight and perspectives about Islam and Muslim communities in Britain today. We draw upon existing scholarship on contemporary Islam and material produced by British Muslims. However, our primary audience is not other academics, but profes-sionals such as teachers, social workers, journalists and politicians working with Muslim communities, frequently bombarded with contradictory images of Islam and British Muslims. We hope this

study contributes to 'religious literacy', a precondition for our religiously and ethnically diverse cities to cohere and flourish. To this
end we have appended a short annotated bibliography of key texts,
as well as useful web resources.

We hope the interested general reader will also enjoy the book.
We share many assumptions which can be captured in three words:
crisis, candour and context. We labour under no illusions that
many parts of the wider Muslim world are in turmoil, especially
the Middle East and South Asia. It is obvious that British Muslims,
with a diversity of transnational, ethnic links are not immune to
such developments. This is not a work of apologetics and Chapter 4
addresses directly the dynamics and scale of radicalisation and
prospects for de-radicalisation. However, the primary focus of this
work is not radicalisation, but rather how different generations
navigate relations across three distinct religious and social worlds:
traditional Islam imported from their relatives' homeland; expressions of Islam drawn from across the Muslim world – the *ummah*
– now accessible at the click of a mouse; and Britain itself, where
among a young generation of graduates and professionals, who are
seeking new and expansive readings of Islam to connect with their
lived experience.

Crises within any minority community can engender candour
and self-criticism, as well as defensiveness and denial. In this book
we quarry from a rich vein of constructive self-criticism which has
emerged in the last ten years, often in surprising places, whether
from within movements usually dismissed as scholastic tradition-
ists, such as Deobandis and Salafis, or the more self-consciously,
politicised movements dubbed Islamist.[2]

Many of the hopeful developments we identify and discuss are
condensed in the term 'context' or better 'contextualising' Islam
in Britain. Inevitably, when Muslim migrants first began to arrive in
large numbers from the 1960s to fill post-war labour shortages in
textiles, foundries and transport, their Islam was embedded in the
ethnic cultures they brought with them. For the first generation of
Muslim migrants, most of whom came from rural areas of South
Asia, culture, religion and ethnicity were unselfconsciously conflated. For their children and grandchildren this would no longer
do, as they faced questions from school friends, neighbours and

colleagues. This forced them to become self-conscious and articulate. As questioning became more relentless and critical, post 9/11
and 7/7, they struggled to get adequate answers from religious
leaders – *ulama*. This exposed systematic deficits in the religious
formation of such leaders, many of whom were either trained
overseas or in 'seminaries' in Britain which were little more than
satellites of an intellectual tradition 'back home'. In short, religious
formation even in British institutions was frequently out of context and did not give the *imam* in the mosque or religious, legal
specialist – the *mufti* – the knowledge and skills to adapt their
teaching to the needs of British Muslims.

For this reason there is much experimentation going on across
different Muslim traditions to contextualise Islam in Britain.
Chapter 2 is devoted to understanding the lively debates around
changes needed in curriculum and methods in 'Islamic seminaries'.
Chapter 3 seeks to rehearse the new thinking and debates about
the relationship between sharia, ethics and public life. This includes
attempts to identify resources within the tradition to live well as a
minority in a non-Muslim country, as well as searching for insights
and perspectives to constrain the excesses of the modern state,
whether in Muslim majority or minority situations. Chapter 4
contextualises the difficult and complex matter of violence in the
name of Islam and situates the current debates about extremist
radicalisation within a historical and political context.

All of these debates indicate an attempt by Muslims to disaggregate Islam from religious and cultural norms deemed dysfunc-
tional in Britain, as well as challenging some of the assumptions of
transnational Muslim movements whether Islamist, Salafi or Sufi.
This task is urgent if Islam is not to appear alien and exotic. When
writing about Islam we wish to escape an unhelpful binary of
good Muslim/bad Muslim and enable a grown-up discussion of
complexity.[3]

As will become clear, we neither assume that British Muslims
are somehow uniquely 'religious' or that Islam in reality impacts
the lives of all British Muslims in the same way. A recent study on
political participation among young British Muslims observed that
they are far from homogeneous as a group. There are 'crucial variations in their strengths of religious and national identities, their

orientations towards British society and their modes of political engagement'. In fact, the author identifies four different sorts of young Muslims:

> [T]hose who downplay their Muslim identification and retain simply a symbolic ethno-religious identity; those with a cosmopolitan, internationalist and multicultural identity; those with a dual identity, thinking of themselves as British Muslims (the largest single group); and finally a small group who prioritise their Muslim identity and for whom a British identity is at best secondary and purely pragmatic, with little emotional attachment to Britain.[4]

For Muslims, as with people of other faiths, religion has to jostle with the demands of other influences that are national, ethnic, political, professional, gendered and cultural. Chapter 5 looks at these new expressions of identity, religion and culture that range from what has been called the 'Muslim Cool', through the performances of young Muslim comedians such as 'Guz Khan', to the normalisation of celebrities from a Muslim background. The latter is demonstrated with England cricketer Moeen Ali and the victory of Nadiya Hussain, who won the BBC's *Great British Bake Off* competition in 2015.[5]

The larger argument of the book is that Muslims in Britain are giving expression to Islam in a new language – English – and that this is contributing to a significant chapter in the modern history of Islam. In its long historical trajectory, Islam has been embodied in a multiplicity of distinct languages and cultures. If we mention only majority Muslim areas, we must speak of at least five main language groups: Arabic, Persian, Turkish, Urdu and Bengali. It is our contention that English today could be as significant as Persian was in the past, as a vehicle for generating new thinking for emerging Muslim elites.[6]

This, in part, is the burden of Chapter 1 which suggests that while reformist Muslim thinking has been around as an intellectual trend for more than a hundred years, the emergence of a newly educated, English-speaking, professional and graduate class – especially women – is beginning to mainstream such progressive thinking into various organisations that draw upon the pioneering scholarship which underpins the ever expanding, international networks of Muslim women's organisations.

Through the medium of English, academics, religious scholars and activists alike are able to apply the insights and methods generated by the social sciences, arts and humanities, to contested contemporary issues. Throughout the book, we contrast such thinking with the traditional pull of South Asian 'schools of thought' 'ideologically and institutionally dominant' in the UK where the medium of instruction remains Urdu.[7] The contrast underlines the centrality of a mastery of English in the process of critical self-renewal of the Islamic tradition now underway.

We would like to thank Carole Hillenbrand, Nicola Ramsey and Kirsty Woods at Edinburgh University Press and the people who were kind enough to respond to queries about the subject matter in this book.

Notes

1. Philip Lewis's last book, with a foreword by Jon Snow, is '*Young, British and Muslim* (London: Continuum, 2007) and he has a chapter coming out in the Routledge *Handbook of Christian Muslim Relations* (2018), edited by David Thomas, entitled 'Muslims and Christians in Britain today: living together, respecting differences?' Sadek Hamid's recent publications include *Sufis, Salafis and Islamists: The Contested Ground of British Islamic Activism* (London: I. B. Tauris, 2016) and *Young British Muslims: Between Rhetoric and Realities* (Abingdon: Taylor & Francis, 2017).

2. See Innes Bowen, *Medina in Birmingham, Najaf in Brent, Inside British Islam* (London: Hurst & Co., 2014) for an accessible overview of the main Islamic traditions in Britain and their transnational links. Also, Sadek's *Sufis, Salafis and Islamists* for inter-generational changes in many of the key movements.

3. The spirit of this work is best captured in the title of a helpful study edited by Andrew Shryock, *Islamophobia/Islamophilia: Beyond the Politics of Enemy and Friend* (Bloomington: Indiana University Press, 2010). This is not to trivialise the phenomenon of anti-Muslim hatred but simply to insist that Muslim communities are not best understood as simply victims.

4. Asma Mustafa, *Identity and Political Participation Among Young British Muslims: Believing and Belonging* (Basingstoke: Palgrave Macmillan, 2015), p. xi.
5. See Charlotte Higgins, 'The Genius of "The Great British Bake Off"' where she notes that Nadiya was 'the first British woman who wears a hijab to have occupied such a positive, joyous role in British mass culture'. *The Guardian*, 6 October 2015.
6. For the importance of Persian as the vehicle for half a millennium – until the mid-nineteenth century – of a distinct Islamic civilisation from the Balkans to Bengal, which sought to create Islamic meaning drawing on literature, Sufism, philosophy rather than simply privileging 'law', see the wonderfully, wide-ranging and stimulating study of the late Shahab Ahmed, *What is Islam? The Importance of Being Islamic* (Princeton: Princeton University Press, 2016).
7. See Sophie Gilliat-Ray, *Muslims in Britain, an Introduction* (Cambridge: Cambridge University Press, 2010), p. 92, where she is speaking of the Deobandis whom we discuss in Chapter 2. Throughout our study we illustrate the continuing influence of South Asian Deobandi scholars by reference particularly to Justice Mufti Taqi Usmani, an influential Deobandi luminary in Pakistan whose works are widely circulated in the UK.

Foreword

Almost everyone and anyone today appears to have an opinion on British Muslims: rarely a day goes by without so called 'Muslim experts' providing commentary on the latest 'Muslim' news story. And yet so often the understanding about the diverse communities that make up Britain's Muslims is limited and shallow.

British Muslims endeavours to provide a more granular account of the most frequently asked questions and topics of discussion around British Muslims. From the role of women, to terrorism from the teaching at religious seminaries, to ideology, this book tries to explore and explain the British Muslim communities as they are rather than as they are reported.

Philip Lewis and Sadek Hamid focus on fact and evidence rather than opinion and judgement. In doing so they provide a wide ranging, non-ideological, informative and often first-hand account of the changing landscape of British Muslim life.

From generation Jihad to generation M this book attempts to get inside the minds and lives of young British Muslims to provide a complex and nuanced picture dispelling the one-dimensional simplistic narrative to which we are more accustomed.

This book will prove to be a useful tool for both practitioners and members of the public who seek out an authentic account of the issues we feel we may know well.

Sayeed Warsi, The Right Honourable Baroness Warsi

Introduction

A mosque managed by women?

A frisson of media excitement was generated in the spring of 2015 when the Muslim Women's Council (MWC) in Bradford announced their intention to establish the first all-women managed mosque in the UK. Their public consultation was carefully crafted. After a meal prepared for the participants, the meeting formally opened, as is usual on such occasions, with a recitation from the Quran. The recitation performed by . . . a young woman.[1]

The background to the project was explained and possible misunderstandings addressed. The mosque was to be Sunni, family friendly, including single mums and young people. An audit of the hundred or so mosques in the city had made clear that such an initiative was necessary as only a few involved any women in their management. Three invited speakers then offered Islamic rationales for such a proposal. The first, a respected traditionalist scholar based in Cambridge; the second, a female academic teaching Islamic Studies at the university of Lancaster; and the third, a lecturer and policy adviser from Leicester, who chairs a liberal reformist initiative, 'New Horizons in British Islam'.

The choice of the traditionalist scholar Shaykh Akram Nadwi was a stroke of genius. Over a ten-year period, this soft-spoken Indian scholar, working at an Oxford Islamic think tank, had compiled a forty-volume dictionary of women scholars of *hadith*.[2] In so doing, he had 'uncovered a long-forgotten history of female Islamic scholarship, blotted out by centuries of cultural conservatism. He discovered nearly nine thousand women,

including ones who lectured, dispensed fatwas and traveled
. . . in pursuit of religious knowledge.'[3] No discipline is more
important than history for the retrieval and critical evaluation of
Islam's complex and multi-layered tradition. No discipline more
corrosive of self-serving myths, passed off as normative.[4]

Dr Shuruq Naguib, a British Egyptian scholar, trained in
Islamic law and anthropology, followed Nadwi. She built on the
shaykh's presentation and provided further examples of women
active and visible in mosques from the earliest days of Islam, as
well as those who had used their wealth to endow and manage
mosques and Islamic institutions. She made clear that there was
support for women's involvement in Islam's master religious science, *fiqh* (jurisprudence). She pointed to the irony of British
women financially supporting mosques, yet excluded from pray-
ing or shunted off to second-rate facilities. Dr Naguib argued that
gendered segregation of prayer space, a familiar feature of many
mosques in Britain, is often rooted in the sectarian particulari-
ties of an imported South Asian Islam. Elsewhere in the Muslim
world, women frequently participate in urban congregations.

The third speaker, Dilwar Hussain, a British Muslim of Bangladeshi heritage, has an intimate knowledge of the British Muslim
scene. For two decades he has worked as a researcher and consult-
ant to government departments and the private sector on social
policy, Muslim identity and Islamic reform. Latterly he has served
as a specialist Adviser to the House of Commons inquiry on Prevent, as well as on the steering group of the 'Contextualising Islam
in Britain' project at the University of Cambridge.[5]

Mr Hussain insisted on the need to re-integrate two key
Muslim institutions, the family and the mosque. He posed a
number of pertinent questions: What does it say to children
when they accompany their parents to the mosque only to find
that that there is no provision or inadequate provision for their
mother? What subliminal message is this giving to male children about the status of women? In a community where female
students are now outperforming boys at school and often doing
better in the job market, how do we address the mismatch
between wider society and the practice in Muslim communities
with regard to gender equality?

Behind the headlines: from avoidance through conflict to accommodation

The MWC is but one example of a new generation of British Muslim professionals developing city and regional-wide organisations to engage critically their own communities and wider society. In Birmingham, the Muslim Women's Network for the UK (MWNUK) chose to tackle the same issue of female exclusion from mosques with a different strategy: they addressed an open letter to the trustees of the Birmingham Central Mosque complaining that none of the thirty-nine trustees were women and warned that they would be lodging a formal complaint with the Charity Commission because of this 'blatant' piece of discrimination.[6]

Alongside female-specific initiatives, other networks are emerging. In 2010, also in Bradford, the Professional Muslim Institute (PMI) was created to support Muslim professionals and to address 'the lack of meaningful and effective leadership within the Muslim community in the district'.[7] Its YouTube videos focus on a range of inspirational speakers attending their dinners from the world of business, politics, sport and literature ranging from Baroness Warsi, Adil Rashid – the Yorkshire and English cricketer – and Qari Asim – a young imam awarded an MBE in 2012[8] – to the Liverpool barrister Zia Chaudhry who launched his engaging autobiography *Just Your Regular Muslim* at one of their dinners.

Such networks are creating spaces to address topics hitherto taboo within the Muslim communities. For example, PMI attracted national media coverage when it brought together a panel of local and national experts to discuss the on-street grooming of young girls. One female Muslim panelist rehearsed grass root research that indicated that those groomed included young Asian Muslim girls, whose voice is usually inaudible, silenced by strict codes of family honour.[9]

Such developments as MWC, MWNUK and PMI reflect a familiar three-generation trajectory for many migrant communities. For many of the first generation, immigration is a 'brutal bargain' – exchanging economic opportunities for a loss over time of the familiar religious, social and cultural worlds left behind.[10]

The first generation often lack the social and linguistic skills to relate to wider society, so they keep their heads down, avoid contact with wider society as much as possible, work hard and invest in their children. The second generation usually enjoys the linguistic skills and cultural competences their parents lacked, while relating differently to their parents' homeland. They begin to ask questions both of the institutions and norms their parents imported and those of wider society, as they seek space for their specific needs.[11] This can generate some tensions but it indicates that the community has moved from avoidance to engagement, and usually by the third generation there is a give-and-take pattern of accommodation with wider society. In the next chapter we will see that this neat three-generational pattern can be impeded by external and internal developments: whether an increase in anti-Muslim hate crime or the creation of a 'first generation in every generation' phenomenon, the result of high numbers of transnational marriages persisting or increasing across the generations.[12]

Mapping seismic changes within the Muslim world: the increased visibility and influence of women

The Muslim Women's Council – the focus of this introduction – has drawn attention to some of the most troubling issues exercising the Muslim world, as well as modelling a way forward. These issues concern first and foremost how the 'cumulative tradition' which is Islam responds to demands for gender equality.[13] The issue of how and why the large majority of mosques in Britain continue to marginalise women with regard to adequate prayer provision and involvement in mosque governance is a sub-set of this larger problem.[14] This invites an exploration of the vexed question as to what counts as religious authority and where it is located today. This is the focus of Chapter 2, but here we will touch briefly on two aspects: first, what pattern of relationship – if any – exists between Islamic scholarship generated by Muslim academics teaching in British universities and those who service the hundreds of British mosques trained in traditional 'seminaries' in Britain or overseas? Secondly, how successful are Muslim communities in dealing with imported sectarianism?

Historically, Muslim and Western Christian worlds have frequently found it hard to understand each other's different attitudes to gender relations. Such mutual incomprehension continues. However, with the invasion of Afghanistan, it could be politicised with part of a justification for conquest to liberate 'oppressed' Muslim women. Unsurprisingly, Muslims frequently respond with their own stereotypes railing against Godless and immoral Westerners. However, the situation facing Muslim women in the West today is altogether more complex. Religious freedom is guaranteed which means that religious affiliation is no longer, of necessity, 'a destiny determined by birth' but 'the subject of a deliberate choice'.[15] Muslim women have also inherited the fruits of several generations of women's struggles. They benefit from gender equality and some are dismayed when their own communities, for religious as well as cultural reasons, seem reluctant to embody such norms. As a result, they are looking for a more expansive and emancipatory reading of their tradition, as evidenced by the MWC.

To tap into the websites of the Muslim Women's Council and the Muslim Women's Network UK is to be signposted to such movements as *Musawah* (Arabic for 'equality'). *Musawah* was formally launched in 2009 in Kuala Lumpur with a huge conference of some 250 attendees, comprising scholars, policymakers and activists – male and female – from almost fifty countries. Its website includes accessible resources, practical and academic, from across the world written by some of the finest female scholars active today, whether the veteran African American scholar Amina Wadud, Asma Barlas or a newer generation such as Kecia Ali.[16] Such scholars writing in English often enjoy tenured positions in Western universities, especially in America, outside the control of the mosque.

Appeal to their work does not go unchallenged. At the same time as the emergence of their networks, many women in Britain appear to have become more not less traditional in their behaviour. This is clear from comments in Professor Mona Siddiqui's recently published memoir. Siddiqui is a specialist in Islamic law and the first person to hold the professorial chair in Islamic and Interreligious Studies at the University of Edinburgh. She observes that gendered segregation has become increasingly common at many social events, accompanied by the wearing of hijab or full face-veil (niqab). She worries that such clothing as a mark of identity, emphasises 'an Islamic otherness' that 'creates a culture of defensiveness and insularity'.[17] She is exasperated that when Muslim women are so often the victims of injustice and abuse of rights 'dress and segregation are projected as the answer to all problems'.[18]

Mapping seismic changes within the Muslim world: religious authority

Professor Siddiqui is aware that there are many reasons for the worldwide, contemporary resurgence of conservative religion. The one which troubles her most is an ongoing intellectual crisis, especially in traditional Islam, which reaches deep into the past but which accelerated with the colonisation of the Muslim world in the nineteenth century. She cites an Algerian scholar, the late Muhammad Arkoun (d. 2010), a lecturer at the Sorbonne in Paris, who wrote a provocative work entitled the *The Unthought in Contemporary Islamic Thought* where he documents how and why the Muslim world increasingly lost touch with intellectual, political and scientific developments in the last few hundred years.[19] This meant the traditional religious leaders, immured in their religious institutions, were unable to describe reality accurately, let alone interpret it Islamically. This could translate into compartmentalising the world between 'religious' and 'secular' domains, with the former privileged. As Siddiqui observes:

> [W]hen I look at some Muslim families today, I see ... the clash between religious knowledge and secular professions, the idea that spiritual growth comes from living apart from this world or that it is only religious knowledge which can strengthen your faith in God. I believe that this has produced a cultural malaise in which basic books of theology suffice as learning and the dissemination of empirical and scientific knowledge, of literature, music and the arts, is seen by some as weakening the faith.[20]

To gain a little perspective on such issues, it is important to recall that Islamic revival and reform in the eighteenth century preceded the impact of European imperialism. In the Arabian peninsula, Iran and North Africa, reform movements emerged as a response to the de-centralisation and growing weakness of the Muslim gunpowder empires – Ottoman, Mughal and Safavid.[21] In Iran, a renewal movement known as Usuli Shi'ism appeared which foregrounded rationalism; in Arabia, Wahhabi Sunnism emerged which stressed theology and a literalist reading of Islam's revered scriptures; in North Africa, Idrisi Sufism developed which emphasised inner knowledge derived from mystically communicating with God or His prophet.

These indigenous reform movements created trends which are with us today: each 'significantly narrowed the field of orthodoxy and they were all critical of popular Sufism'.[22] Two of the three reform movements – the exception is Idrisi Sufism – 'declared infidelity (*takfir*) on their Muslim enemies' thereby justifying violence to eliminate them.[23] While the intra-Muslim fault lines between Sunnis, Sufis and Shi'i are almost as old as Islam, the reform movements gave them a new virulence. Finally, how to interpret and apply revered texts was contested with appeals variously made to textual literalism, reason or mystical knowledge. Overall, the legacy of Wahhabi Islam was the most worrying. Its founder's 'acts of destruction and puritanical interpretations de-emphasized the peaceful, pluralistic dynamism of Islam ... widespread between the eleventh and eighteenth centuries'.[24]

If such movements sought to address problems internal to the Muslim world, these were relatively straightforward compared to the problems posed by colonialism, where Muslim thinkers had, from a position of weakness, to confront a confident and expansive civilisation which left 'its cosmology of truth shattered'.[25] One baneful result of this encounter was the fracturing of Muslim education into two parallel systems: one that of traditional Islamic 'seminaries' which trained the *ulama* – Islam's religious scholars – who staff the mosques and other Islamic institutions; and the other, Western colleges and universities which taught modern disciplines to Muslim elites.

The need to bridge this gulf has been recognised for more than a hundred years. The urgency to do so was spelled out more than thirty years ago in a seminal text by Fazlur Rahman.[26] The fact that it has not been adequately addressed is part of the rationale for an imaginative new initiative – the Centre for Research and Evaluation in Muslim Education (CRÈME) – launched in the Institute of Education at London University in 2012. CRÈME's director, Dr Panjwani, points out that 'many experiments have been made to find ways to combine these [two intellectual traditions] but so far no satisfactory resolution ... has been found'.[27]

The alumni of these two educational systems are frequently suspicious, even contemptuous, of each other. Those educated in modern disciplines often have the most superficial understanding of the classical Islamic tradition; while those educated in traditional Islamic institutions, often have little understanding of the modern world. A Muslim doctor confronted with an authentic *hadith* which seemed to contradict 'everything ... learned about disease and standards of hygiene' at his medical school finds his confidence in the former's authority shaken.[28] He is not reassured by the teaching of *ulama* 'parroting their medieval forefathers' which embodies a vision of religion that the world seemed to have outgrown.[29]

Unsurprisingly, the *ulama* respond in kind. One example will suffice. Professor Ebrahim Moosa, a South African and one of America's leading Islamic scholars, was initially trained in a traditional 'Deobandi' seminary in India – the Deobandi franchise is the largest in the UK.[30] Moosa recently returned to India to research whether the curriculum of Deoband and other Islamic 'seminaries' had changed in the three decades since he graduated. His conclusions are sobering:

> No [seminary] integrates modern science, social science, and the humanities ... in conversation with the core traditional curriculum ... [The] objection to [such] new disciplines ... is associated with a fear and loathing of a materialistic West whose knowledge traditions are viewed as poisonous ...[31]

We will look at attempts to bridge this chasm in Chapter 2. But first, we must touch on the escalating, intra-Muslim sectarianism which threatens such initiatives. Its ubiquitous nature is clear from a range of Muslim commentators. Baroness Warsi considers it 'one of the most rapidly growing internal challenges' facing British Muslims and is shocked by the 'deep-rooted animosity' it reveals.[32] Sameer Rahim, the arts and books editor of *Prospect* – a political and intellectual monthly – contributes a piece entitled 'Who Speaks for Islam in Britain?' In the context of pointing out that Sunni Islam is a decentralised religion with no official structure of legitimate authority, he comments that most mosques are organised around discrete ethnic groups and characterised by 'different sects [which] barely speak to each other'.[33]

An excellent blog by a Bradford Muslim councillor, when discussing the MWC's proposal for a women's managed mosque, observes that in most of the city's mosques, 'leadership is largely men from the first generation . . . [who] remain to a large extent trapped in a time and place that belongs somewhere else . . . [driven by] by secular clan/caste based politics, *religious sectarianism* and/or dogma'.[34] The implications are spelled out by the Dean of Cambridge's Muslim College, Shaykh Abdal Hakim Murad (Tim Winter), in a panel discussion on 'Trust in Religious Leadership' shared with the Archbishop of Canterbury and the Chief Rabbi. Asked whether the time was ripe for the emergence of a Muslim equivalent to the Chief Rabbi, he explained that Muslim communities were 'not yet sufficiently mature to accept as a figurehead someone not doctrinally or ethnically of their background'.[35]

Mapping seismic changes within the Muslim world: a place for women as leaders?

Within many Muslim communities there remains a deep-seated reluctance to acknowledge the legitimacy of women as leaders, whether in religious or political institutions. One reason, touched on already by the Bradford Muslim councillor, is the continuing vitality of patriarchal attitudes embedded in an imported ethnic politics, which he refers to as 'clan/caste based politics'; especially in contrast to the professionalism expected of a modern political

party and its local councillors and MPs. In Chapter 3, we will discuss other examples of how religious rhetoric has been recruited
by ethnic leaders to entrench their political influence and exclude
or marginalise Muslim women.

Another reason for antagonism to women having a leadership
role is an ambivalence expressed within the Islamic tradition itself.
As with so many contemporary issues there are a number of possible positions amongst Muslims. Thus, in Bradford in 2012, the first
female Muslim Lord Mayor hosted an inter-faith gathering in the
Town Hall to introduce her spiritual guide, a Sufi leader, visiting
from Pakistan. She went on to commend him for his unreserved
support for female education and his prayers for her new public
and civic responsibilities.[36] In 2015, the city elected its first female
Muslim MP, Naz Shah. This was less the result of a change of heart
within the powerful, patriarchal Kashmiri clans in Bradford – as
will become evident in Chapter 3 – than the fruit of the Labour
party's policy to designate all-women shortlists in certain constituencies.

In contrast to the support for the Lord Mayor extended by
her Sufi guide, the teaching of a local, British-trained, traditional
scholar is quite different. Mufti Saiful Islam's legal judgements were
published in 2010 in a book (*Your Questions Answered*) with a significant print run of 5000 copies. The mufti is patron in Bradford
of two private Islamic schools, one primary, the other secondary,
and runs a non-residential Islamic seminary for those with jobs
and family responsibilities. Belonging to the influential Deobandi
tradition, his judgements are mainstream rather than eccentric.

The mufti's views on gender relations can be gauged from his
answer to the following question: 'Many Muslim sisters travel to
far towns and cities and even to different countries for higher
education or employment without a *mahram* [a person to whom
marriage is not permitted] . . . Is it permissible for them to travel
without a *mahram*?' His views are unequivocal:

> [A] woman is prohibited from travelling alone . . . even when
> going . . . to perform *hajj*. In comparison to this, travelling
> for higher education or employment are of lower degree of
> importance . . . [since] Islam has placed the responsibility of

a woman's maintenance on her father before her marriage
and on her husband after her marriage, and has not allowed
women to leave their homes without any urgent need.
Therefore travelling for higher education or for employment purposes without a *mahram* is not permissible.[37]

With regard to political leadership, there is a much discussed
hadith which reads: 'A community that entrusts its affairs to a
woman will not flourish.' This underpins the fact that all Islamic
schools of law hold that women can 'not legitimately rule a country'.[38] Such teaching has become a storm centre of debate across
the Muslim world. However, notwithstanding the textual ingenuity
of one of Egypt's greatest traditional scholars, Muhammad Ghazali
(d. 1996), who felt that empirical experience – whether a Golda
Meir, an Indira Gandhi or a Margaret Thatcher – clearly contra-
dicted its plain meaning, his arguments were not able to carry the
day. Even his friend, the influential Islamist scholar Yusuf Qaradawi,
distanced himself from such re-thinking.[39] If we may argue from
silence, Mufti Saiful Islam has no interest in re-opening this issue.

The mufti, for his part, reminds his readers that one of the signs
of the Day of Judgement is that 'businesses will expand to the
extent that the wives will begin to assist their husbands to conduct
trade'.[40] In Chapter 2 we will return to the mufti's views, whether
on family planning, how Muslims should conduct themselves with
regard to wider society or his attitude to evolution.

For the peace of the city: the MWC navigating a difficult path forward

The Muslim Women's Council set out their stall in 2011 with
a regional 'Daughters of Eve' conference, at which the keynote
address was delivered by Pakistan's veteran activist and feminist,
scholar of the Quran, Professor Riffat Hassan, then lecturing at
an American university. The council clearly has two broad aims.
The first is unapologetically empowering Muslim women. The
second, to bridge the many divides within Muslim communities –
whether ethnic, sectarian, gender or inter-generational – and with
wider society.

This is certainly the vision of their Director, Bana Gora, who envisages their proposed centre of excellence for women as providing a safe space for such discussions, drawing inspiration from the 'big tent' of St Ethelburga's peace and reconciliation centre in London.[41] This builds on the work of key members of the MWC core team who have for some years been involved in peacemaking initiatives in Bradford along with the bishop, police and personnel from the Peace Studies Department at the local university.[42] Research across the world has shown how critical women's involvement is in successful, localised peacemaking, not least Muslim women.[43]

The community consultation organised by the MWC to explain and elicit responses from all communities to their mosque and centre of excellence proposal, included a number of dimensions which bode well for the future. First, instead of succumbing to the temptation to parade their anger and exasperation with the male leadership of most of the city's mosques which excludes them, they held preparatory meetings with representatives of the Bradford Council for Mosques (BCM). Here possible misunderstandings were laid to rest. The BCM was reassured that the proposed mosque would be Sunni, gender inclusive and 'mixed congregational prayers would be led by a male Sunni Imam'. Further, they took heart that the MWC were committed to consulting with local, respected *ulama*. This enabled the BCM to support the venture and their letter of support was read out at the consultation.[44]

The MWC wisely resisted any temptation to sideline the BCM, the only umbrella organisation for mosques in the city, which, since its inception thirty years earlier, has sought to incorporate all sectarian traditions. There was goodwill on both sides. However, it was clear that the MWC would maintain its independence of action. Further, it was not limited to working with the leadership of mosques. It could and did spread its net widely, drawing on the best available scholarship, male and female, looking beyond familiar ethnic and sectarian horizons. It was free to draw on academics, religious scholars, policymakers, traditionalists and reformists alike.

It is evident that there is much enthusiasm locally, nationally and internationally for this imaginative venture. Should the MWC succeed in the next few years, it could radically challenge the ethos and governance of mosques and Islamic institutions. Their willingness to pioneer such a controversial proposal is indicative of a new confidence among this generation of British Muslim women. The activities and impact of such women is one of our major themes.

In the rest of this book we will describe and evaluate some of the many attempts to move beyond ethno-Muslim identity politics; to quarry and retrieve forgotten resources in the Islamic tradition to orientate Muslims to live well as a minority in Britain today and to provide a new generation of religious leaders with a religious formation contextualised within the British situation. We will hear many new voices from across the Muslim world, some of whom are now resident in the UK. A precondition for all such initiatives is the importance of English as a shared language. In all, a more hopeful narrative of positive co-existence across different communities, Muslim and non-Muslim, is emerging.

Notes

1. The following account is based on attendance at the public consultation held on the 2 August 2015 and discussion with participants and speakers. Some 150 people attended. There is much interesting additional material on their website, www.muslimwomenscouncil. org.uk.
2. Non-Muslims are often unaware that Islam has two sources of revelation: the Quran, a short work two-thirds the length of the New Testament, and the Sunna, normative behaviour of the Prophet Muhammad, who is considered the 'living Quran'. The Sunna comprises traditions − *hadith* (singular) − compiled in six revered and voluminous collections a couple of centuries after the death of the Prophet. The two most famous are referred to as *Sahih Bukhari* and *Sahih Muslim*. The six respected collections do not exhaust the sources of *hadith* used in developing Islam's legal schools. In the contemporary Muslim world, as well as academic scholarship, the reliability and authenticity of *hadith* is a contentious issue. A good way into these debates are two excellent works by an American Muslim academic, Jonathan A. C. Brown, *Hadith: Muhammad's Legacy in the Medieval and Modern World* (London: Oneworld, 2009) and *Misquoting Muhammad, The Challenge and Choices of Interpreting the Prophet's Legacy* (London: Oneworld, 2014).

3. Carla Power, *If the Oceans were Ink: An Unlikely Friendship and a Journey to the Heart of the Quran* (New York: Henry Holt and Company, 2015), p. 8. A fatwa is a legal opinion given by a legal scholar – a mufti – in answer to a question about Islamic law.

4. For a well worked out example, see M. Riexinger's 'The Ottoman Empire as harmonious utopia: a historical myth and its function', in I. Weismann, M. Sedgwick and U. Martensson (eds), *Islamic Myths and Memories, Mediators of Globalization* (Farnham: Ashgate, 2014), pp. 35–52.

5. The 'Contextualising Islam in Britain' project brought together traditional, religious scholars, academics and activists, male and female, to discuss contemporary challenges in the UK facing Muslim communities and how resources might be found within the Islamic tradition to meet them. Two reports were published in 2009 and 2012. It was funded by the UK Department for Communities and Local Government and run by the Cambridge Centre for Islamic Studies.

6. We are grateful to the Executive Director of MWNUK, Faeeza Vaid, for giving us a copy of this letter dated 28 January 2016. We shall return to this episode in Chapter 3 since it also involved a full frontal attack on the clan/caste loyalties dominating much local Muslim politics and mosques alike.

7. 'Muslim Group in Launch in Lords', *Keighley News*, 27 March 2010.

8. Qari Asim is unusual in being an imam in a Leeds mosque while also a practising solicitor. His MBE was awarded when thirty-four years old for services to inter-community and inter-faith relations in the city.

9. The PMI invited Shaista Gohir, the chair of the Muslim Women's Network for the UK (MWNUK), to share the findings of an excellent piece of research which they had conducted with thirty-five victims, entitled 'Unheard Voices – sexual exploitation of Asian girls and young women'. This can be downloaded from their website.

10. P. Scheffer, *Immigrant Nations* (Cambridge: Polity Press, 2011), pp. 8, 36.

11. One struggle was to get state schools to provide *halal* school meals to enable Muslim pupils to access them. This occasionally ran up against opposition from animal rights activists.

12. See Dame Louise Casey's *The Casey Review: a review into opportunity and integration* (December 2016), https://www.gov.uk/government/publications/the-casey-review-a-review-into-opportunity-and-integration; pp. 138–40 for data on the increase of anti-Muslim hate crime and p. 32 for data on transnational marriage, which cites, *inter alia*, one localised study indicating that between 2007 and 2011,

80 per cent of babies of Pakistani ethnicity born in Bradford's one local maternity hospital had at least one parent born outside the United Kingdom.

13. More than fifty years ago, the Canadian scholar of religion and specialist on Islam, Wilfred Cantwell Smith wrote a landmark work in which he argued that all world religions have two inescapable dimensions. What he called 'faith' and 'the cumulative tradition': '"By faith" I mean personal faith . . . an inner religious experience or involvement of a particular person; the impingement on him of the transcendent, putative or real. By "cumulative tradition" I mean the entire mass of overt objective data that constitute the historical deposit . . . of the past religious life of the community in question: temples, scriptures, theological systems . . . legal and other institutions, conventions, moral codes, myths, and so on. . .': *The Meaning and End of Religion* (New York: Macmillan, 1962), pp. 156–7.

14. The most reliable source of data on mosques in the UK, their ethnic and sectarian makeup, as well as a range of insightful essays on related topics, is the remarkable website put together in his spare time by Mehmood Naqshbandi, a convert to Sufi Islam many decades ago. See, for example, www.MuslimsinBritan.org/reources/masjid_report.pdf.

15. Mona Siddiqui, *My Way: a Muslim Woman's Journey* (London: I. B. Tauris, 2015), p. 175.

16. Women from both MWC and MWNUK have commended the volume commissioned by *Musawah* and edited by Ziba Mir-Hosseini, Mulki Al-Sharmani and Janna Remminger, *Men in Charge? Re-thinking Authority in Muslim Legal Tradition* (London: Oneworld, 2014). The MWNUK sell discounted copies of this seminal study.

17. Siddiqui, *My Way*, pp. 62–4. Siddiqui wearies at the extent to which such external piety can mask a culture of deception with some *niqabis* depicted as going to their female tutor at university asking for 'the morning after pill', p. 65.

18. Ibid. p. 64.

19. Translated into English in an expanded edition under the title *Islam: to Reform or to Subvert?* (London: Saqi Books, 2006).

20. Siddiqui, *My Way*, p. 21.

21. See Zachery M. Heern, *The Emergence of Modern Shi'ism: Islamic Reform in Iraq and Iran* (London: Oneworld, 2015).

22. Ibid. p. 132.

23. Ibid. p. 132.

24. Ibid. p. 148.

25. Brown, *Misquoting Muhammad*, p. 13.
26. See Fazlur Rahman, *Islam and Modernity: Transformation of an Intellectual Tradition* (Chicago: University of Chicago Press, 1982).
27. See Dr Panjwani, *Centre for Research and Evaluation in Muslim Education, Annual Report, August 2012–May 2013* (London: UCL Institute of Education, 2013), p. 3. CRÈME, after wide consultation, has defined 'Muslim Education in three inter-related dimensions: the experience of Muslims in education; educational thought and practice in Muslim history and its relevance to Muslims and beyond; and the quality of teaching and learning about the histories and cultures of Muslims' (p. 2).
28. The *hadith* in question reads: 'If a fly lands in your drink, push it all the way under, then throw the fly out and drink. On one of the wings is disease, on the other is its cure', cited in Brown, *Misquoting Muhammad*, p. 69, where he rehearses the dismay of a pious Egyptian doctor at the turn of the twentieth century on discovering such a *hadith*.
29. Ibid. p. 113.
30. See the first chapter in Innes Bowen's *Medina in Birmingham, Najaf in Brent, Inside British Islam* (London: Hurst & Co., 2014). The entire book offers an accessible insight into the main Islamic traditions operating in the UK and the transnational links of each, along with informative comments on their respective attitude to gender, relations with wider society and violence.
31. Ebrahim Moosa, *What is a Madrasa?* (Edinburgh: Edinburgh University Press, 2015), pp. 50–3.
32. Sayeeda Warsi, *The Enemy Within: A Tale of Muslim Britain* (London: Allen Lane, 2017), pp. 164–5.
33. *Prospect*, January 2016, pp. 19–20.
34. See 'Muslim Women's Mosque', 1 June 2015, http://cllrshabbir.blogspot.co.uk; italics ours.
35. 'Christian, Jewish, and Muslim panel debates collective mistrust', *The Church Times*, 20 November 2015, p. 13.
36. See Philip Lewis, 'The civic, religious and political incorporation of British Muslims and the role of the Anglican Church: whose incorporation, which Islam?', *Journal of Anglican Studies*, 13:2 (2015), pp. 189–214; pp. 189–90.
37. Saiful Islam, *Your Questions Answered* (Bradford: JKN Publications, 2010) p. 244.
38. Brown, *Misquoting Muhammad*, p. 134.
39. Ibid. p. 140.

40. Islam, *Your Questions*, p. 284.
41. Conversation with Bana Gora, 24 August 2015. St Ethelburga's was the church in the city of London bombed by the IRA and rebuilt as a centre for peace and reconciliation. One of the young women in the MWC network is also part of a national Christian Muslim Forum which has held meetings at St Ethelburga's.
42. See Philip Lewis, 'Muslims in Britain: researching and addressing conflict in a post-secular city', in John Wolffe (ed.) *Irish Religious Conflict in Comparative Perspective: Catholics, Protestants and Muslims* (London: Palgrave Macmillan, 2014), pp. 191–205. This chapter reviews the many peacemaking initiatives in Bradford in the last twelve years – whether developing a city-wide civic network to mitigate the impact of terrorism, providing leadership training for young leaders drawing on all communities, to a women's peace network.
43. See Yasmin Saikia and Chad Haines (eds), *Women and Peace in the Islamic World: Gender, Agency and Influence* (London: I. B. Tauris, 2015).
44. We are grateful to the BCM for letting us have a copy of the letter.

1

Muslims in Britain: A Changing Landscape

New data

Muslim organisations are beginning to draw on the best insights of the social sciences and humanities to explore the changing nature of Britain's Muslim communities: their ethnic make-up, geographical location, educational and economic profile, inter-generational shifts; positive aspects which can be celebrated and challenges which need to be addressed.[1] Typical in this regard is *British Muslims in Numbers*, a polished and professional report produced by the Muslim Council of Britain in 2015. It reflects Muslim aspirations and anxieties as it targets a number of audiences: media commentators, community organisers in the Muslim voluntary and social enterprise sector, researchers and decision-makers in social policy.[2]

British Muslims in Numbers maps a number of important changes between 2001 and 2011 drawing on multiple sources of information, including census data. The Muslim population has grown from 1.55 to 2.71 million within the decade. It is a very young population with 33 per cent fifteen years or under, compared to 19 per cent in the overall population. While the Muslim population accounted for 4.8 per cent of the general population, in the 0–4 age range this was 9.1 per cent and in the 5–15 age range 8.1 per cent. This latter cohort will translate to approximately 300,000 Muslim teenagers by 2021.

Just less than half of Muslims are UK born and the report makes it clear that no one is a Muslim-in-general but rather people belong to a diversity of ethnic communities and religious traditions.[3] Around 68 per cent have roots in South Asia which include just over 1 million with origins in Pakistan, 400,000 in Bangladesh and 200,000 in India. For the first time an 'Arab' ethnic category was used in the 2011 census which produced a figure of approximately 180,000. The category 'black' includes more than 200,000 black African, 7,000 black Caribbean and some 60,000 'other black'. The broad category 'white' comprises more than 200,000 of whom more than 75,000 are British, 2,000 Irish and the vast majority – 130,000 – 'other white'.

Many of these categories are too undifferentiated to provide precise numbers for different communities: the oldest settled Muslim communities in Britain, the Yemenis, are subsumed within the undifferentiated 'Arab' category.[4] Similarly, we have no precise figures for the growing Somali community, part of the 'black African' figure. Indeed, the report offers four different figures drawing on different sources which range from 46,000 to 250,000! As regard to the 'other white' category, this does not disaggregate the mainly Turkish Cypriot community in North East London from the growing eastern European communities.[5]

Some welcome socio-economic and educational developments are flagged up in the report. For example, those with no educational qualifications fell from 39 per cent to 26 per cent in the decade 2001–11. The proportion of Muslims in the 'higher professional occupation category' is 5.5 per cent, not too far adrift from the figure in the general population of 7.6 per cent. The percentage of Muslims with 'degree level and above' qualifications at 24 per cent is only 3 percentage points from the figure for the overall population. Some 43 per cent of the 330,000 Muslim students in further education are now female. The contrast with low levels of further education for women in many Muslim majority countries, not least Pakistan, is striking. The potential of Muslim women as agents of religious and social change in Britain is one of the main themes of this book.[6]

These positive changes need to be qualified by a number of observations. A perceptive Muslim commentator worries about 'cultural illiteracy amongst Muslims'. This he explains in terms of most graduates pursuing careers in the

technical, scientific, medical, financial or legal professions . . .
There are relatively few Muslim graduates in the humanities and social sciences . . . By default the career choices of
our best and brightest means we remain culturally delin-
quent and unable to recognise the subtleties required for
the art of persuasion.[7]

Secondly, a study of 5,523 Pakistani and Bangladeshi heritage
students of business studies noted that 'British Muslims get com-
paratively low A-levels grades, overwhelmingly enter post-1992
universities (former polytechnics), live at the parental home during term-time, and are decreasingly satisfied with the quality of
the higher education they receive'.[8] This translates into much
lower representation than other faith communities amongst civil
servants, solicitors and journalists.[9]

Muslims in poverty: declining across the generations?

More than a fifth (21.3 per cent) of all Muslims between six-
teen and seventy-four have never worked (this figure excludes
students); this compares with 4 per cent in the overall population.
Eighteen per cent of Muslim women aged 16–74 look after the
family home compared to 6 per cent in the population at large,
and 29 per cent of Muslim women aged 16–24 work as compared
to about half of the general population. With regard to this pattern of young, female underemployment, the authors comment
that, 'for many this is because family responsibilities after marriage
take priority'.[10] However, *British Muslims in Numbers* also cites
research that:

> [t]he majority also want to return to work after having
> children and combine family life with a career. Some of
> the barriers which affect British Muslim women affect all
> women, such as gender discrimination, inflexibility, and
> lack of childcare. But British Muslim women also face
> additional challenges, including discrimination based on
> clothing and faith.[11]

This raises the question of the extent to which Muslims may suffer from a double penalty which impacts their employment chances, and thus deepens their poverty, namely racial and religious prejudice. Here we must mention the increased incidence of anti-Muslim hate crimes, not least as it disproportionately impacts Muslim women, whose dress codes often render them more visible than men. The escalation in such hate crimes is clear from government, police and academic research which inform recent reports, for example, the Citizens Commission – *The Missing Muslims: Unlocking British Muslim Potential for the Benefit of All* produced by Citizens UK in 2017.

The Commission rehearsed 2014 data from the Metropolitan Police showing a 70 per cent year-on-year increase in attacks on Muslims and police data for 2015–16 that highlights the fact that across England and Wales 'the volume of hate crime against British Muslims surpasses that of all other religious groups'. Muslim women are more likely than men to feel unsafe. 'Verbal and, particularly, physical assaults contribute to making public space unsafe for women, and this in turn cannot help women participate in the life of their community or wider British society.'[12]

This broad conclusion is supported by the Casey Review which cited the findings of Tell MAMA – a confidential third-party reporting service for individuals who experience anti-Muslim hate crimes – and reported 'a 200% increase in offline Islamophobic incidents in 2015', with more than 60 per cent of victims female. 'The three most common places where attacks occurred were public areas (26%), the transport network (20%), and places of business (12%).'[13]

The impact of such factors is addressed obliquely in research commissioned by the Joseph Rowntree Foundation (JRF) to support their anti-poverty strategy which, for the first time, systematically reviews the relationship between religion and poverty – where poverty is measured as 'falling below 60% of the median income'.[14] The bald data is striking: people from Muslim communities are most likely to be poor – 50 per cent, where the overall rate is 18 per cent. Christians are generally less likely to be in poverty, although there are differences between Anglicans (14 per cent) and Catholics (19 per cent).[15] However, the most important and encouraging finding was the huge decline in poverty across generations. For first-generation Muslims 54 per cent were in poverty, for the second generation 48 per cent and for the third generation 25 per cent. 'This suggests that third generation Muslims have almost caught up with the society as a whole in avoidance of poverty and that with the passage of time, the marked Muslim differences . . . might be substantively reduced.'[16]

The drivers of poverty for the first generation are contingent upon many Muslim migrants coming from countries with under-developed educational and economic infrastructure. This means that they often have limited English, few transferable social skills and limited employment prospects. Many also have traditional attitudes to gender roles with women expected to marry early. This is consistent with the data:

> First and second generation Muslims have more dependent children than . . . other religious groups, and are over twice as likely to be unemployed or economically inactive as the national average. 68% of first generation and 44% of the sec-ond-generation Muslim women are economically inactive.[17]

However, as we should expect, by the third generation the differ-entials are much less marked.

The JRF research factored in one other variable, namely, the extent to which different religions developed 'bridging social capital'. The American social theorist Robert Putnam had devel-oped this terminology from his research in America which sug-gested that membership of churches might mitigate or protect from poverty. This is:

> because church members are more likely than non-mem-bers to belong to and participate in a range of voluntary and civic organizations . . . [with people] *outside their own immediate social circle* . . . [this] may also help people to learn various skills and develop self-confidence. . . [and] help them in the labour market.[18]

The authors of the working paper noted that with regard to civic engagement in a range of different activities, 'Muslim groups were below the national average in terms of both the propensity to join and the density of engagement'.[19] Unsurprisingly, the authors pointed to the desirability of increasing such engagement. By generating 'bridging social capital', resilience and confidence are enhanced. This, in turn, might create supportive networks to circumvent discrimination. This is also the burden of many of the recommendations of the Citizens Commission – *The Missing Muslims* report. Another encouraging finding of the JRF working paper was that the most recent research looking at 'religious differences in earning among people who have accessed jobs in the salariat (professional and managerial occupations) did not find convincing evidence of any general Muslim pay gap at this level of the occupational structure'.[20]

British Muslims in both hyper-diverse and bi-cultural towns

Geographically, Muslim communities are unevenly spread across the country. Some 75 per cent live in four regions: Greater London, West Midlands, North West and Yorkshire and the Humber. The rest live in the remaining five English regions, along with relatively small numbers in Wales and Scotland. Within the four regions where most Muslims live, there is increasing concentration within certain urban areas. For example, while less than 7 per cent of the West Midlands population is Muslim, some two-thirds (more than 230,000) live in Birmingham. This represents just over one-fifth of the overall population of Birmingham.

Within Birmingham, there is further concentration within five wards: Washwood Heath, Bordesley Green and Sparkbrook all have more than 70 per cent with Aston and Springfield in excess of 50 per cent. The number of 5–15-year-old school pupils is even higher in these five wards, ranging from 69 per cent in Aston to 86 per cent in Washwood Heath. In a further four wards, the pupils comprise 50 per cent or more. The varied data in *British Muslims in Numbers* suggests two distinct spatial developments are happening at the same time. At one level, a successful professional and middle class is emerging, enjoying a measure of social mobility, moving out of inner city, ethno-Muslim enclaves. This enables the report to rehearse research that points to all ethnic minorities as 'more evenly spread in 2011 than in 2001'.[21]

At the same time, the report notices that between 2001 and 2011 the number of Muslims living in the most deprived local authority districts (LADs) in England grew from 33 per cent to just under half (46 per cent or 1.22 million).[22] This is consistent with the description of inner city wards in Birmingham, above. The same is happening within the other three English regions where the Muslim population is concentrated.[23] Whether in Tower Hamlets or the northern mill towns, the situation is more accurately characterised as bi-cultural than hyper-diverse. Here, 'there is not a range of groups but often just two, for example, Asian Muslims and whites'.[24]

This has led the sociologist Bryan Turner to worry that across many cities in Europe the creation of an enclave society is emerging, where Muslim 'rituals of intimacy' – food and dress codes, marriage norms – intensify a web of exclusion. This means that easy talk of different religious and ethnic communities interacting and constructing an 'overlapping consensus' in public and civic life presupposes the overlapping of social groups. In its absence, we find 'separate and sequestered communities'.[25]

Whilst Turner exaggerates the degree of willed apartness, his concerns are not without substance. This is clear in a fine comparative study by Eren Tatari, an American Muslim political scientist, of three Labour-dominated London boroughs with the highest percentage of Muslims. Professor Tatari was concerned to identify the extent to which Muslim councillors have enabled their respective local governments to be responsive to Muslim needs. We will focus on just two of the three boroughs which offer an illuminating contrast between one borough which approximates to the bi-cultural model – Tower Hamlets – and the other – Newham – 'the most ethnically diverse local authority in England and Wales'.[26]

In Newham, there is no dominant ethnic minority and there are minimal racial or religious tensions between its diverse communities. The white communities are over 39 per cent and a similar size to the South Asian communities which have a rough equivalence of Indian, Pakistani and Bangladeshis. In addition, the black communities comprise some 20 per cent.

In the 2006–10 period, the number of Muslim councillors (thirteen of sixty) reflected both the percentage of Muslims in the borough (24 per cent) and its South Asian mix. The councillors were successfully incorporated in the political process holding between them, 'six leadership positions and twelve prestigious committee assignments'.[27] Professor Tatari distinguishes between two styles of minority representation: the 'balancers' seek to represent both their Muslim constituents and advance the interests of all constituents; in contrast, the 'group' style simply advances its own interests. With regard to Newham, she concludes that Muslim and non-Muslim councillors alike are generally 'balancers' and Muslims have generally been well served by this style of representational politics.

This is in marked contrast to Tower Hamlets where over a third of the borough is Bengali with no other significant Muslim communities. Further, the white communities constitute more than 40 per cent of the population, yet in 2010 thirty-three of the fifty-one councillors were Muslim and all but one of these were Bengali. Professor Tatari is very critical of Bengali politicians, most of whom are first generation with poor English and who pursue a

Bengali style politics through patronage and kinship ties. The primary reason for this is that the large Bengali community ... is [self-contained] with its shops, businesses, media outlets, schools and social and political organizations, with little need to interact with the British society or learn to speak English fluently.[28]

Professor Tatari characterises such politics as embodying an aggressive 'group' style. Since the Bengali councillors can count on the bloc votes of fellow Bengalis, they do not have to 'worry about offending the non-Muslim voters ...[their] majority in the council enables them to secure Muslim-friendly policy outcomes despite disgruntled opposition ... [notwithstanding the fact that] these dynamics hurt social harmony and are counterproductive to conflict resolution'. She concludes with a quotation from a non-Muslim councillor who worries that:

The trouble with that kind of politics ... is that [the] white working class community feels marginalized. A lot of people I speak to, who complain that they got three Bengali councilors, feel marginalized and that their needs are not met. That's when people start voting for the BNP ...[29]

The study indicates that where Muslim councillors operate within a context of hyper-diversity, they learn the bridging skills to work at alliances across ethnic and religious groupings to effect positive change. However, as a footnote to this discussion, she observes that hyper-diversity does not work to the advantage of the Muslim councillors in Hackney. This is because they are fragmented according to inter-generational tensions, sect, ethnicity and gender: four are of Indian heritage, three Alevi Kurds, one Sunni Turk and one of Pakistani heritage. Three of the councillors are young women and more secular than the South Asian male councillors, who are all in their sixties or older.

In British Muslims in Numbers, it is remarked that '[i]n assessing the potential of the "Muslim vote", it should be noted that voter registration and voter turnout is lower with BME communities in comparison with the rest of the population'.[30] Yet they still give the percentage of 'Muslim' votes in a detailed appendix of thirty-three marginal constituencies. This obscures what Tatari makes clear, First, that in some bi-cultural contexts, ethnic politics tends to be a proxy for Muslim politics. Secondly, within contexts of hyper-diversity, Muslim communities in the UK come from very different parts of the world, are carriers of variable social capital, and embody a variety of sectarian allegiances, as well as migration histories. To homogenise this experience with talk of a 'Muslim vote' obscures rather than illuminates a complex picture.

This is clear in the following comments by a Turkish councillor in Hackney:

I joke with my Turkish friends to turn off their Turkish TV. They must learn the language, go to the library, read children's book, and listen to radio ... they see themselves as

guests here. They don't want to get involved in politics here
but earn enough and leave. But they cannot leave either [as]
their children are born and raised here.[31]

Many in his community still cling to the first-generation myth
of return, yet other Muslim communities are now embedded in
British life, and two or three generations away from the pioneer
migrant generation. They are decidedly British and not 'guests'.
However, such categorical distinctions between Muslims who
belong to first, second or third generations can be blurred in
practice.

New questions: language proficiency

It is assumed that a three-generation migrant trajectory from
avoidance, through engagement to accommodation is typical of
most migrant communities.[32] The standard pattern is that by the
third generation, as a result of education and socialisation, migrant
communities begin to reflect the socio-economic range of wider
society, thereby achieving a measure of social mobility. As we
have seen, there is some encouraging evidence that this is true for
Muslim communities. However, it may not hold true for all
Muslim communities to the same extent.

British Muslims in Numbers makes clear that the largest Muslim
communities – the Pakistani and Bangladeshi communities – still
include about half its number born overseas. In each of these
latter cohorts, sizeable majorities – two thirds of the Pakistani
and three quarters of the Bangladeshi – declare that their main
language is not English. One in five of the Pakistani cohort either
does not speak English well or not at all; the figure for Bangladeshis is one in four.[33]

We can dig a little deeper with regard to the British Pakistani community. An anthropologist argues that this community is unlike the generality of Europe's Muslim communities
in embodying three specific practices. The vast majority marry
co-ethnics; transcontinental marriage has remained stable across
the generations accounting for 57–69 per cent of all marriages
and the community prefers to marry 'close' relatives in two senses:

'more than one-half marry first cousins, and most Mirpuris Muslims (the majority of British Pakistanis) marry someone from the
same village ... [Indeed], rates of close-cousin marriage appear
to be rising.'[34]

One innovative health project – 'Born in Bradford' (BiB),
located in that city's one maternity hospital – conducted research
from 2007 to 2011 amongst mothers of babies born in that period,
to consider the extent to which different communities presented
with distinct neo-natal problems. What was surprising was that data
from the BiB project suggests that of the 4,649 babies with Pakistani origins, only 11 per cent had both parents born in the UK
and 49 per cent had one parent born in the UK.[35] This leaves a
large majority with one or both parents born overseas, even though
the parents were assumed to be third- or fourth-generation British
Pakistani.

This phenomenon of 'the first generation in every generation' when allied to other variables, suggests that educational disadvantage can be trans-generational. In the case of the Mirpuri
community, the other factors turn on the specifics of language
politics of Azad Kashmir as they continue to impact communities
in the UK, demographic density and after-school programmes
at the mosque. With regard to the linguistic complexity, children
are expected to work across four languages: English at school, an
oral Punjabi dialect at home, Quranic Arabic in the madrasa –
often learned by rote without understanding its meaning – and
Urdu, the language through which Islamic studies are taught in
the mosque.[36]

Bradford has similar patterns of ethno-Muslim clustering as
Birmingham. The Metropolitan district of Bradford comprises
some 25 per cent Muslim, with some 43 per cent of all school
children. In 2012 the city had about forty primary schools and
ten secondary schools where 85 per cent of the pupils were of
Pakistani heritage, most within or adjacent to nine inner city
wards where the communities live.[37] These data mean that many
youngsters at school and at home largely socialise with those of
the same ethnicity and enjoy limited opportunities to develop
the linguistic, cultural and social skills to interact confidently
with those outside their immediate community.[38]

Finally, most Mirpuri youngsters can spend up to two hours a day after state school in a madrasa learning Quranic Arabic, five days a week, from six years old for a minimum of five or six years. While there are some excellent examples of British-trained *ulama* (Islamic religious specialists) also acquiring training in state schools, thereby enabling a convergence of educational methods in both institutions – as we will explore in the next chapter – such personnel remain the exception to the rule.[39] This means that the pedagogy of a majority of madrasas is traditional – rote learning with instruction in Urdu – which many youngsters do not fully understand.

One of the few academic studies of the impact on twelve-year-old Mirpuri boys of six years learning the Quran in a British madrasa concludes that, in comparison with the time they spend learning to read English in school, much more 'real time and personal effort' was spent learning to read the Quran by rote, an activity deemed to carry considerable religious merit.[40] Despite this, after six years most were unable to explain the meaning of the opening chapter of the Quran in English.

The researcher Dr A. Rowosky points out that it usually requires 'a five to seven year period' for bilingual pupils to bridge the language gap with their monolingual peers.[41] However, the plight of the Mirpuri is exacerbated because of the lack of a developed literacy in their mother tongue, Mirpuri Punjabi. Moreover, many parents, not proficient in English themselves, exaggerate the success of their children in English by confusing what linguists dub 'conversational language proficiency' with 'academic language proficiency'. With the former, children quickly acquire that which enables them to interact and fit in; academic proficiency, however – which enables them to do well in examinations – takes much longer to acquire.

What is surprising is the absence of research into the cumulative impact of the various factors on educational achievement. It might be that a child can do well if, say, only two of the possible four variables operate: one or both parents from rural Pakistan with little if any formal education; spending two hours a day in a madrasa with a non-English speaking teacher; expected to learn three or four languages; living and socializing in a mono-ethnic home and school environment.

New questions: homeless and prison population

British Muslims in Numbers points out that while 2.2 per cent of the overall population are in hostels or temporary shelters for the homeless, the figure for the Muslim population is 5.1 per cent. Similarly, while Muslims account for 4.8 per cent of the population, the figure for the prison population is 13 per cent, of which more than 30 per cent are 'black British'.

The authors observe that 'the higher proportion of Muslims in hostels for the homeless and in prison is an unwelcome social reality, requiring urgent attention by mosques and Muslim civil society.[42] Two very different pieces of work indicate that a beginning has been made to address such issues. The first is a subtle and thoughtful article reviewing the Islamic tradition to identify theological resources to undergird 'religious professionals offering pastoral support to Muslims suffering from substance abuse'.[43] The second, is a bold and imaginative project aimed at understanding and addressing the 'silent suffering' of Muslim women in prison, modelling an innovative pattern of collaboration across Muslim civil society.[44]

Dr Mansur Ali's article 'Perspectives on drug addiction in Islamic history and theology' is rooted in ground-breaking research he has conducted on the role and impact of Muslim chaplains, especially in prison.[45] He and his co-author observe that 'after mosques and Islamic Centres, the Ministry of Justice/Prison Service is now probably the largest single employer of Muslim religious professionals in Britain. Over 200 Muslim chaplains work in British prisons ... [which] includes 12 women, mainly serving in all-female establishments.'[46]

Dr Ali's study is necessarily explorative and 'tentative' given that 'the literature examining the theology of substance addiction in Islam is scarce' and that most theological models to explain addiction are 'found in Christianity'.[47] In seeking to fill a significant gap in Muslim theological and pastoral reflection he draws on an American Muslim initiative – Millati Islam (MI) – and points out that traditional Muslim societies are mainly shame-based cultures rather than guilt-based cultures.

Shame-based cultures have their deterrent mechanisms . . .
[external] to the person. 'What will people say?' is a common feature of a shame-based culture. The fear of being
negatively exposed in front of people stops one from doing
wrong. In contrast, guilt-based cultures have their mechanisms built in to the individual conscience, which leads to
remorse, pity, and reparative action.[48]

The first two Islamic models he explores and evaluates operate within such a shame-culture. The first – addiction as 'crime' –
treats recreational drug taking as an analogy with the prohibition
on alcohol as both a sin against God and a crime. As with alcohol
in Islamic law it carries an exemplary punishment meant to deter.
However, as Dr Ali observes, most Muslim countries today do not
enact such punishments and 'the ones that do are discriminatory
and selectively biased'.[49] The second model – addiction as a 'spiritual
disease' – presents the use of intoxicants as severing the relationship
with God, family and community. He considers that both of these
models will encourage the practising and devout to abstain from
substance addiction. However, neither really helps those already 'suffering from drug addiction nor instrumental in changing people's
attitudes towards those who are addicted'. Rather, a 'practical model,
based on guilt-culture and personal redemption, can work better for
people wanting to escape from addictive disorder'.[50]

This is where Dr Ali commends the Millati Islam. MI is a
fellowship founded for Muslims suffering from addiction in the
USA in 1989. MI has adapted the twelve-step Alcoholics Anonymous (AA) model to make it responsive to Islamic imperatives
and perspectives. While there is a significant overlap between the
Christian inflected 1935 version and MI's adaptation, there are
also important changes in detail. For example, in the original AA
document point 3 reads: '[We] made a decision to turn our will
and our lives over to the care of God as we understood Him.' In
MI, this now reads: 'We made a decision to submit our will to
the will of Allah.' In his detailed commentary on such changes
he argues that the authors of MI omit the phrase 'as we understood him' since, for them, 'in Islam, God is transcendent beyond

all comprehension'. He admits that this may be theologically correct but

> lacks the personal closeness of God that one needs during times of crisis . . . [Therefore] God's immanence needs to be reclaimed back from his transcendence if we are to develop a model of pastoral care that emphasizes God being with people, rather than aloof from them.[51]

In all, this is a bold foray into a contested area. Ali is clear that if Muslims are to develop an adequate theory and practice of Islamic pastoral care for addicts, Islamic law will have to be complemented by developing an Islamic theology which draws on the best of the social sciences and Islamic history, in a critical conversation with other religions.

The second example highlights Muslim civil society itself taking ownership of a sensitive issue, with a pioneering project – *Muslim Women in Prison* – written up and reported in April 2015. It is a hard-hitting pilot study of seventeen Muslim women in two prisons and the particular vulnerabilities they face during confinement and post-release.[52] Maqsood Ahmed – formally the Senior Government Advisor for Muslim Chaplaincy at HM Prison Service – in commending the report, observes that Muslim communities tend to be in denial about the phenomenon, since 'the subject is embroiled in stigma, taboo and shame. There is the attitude that these women are "bad eggs" and should not be discussed or supported let alone rehabilitated. . .'[53] At the same time, service providers are unaware of distinct socio-cultural and religious norms which impact their lives.

Because Muslim women bear the burden of family honour, in prison they frequently suffer additional isolation and depression, with families often unwilling to visit them. Moreover, when they leave prison, many cannot be reintegrated into family and community because of fear of rejection, criticism, even violence. The study cites a pregnant woman who presses for her baby to be born outside the prison, since she did not want the baby to carry the stigma, shame and dishonour of being a 'prison baby'. She emphasised that she did not mind being punished for a crime, but it would be totally unfair for her baby to suffer from bullying and taunts from the wider community for the rest of the child's life.

In the event, the female researcher intervened successfully with the prison authorities for the baby to be delivered outside the prison.[54]

In addition to the normal difficulties of resettlement, Muslim women ex-prisoners have a multiplicity of additional needs with respect to Islamic divorce, inheritance, access to children, legal matters in countries of origin and immigration status. Although half of the cohort entered prison married, most are divorced while in prison. With regard to crimes committed, the researcher identified 'a theme of family loyalty . . . where the female prisoner may have been connected to a crime which is linked with other family members.' A poignant example is given, where a prisoner was imprisoned following a sham marriage charge. She claims that one of her cousins from Pakistan tried to submit a case as her spouse and forged documents to that effect.[55] Here the claims and power of her extended family – *biraderi* – are presented as trumping legality.[56]

The *Muslim Women in Prison* report represents a model collaboration of different Muslim organisations willing to recognise a problem and fund research to develop the knowledge to begin to address it. Significantly, the research was funded by a well-known Muslim charity – Muslim Hands – working through a local organisation, the Huddersfield Pakistani Community Alliance (HPCA). Muslim Hands is headed by a respected Islamic scholar, which means that other religious scholars – *ulama* – are more likely to give their research a sympathetic hearing.

The lead researcher was a youth and development worker, Sofia Buncy, who had spent ten years patiently developing the trust of the local Muslim communities to enable her to develop leadership and youth training for young men and women with HPCA. The final report was co-authored by Ishtiaq Ahmed, a member of the

Bradford Council of Mosques. This guaranteed that the findings of the report would be circulated among relevant bodies.

Traditionally, Muslim charities have raised money in the UK and funded projects across the Muslim world. However, Muslim Hands, by funding such British-based initiatives, is a positive acknowledgement of local needs having a legitimate claim on donors. HPCA already has a reputation for innovative and edgy youth and development work, developing capacity and leadership across different communities.[57]

Further, the project could draw on the expertise and contacts within the prison service developed by Maqsood Ahmed. It is testimony to the seriousness with which Muslim Hands have taken on this project that subsequently they have employed Sofia Buncy as their first 'community development and prison rehab coordinator' across the north of England.[58] In all, it is an exemplary case study of inter-generational collaboration across genders, including a diversity of organisations, to tackle an issue hitherto taboo in many Muslim communities.

New questions: tight-knit communities beginning to unravel?

Probably the most startling data in *British Muslims in Numbers* was that alongside 260,000 married Muslim households with dependent children, there are 77,000 Muslim lone parent families with dependent children and 135,000 one-person Muslim households. This 'surprisingly high' figure for single households and lone parent families was recognised by the authors of the report as posing a significant challenge to Muslim civil society. With little systematic research into rising divorce rates and issues of social isolation, 'imams require briefings on such social realities'.[59]

Since there is little research, the most that can usefully be done here is to point to possible lines of inquiry, much implicit in what has already been said. Clearly, traditional patterns of arranging marriage within many Muslim communities are proving inadequate and new forms are emerging. Typical in this regard are comments taken from an article − 'The trouble with marriage' − in a popular Muslim magazine a few years ago. The journalist Shelina

Janmohamed regrets that 'a woman in many Muslim communities only seems to acquire social standing after her marriage. She is advised that she will be given her freedoms once she has arrived at her husband's home and becomes his responsibility.' Janmohamed remarks that parents routinely pressurise their children by posing them with a false dichotomy: either you 'choose your own spouse or [remain] loyal to your parents and culture'. Moreover, cultural factors are often privileged over Islamic norms:

It's about picking the 'right' family . . . the 'right' caste . . . the 'right' job . . . [or] picking someone from 'back home' as the 'right' thing to do – to find a more compliant wife; to transport the extended family over to Britain; or to ensure that undue pressure can be exerted in internal family matters.

Janmohamed observes that, in addition, new challenges are beginning to emerge. 'Despite the pressure to marry "within" the culture, traditional networks of extended families and matchmakers are breaking down, unable to connect prospective spouses who are a good match for each other.' She then evaluates some of the alternatives, 'such as online matrimonial sites, speed dating, or marriage events'. She worries about the lack of space to articulate and manage different marital expectations. Too often 'the wedding becomes the big event instead of the marriage'. She urges families and *ulama* to invest in 'pre-marital counselling'. To 'reverse the tide of difficulties' in spouse selection and rising divorce rate requires 'change in our cultures and attitudes'.[60]

However, changing cultural and attitudinal norms is far from straightforward. This is evident in the avalanche of anguished commentary across the Muslim blogosphere which followed the publication of the *Jay Report*, the *Independent Inquiry into Child Sexual Exploitation in Rotherham in 2014*.[61] Such commentary illuminates many of these intractable issues around gender within sections of some ethno-Muslim communities in Britain, which render stable marriages precarious. The Muslim councillor from Bradford, cited in an earlier chapter, makes an important observation in his blog – *Stop this madness* – where he urges Muslims to openly debate the wisdom of continuing to bring partners and spouses over from

Pakistan since the 'cultural gap' between the young people here and abroad is 'vast':

> There exists a chasm ... [in] understanding [ranging from] the meaning of a joke, communicating ... [or how] to be intimate ... [which leads to] emotional, intellectual and sexual [frustration] in young people's lives. Furthermore both men and women are not taught about sex and lovemaking ... Conversation needs to be more than just what is 'halal and haram' (permissible and forbidden) but ... [include] exploration of one's sexuality.[62]

A Salafi imam and youth worker, Alyas Karmani, who has pioneered de-radicalisation work in West Yorkshire and London, draws attention in published sermons to the paucity of institutional spaces where Muslim youth could discuss issues of immediate concern: drugs, alcohol consumption, 'gangsta lifestyle' and the popularity of a rap culture which reduces women to sex objects.[63] He lambasts mosques and families alike: 'We don't even talk about these issues. We don't give any guidance to our children on sex education.'

What would count as sex education is less clear. Karmani rehearses traditional teaching:

> we don't have free mixing in our *deen* [religion]. You put men and women together in an environment ... we know what happens because of this. That's why we have purdah [the practice of concealing women from men], that's why we maintain this hijab. Allah has prohibited free mixing.

At the same time, he is aware that Muslim youngsters have internalised wider society's norms to the extent that

> they don't have any problem now with this idea of a boyfriend and a girlfriend and 'Let's go out on dates'. It's a mass trauma in our community, an identity conflict. On the one hand we have our community life which is nice and respectable. On the other hand there is a double life going on.[64]

If young men and women can feel trapped by the pressure of the extended family to marry someone, often a cousin, from 'back home', this can generate a set of responses – themselves gendered – which further disables trusting relationships. This is clear in the blog of a young woman in her twenties, the communities reporter for BBC Look North. Sabbiyah Pervez details how the persistence of 'a culture of shame' makes it difficult to discuss a range of sensitive issues within Muslim communities. For example, women vulnerable to abuse are often cowed into silence. If they do broach the topic, they know that they will be blamed with comments such as 'That's what happens when you wear jeans and no dupatta'. If she speaks out about abuse, 'she is the one who is ostracized . . . named a whore . . . who has brought dishonour [to the family]'.[65] Pervez particularises the issue by referring to her own community within which

> men are brought up as kings, with their dishes cleaned, beds made, clothes ironed and shoes polished from the day they are born to the day they die. The servitude begins with the mother and the unfortunate sisters and then passes on to the wife and the subsequent daughters . . . If a man has an affair, the wife is blamed for being too fat or unattractive . . . I know so many cases where young lads have got married to a girl their parents wanted them to marry but then kept 'a girl on the side' to keep themselves happy . . . There is a clear conflict between duty and autonomy . . . [with young men raised] to serve the expectations of the extended family network, however at school . . . they are taught to express themselves, to be independent. As they grow older this conflict grows stronger . . . This is where you get men who are committing adultery, who are marrying women from the sub continent but still dating other women . . . It is essentially a massive identity crisis.[66]

She concludes that change is coming with her generation, not least through supportive male role models. As with other commentators, she labours under no illusions as to what is required: nothing less than 'a fundamental change in the way women are

perceived and treated ... [no longer] as objects of honour and
shame ... bargaining tools used to play politics via ... marriage ...
[or] treated as slaves of the house'.[67]

Now, of course, such comments paint only part of a complex
picture. There is inevitably a dissonance between such cultural
notions of male superiority and the fact that, as with all communities, young Muslim women are outperforming their brothers.[68] This
can lead to a different sort of problem, namely finding educated
husbands for better educated women. On the one hand, female
Muslim graduates are

> asserting their agency at every stage of the matrimonial
> process – from their very decisions to look for a mar-
> riage partner, how they decide which form of matrimonial
> service(s) they will engage with, to negotiating marriage
> contracts and asserting their rights as Muslim women and
> wives within marriage.[69]

The author of these remarks – Dr Fauzia Ahmad – also observes
that some parents are open to the possibility that their daughters
will meet potential partners at university or work. On the other
hand,

> Muslim women often complain about a lack of suitably
> educated and professionally employed men on matrimonial
> websites and at the various matrimonial events held across
> the UK, Europe and North America ... Some commentators
> have described the rise in the numbers of single, professional
> Muslim women, as the '*Muslim spinster crisis*' ... or more gen-
> erally as the '*myth of the happy celibate*'.[70]

If Muslim communities are in the midst of rapid social changes
which are reconfiguring how gender relations are understood,
the most challenging aspect is the extent to which Islam itself has
to be rethought if patriarchy and misogyny are to be addressed.
The contributors to a sparkling collection of essays in a recent
volume of *Critical Muslim* are in no doubt that such a task is inescapable and urgent. The editorial refers to one day's international

news drawn at random from a British broadsheet in 2013 that featured the systematic abuse of Muslim women in Egypt, Iran, Saudi Arabia and Nigeria. The editor concludes that 'this is clear evidence of a culture gone pathological'.[71]

By way of partial explanation, the editor reminds his readers that Muslim scholars have divided the names of God into two categories: Names of Majesty, which reflect the masculine attributes; and the Names of Beauty, which reflect the feminine attributes. The Islamic tradition as it developed emphasised the former. 'Given that fear, vengeance, and brute force are seen as the prime attributes of God, it is not surprising that they have become the dominant themes of Muslim societies.'[72] Predictably, a way back to sanity is presented as rediscovering and embodying His Names of Beauty. As with Mansur Ali's reflections on how to address substance abuse, where he argues for a re-thinking of the relationship of divine transcendence and immanence, so here with the issue of gender relations, Muslim scholars are realising that how God is construed has implications for the sort of society that is created. This is opening up space for some imaginative, new thinking in the field of Islamic theology.

Notes

1. The confidence to draw on such disciplines is in marked contrast to the Islamic seminaries in South Asia – see Introduction – and in Iran where Kamran Daneshjoo, a recent Minister of Higher Education, rehearses the fears of the Supreme Leader who 'repeatedly warned of the dangers of Western values infiltrating Iranian society through social sciences and humanities. Daneshjoo labelled these academic fields as "dangerous", since they can breed "secularism, liberalism and materialism", thereby undermining the foundations of the Islamic Republic.' Afshin Shahi and Alam Saleh, 'Andalusiasation: is Iran on the trajectory of de-Islamisation?', *British Journal of Middle Eastern Studies*, 42: 4 (2015), pp. 500–19; 508.

2. *British Muslims in Numbers, a demographic, socio-economic and health profile of Muslims in Britain drawing on the 2011 census*, published in January 2015 by MCB's Research and Documentation Committee, London, with the named lead analyst a young female sociologist who lectures at Oxford University, Dr Sundas Ali, p. 12.

3. For most first-generation Muslims, Islam was an aspect of their ethnic identity, and faith adherence was concerned with participating in communal life and less about personal religiosity. This has changed significantly for second and third generations. Most South Asian British Muslims are from Sunni theological backgrounds that consist of a range of sectarian traditions. Among these, four major religious traditions predominate: the devotionalist Barelwi Sufi tradition, the scriptually oriented reform of the Deobandis, the Islamist Jamaat-e-Islami (JI)-inspired institutions and the Ahl al-Hadith mosque network. For further background, see Sadek Hamid, *Sufis, Salafis and Islamists: The Contested Ground of British Islamic Activism* (London: I. B. Tauris, 2016).

4. For the Yemenis, see Mohammad Siddique Seddon, *The Last of the Lascars: Yemeni Muslims in Britain, 1836–2012* (Markfield: Kube Academic, 2014).

5. T. Kucuken's *Politics of Ethnicity, Identity and Religion: Turkish Muslims in Britain* (Farnham: Ashgate, 1999) estimated that already in the late 1990s there were some 125,000 Turks in London (p. 63).

6. The shockingly low level of state education for women in Pakistan, especially in rural areas where 60 per cent of the population live, is laid bare in Anatol Lieven's, *Pakistan, A Hard Country* (London: Allen Lane, 2011). At its most extreme, in the Federally Administered Tribal Areas, male literacy is 30 per cent and female 3 per cent. A local activist is cited who argues that for the Pukhtoons more generally, 'female education is disliked by the majority … The empowerment of women anathema …' (pp. 383–4).

7. S. M. Atif Imtiaz, *Wandering Lonely in a Crowd: Reflections on the Muslim Condition in the West* (Markfield: Kube, 2011), p. 57.

8. D. Hussain and S. McLoughlin, 'United Kingdom', in J. S. Nielsen (ed.), *Yearbook on Muslims in Europe*, vol. 5 (Leiden: Brill, 2013), pp. 692–3.

9. For details see Citizens Commission, *The Missing Muslims: Unlocking British Muslim Potential for the Benefit of All* (London: Citizens UK, 2017), pp. 17–18.

10. MCB, *British Muslims in Numbers*, p. 63.

11. Ibid. p. 63.

12. Citizens Commission, *The Missing Muslims*, pp. 50–1.

13. L. Casey, *The Casey Review, a Review into Opportunity and Integration* (London: UK Government, 2016), pp. 139–40. An accessible and well-argued exploration of Islamophobia is provided in chapter 6 –

'Islamophobia' – in Sayeeda Warsi's *The Enemy Within: A Tale of Muslim Britain* (London: Allen Lane, 2017).
14. The paper is produced by the Centre for Social Investigation (CSI) – CSI Working Paper: 2015-01 – Nuffield College, Oxford, by Anthony Heath and Yaojun Li, entitled *Review of the Relationship between Religion and Poverty – an Analysis for the Joseph Rowntree Foundation*, http://csi.nuff.ox.ac.uk/, p. 53.
15. Ibid. p. 2. For Jewish people the figure is 13 per cent, for Sikhs 27 per cent and Hindus 22 per cent.
16. Ibid. p. 16: 'The first generation refers to immigrants who were born abroad and who came to the UK after 6 years of age. The second generation refers to those who were born in the UK or who came before the age 6. The third generation or above refer to those whose parents or at least one of their grand-parents were born in the UK.'
17. Ibid. p. 22.
18. Ibid. p. 19, italics ours.
19. Ibid. p. 29.
20. Ibid. p. 11. As with most research new questions are also thrown up. It is not clear, for example, why there are marked differences in unemployment levels across genders and communities. So the unemployment rate for women seeking work varied between 37, 13, 27 and 22 per cent for Muslim women in black African, Indian, Pakistani and Bangladeshi ethnic groups respectively (p. 41). The Citizens Commission's *Missing Muslims* report also points to a significant difference between Somali and Pakistani women's inactivity levels which require an explanation (p. 18).
21. MCB, *British Muslims in Numbers*, p. 26.
22. Deprivation refers to neighbourhoods characterised by 'seven dimensions of deprivation: income, employment, health, education, barriers to housing and services, crime and living environment'. Ibid. p. 48.
23. For example, Yorkshire and Humber has 6 per cent Muslims across the region but this is concentrated within in a few urban areas. So the Metropolitan district of Bradford comprises some 25 per cent Muslim, with some 43 per cent of all school children.
24. Tariq Modood, *Post-immigration 'Difference' and Integration: The Case of Muslims in Western Europe* (London: British Academy Policy Centre, 2012), p. 34.
25. Bryan S. Turner, 'Revivalism and the Enclave Society', in Amyn B. Sajoo (ed.), *Muslim Modernities: Expressions of the Civil Imagination* (London: I. B. Tauris, 2008), p. 148.

26. Eren Tatari, *Muslims in British Local Government: Representing Minority Interests in Hackney, Newham, and Tower Hamlets* (Leiden: Brill, 2014), p. 142.
27. Ibid. p. 155. Key positions involve responsibilities, for example, for budget, planning and scrutiny of policy.
28. Ibid. p. 132. The reality of a relatively enclosed ethnic enclave, enabling the import of a particular style of ethnic politics to take root, is only part of the Tower Hamlets story. The borough has seen a quite remarkable turnabout in education. In 1998, 'Only 47% of pupils achieved level 4 in Key Stage 2 English tests, compared with 63% nationally.' By 2012, primary schools in Tower Hamlets have 'improved at rates in line with and better than nationally, particularly in writing from 64% in 2006 to 85% in 2012, gaining 21 points compared with a 15-point improvement nationally.' This improvement is built on a number of factors including peer mentors to build links between younger and older residents; an innovative schools and business link with volunteers supplementing literacy and numeracy skills; the local Inter-Faith Forum promoting understanding across the different religions; and multiple partnerships with local faith communities, for example, mosques educating their congregations not to take children out of school for long visits to Bangladesh given its deleterious impact on educational achievement: see Professors David Woods, Professor Charles Husbands and Dr Chris Brown, *Transforming Education for All: the Tower Hamlets* Story (London: Mayor of Tower Hamlets Office, November 2013). We are grateful to Dr Dan DeHanas of King's College, London University for drawing our attention to this report. It can be downloaded from www:thomasbuxton.towerhamlets.sch.uk/files/press/transforming-education.pdf.
29. Tatari, *Muslims in British Local Government*, p. 141.
30. MCB, *British Muslims in Numbers*, p. 30.
31. Tatari, *Muslims in British Local Government*, p. 179. Emphasis ours.
32. The first generation with little knowledge of the language and culture of the host community keeps its distance; their children, at ease with both, are able to make claims on the new society, which can generate some conflict but this is a measure of engagement, and by the third generation they are at home with mutual accommodation between minority and majority the norm.
33. MCB, *British Muslims in Numbers*, p. 35.
34. John Bowen, *On British Islam: Religion, Law, and Everyday Practice in Shari'a Councils* (Princeton: Princeton University Press, 2016),

p. 19. Trans-continental marriages have been reduced with the introduction of a residential requirement of a Minimum Income Requirement (MRI) of £18,600 in 2012 (see Casey, *Casey Review*, p. 32).

35. J. West *et al.*, 'UK-born Pakistani-origin infants are relatively more adipose than white British infants; findings from 8704 mother-offspring pairs in the Born-in-Bradford prospective birth cohort', *Journal of Epidemiology and Community Health*, 67: 7 (2013), pp. 544–51. In discussion with the analyst of this data, his 'guestimate' was that half of the mothers born in South Asia, came to the UK as children and so much of their schooling was here.

36. The Mirpuri Muslim experience contrasts with the Punjabi Sikhs who only have to operate with one language additional to English, Punjabi, which is both a written language and the language of their holy book. Moreover, unlike Muslim children, they do not spend up to two hours a day after school, five days a week, learning about Sikhism. This is usually confined to Saturday morning gurdwara school.

37. These figures were extrapolated from Local Authority figures obtained in 2012.

38. See Paul Collier, *Exodus, Immigration and Multiculturalism in the 21st Century* (London: Allen Lane, 2013), pp. 88–92, for a case study.

39. See Ron Geaves, 'Drawing on the past to transform the present: contemporary challenges for training and preparing British imams', *Journal of Muslim Minority Affairs*, 28: 1 (2008), pp. 99–112.

40. A. Rosowsky, *Heavenly Readings: Liturgical Literacy in a Multilingual Context* (Bristol: Multilingual Matters, 2008), p. 55. It is worth pointing out that Dr Rosowsky is both an Arabic speaker, having lived in the Arab world, and is himself a Muslim who has taught such pupils.

41. A. Rowosky, 'Decoding as a cultural practice and its effects on the reading process of bilingual pupils', *Language and Education*, 15 (2001), p. 69.

42. MCB, *British Muslims in Numbers*, p. 43. The study provides a good example of an imaginative project addressing such issues: the Date Palm Project (DPP) is a an eight-bed supported housing project in the borough of Brent which accommodates and supports young Muslim prison-leavers, helping them readjust to life outside, assist their rehabilitation and break the cycle of re-offending. DPP provides specialised mentoring and career development delivered within an Islamic household environment.

43. Mansur Ali, 'Perspectives on drug addiction in Islamic history and theology', *Religions*, 5 (2014), pp. 912–28; 912 (doi:10.3390/rel5030912 – open access).

44. *Muslim Women in Prison [Second Chance Fresh Horizons]: A study of the needs and experiences of Muslim women in prison at the HMP & YOI New Hall & Ashham Grange Prisons during custody and post release*, December 2014, a Joint Muslims Hands and HPCA project, written by Sofia Buncy and Ishtiaq Ahmed. It can be downloaded from https://muslimhands.org.uk/_ui/uploads/87djpw/MWIP_Report.pdf p.5.

45. See Sophie Gilliat-Ray, Mansur Ali and Stephen Pattison, *Understanding Muslim Chaplaincy* (Farnham: Ashgate, 2013) and Mansur Ali and Sophie Gilliat-Ray, 'Muslim chaplains: working at the interface of "public" and "private"', in W. Ahmad and Z. Sardar (eds), *Muslims in Britain: Making Social and Political Space* (London: Routledge, 2012), pp. 84–100.

46. Ali and Gilliat-Ray, 'Muslim chaplains', p. 85.

47. Ali, 'Perspectives on drug addiction', p. 913.

48. Ibid. p. 917.

49. Ibid. p. 919.

50. Ibid. p. 921.

51. Ibid. p. 923.

52. The case study is drawn from women from a variety of ethnic backgrounds: Indian, Pakistani, Kashmiri, Arab and white British – five converts are among the group.

53. Buncy and Ahmed, *Muslim Women in Prison*, p. 3.

54. Ibid. pp. 20, 22.

55. The case reads like an airport novel: living in Pakistan at the time with her two young children and an abusive husband – aided and abetted in this abuse by her mother-in-law. Eventually, resisting advice to stay with her husband, so as to avoid the shame and dishonour of separation, she returns to Britain. Meanwhile, her two children are kidnapped and spirited back to Pakistan. Her freelance-assassin husband is murdered, but she cannot get a death certificate. Attempts by the British embassy to get her children back fail because of the passing of bribes by her family to the police to forestall the hand-over. Ibid. p. 19.

56. For the pervasive and frequently poisonous impact of *biraderi* on politics and family life in Pakistani and British society, see Philip Lewis, *Young, British and Muslim* (London: Continuum, 2007), pp. 46–53. *Biraderi* – literally meaning 'brotherhood' – can be briefly

defined as locally inter-marrying caste groups organised hierarchically, with land-owning castes at the top and artisan castes at the bottom.

57. Conversation with one of the two authors of the report, Mr Ishtiaq Ahmed.

58. Telephone conversation with Sofia Buncy, 17 March. Much of the analysis offered here draws from that conversation.

59. MCB, *British Muslims in Numbers*, pp. 36, 17.

60. Shelina Janmohamed, 'The trouble with marriage', *Emel*, 75 (December 2010). Janmohamed has developed these ideas in an engaging and amusing memoir, *Love in a Headscarf* (London: Aurum Press, 2014). Her blog is at www.spirit21.co.uk.

61. The enquiry highlighted the child sexual exploitation of over a thousand children by a number of mainly Pakistani heritage men which took place between 1997 and 2013.

62. *Stop this madness*, 13 November 2014, http://cllrshabbir.blogspot.co.uk. In this blog Shabbir adds that the continuing racism and Islamophobia translates into many lacking a sense of belonging and welcome that reinforces the desire to maintain family links with Pakistan.

63. Karmani helped develop the innovative work in the Brixton mosque in London profiled in Abdul Haqq Baker's monograph, *Extremists in our Midst: Confronting Terror* (Basingstoke: Palgrave Macmillan, 2010).

64. See 'Alyas Karmani is an imam and academic . . .', *The Times*, 4 November 2011.

65. 'Culture of shame aids groomers', 12 September 2014, http://sabbiyah.co.uk.

66. Ibid.

67. Ibid.

68. For example, 51 per cent of Pakistani boys and 60 per cent of Pakistani girls achieve five or more A* to C grades including English and Maths at GCSE, in comparison to the national average of 56 and 66 per cent for boys and girls, respectively. See Department for Education, *GCSE and Equivalent Attainment by Pupil Characteristics* (London: Department for Education, 2014), https://www.gov.uk/government/uploads/system/uploads/attachment_data/file/280698/SFR05_2014_National_and_LA_tables_updated.xls.

69. Fauzia Ahmad, 'Do young British Muslims need rescuing?', in Sadek Hamid (ed.), *British Muslim Youth: Between Rhetoric and Real Lives* (Abingdon: Taylor & Francis, 2016), p. 19.

70. Ibid. pp. 19–20.

71. Ziauddin Sardar, 'Men in Islam', *Critical Muslim*, 8 (October–December 2013), p. 5.
72. Ibid. p. 7. The following example is given of such scholarship: 'Yusuf al-Qaradawi – seen by many as one of the most influential Sunni clerics in the Middle East – told his television audience: "if they had gotten rid of the punishment for apostasy [death], Islam would not exist today". There is no moral qualm here; indeed, there is no notion of morality at all. To kill apostates is the most natural thing to do. It is after all part of God's design and law. Al-Qaradawi's sentiments would be echoed by conservative Muslim scholars from Saudi Arabia to Iran, Pakistan to Indonesia. And it is the same fear that is used to keep women in their prescribed position . . .'

2

The Islamic Seminary: Between Crisis and Renewal

Shaking the foundations

Historically the responsibility to transmit, interpret and apply the Islamic tradition lay with the religiously 'learned' – the *ulama*.[1] Their natural milieu was the city where illustrious scholars would attract students from across the Muslim world. Initially, such a network of teachers and students was 'personalised, fluid and unstructured' with students attending lessons in the scholar's home or mosque.[2] The learned were often traders and merchants, men of independent means. The professionalisation of the *ulama* only began in the eleventh century with the creation of a distinctive institution, the Islamic seminary, the madrasa.[3]

When Muslim migrants established themselves across Western Europe in significant numbers in the 1950s and 60s, they initially brought with them *ulama* trained in madrasas in their home countries. In Britain, the first madrasa was established by the mid-1970s.[4] Today, these have proliferated, with one South Asian 'school of thought' – the Deobandis – dominating the madrasa landscape in the UK.[5] The fact that an institution embodying 'a late medieval form of conservatism' has become entrenched in Britain is without parallel elsewhere in Europe.[6] It reminds us that no one is a Muslim-in-general and that Muslims in the UK are, to some extent, outliers in Western Europe.[7]

Such institutions face the daunting challenge of helping Muslims live Islamically as a minority in Western societies and managing, over time, ever widening inter-generational differences. This raises difficult issues for a majority of madrasas

which continue to look to a mother house in South Asia for
their exemplars in scholarship, curriculum and ethos. One contentious issue remains the language of instruction. To this day,
the majority of such madrasas continue to teach through the
medium of Urdu rather than English.

In addition, the madrasas have to operate within a context of
religious pluralism and secularism, where as a minority they cannot dictate the terms on which co-existence is regulated. Cities
such as London, Birmingham and Manchester are marked by a
super-diversity of ethnicities and religions, and a proliferation of
Muslim trends. Where perhaps two Islamic 'schools of thought'
enjoyed something approximating to a monopoly of influence
and expression in South Asia, in Britain their respective claims
to embody true Islam are relativised and contested, not least by
expressions of Islam imported from the Arab world and beyond.[8]
Perhaps no 'school of thought' has done more to inflame intra-
Muslim sectarianism than the Salafi – also referred to as Wahhabis
– whose influence has been projected world-wide by Saudi petrol
dollars, notorious both for their claim to be the one true sect saved
from Hell and their frequently disparaging comments about other
Muslims.[9]

Notwithstanding this ever increasing diversity of Muslim communities, a recent analysis of the 1700 mosques in the UK by
ethnicity and sectarian affiliation indicates that about 70 per cent
belong to one of two South Asian Sunni 'schools of thought': 43
per cent Deobandi (779) and 25 per cent Barelwi (447). However,
the biggest growth in the last few years has been in the Saudi-
oriented Salafi tradition, which although representing less than
10 per cent, now numbers some 155 mosques.[10] More than 80
per cent of the mosque committees draw exclusively from one
of three national communities: Pakistani, Bangladeshi or Indian.[11]

Madrasas have not been without their internal critics. Within
South Asia, Deobandi voices such as 'Ubayd Allah Sindhi (d. 1944)
and Manazir Ahsan Gilani (d. 1956) developed powerful critiques.
Sindhi, a convert from Sikhism, stressed the importance of taking local contexts much more seriously into account in applying
ancient texts; seeking common ground with non-Muslims; giving
attention to socio-economic justice: and the need for students to

learn English and the Western sciences. In all, he offered a 'more nuanced view of the West than the caricatures that many of his contemporaries traded in . . .'[12] Gilani – the author of a two-volume study of Islamic education in South Asia in both the medieval and modern world – sought to make room for new texts and new disciplines by thinning out the curriculum, insisting that there was 'nothing sacrosanct about much of what is taught in madrasas . . .'[13]

In South Asia such internal criticism proved 'a fragile enterprise' with critics marginalised.[14] In Britain, as we will discover, internal critics are increasing as the drivers for change multiply: whether because of the paucity of career prospects for madrasa graduates; the development of a safe space within the expanding chaplaincy sector for *ulama* to experiment and develop new skills; or the move of the more able into universities where they are assimilating new disciplines. Some are setting up new educational institutes where they seek to bridge the separate intellectual worlds of madrasa and university.

The madrasas are also exposed to a rising chorus of Muslim criticism from those educated outside their institutions. Two examples will provide the tenor of such criticism. An American Muslim academic researching Muslim youth in a northern city observed that many

> feel alienated from the messages espoused from the pulpit . . . sermons privileging Pakistani issues leave the youth with an abject lack of contextuality. Lamentations over the great and lost civilization, coupled with a continued contempt for the British believed to be responsible for the post-colonial Pakistani morass, leave the youth with little inspiration . . . [This translates into] cynicism and disdain . . . towards the mullahs . . .[15]

The response of Muslim professionals to such preaching is increasing exasperation. This is clear in the title of a recent essay 'Creating a society of sheep?' which, in addition to many of the above points, laments the 'masculinisation of mosques' – only 2 per cent women on mosque committees – and the persistence of 'de-contextualised and dehistoricised' male interpretations of sacred texts which 'diminish women's position in Islam'.[16] In South Asia – especially in Pakistan, where state educational provision is patchy and under-resourced – the madrasas

> still mostly attract the lower strata of society from a largely rural background. For those who see no other option of advancement, graduation from one of the major religious seminaries is key to upward mobility, the only way out of the narrow confines of their village and its poverty.[17]

In the UK, with state education universal and free, the future of the madrasas may well depend on their ability to modify and expand their curriculum, not least to guarantee a greater range of viable career options.

Some *ulama* are aware that British Muslims are looking for religious guidance outside the traditions imported by their parents and grandparents. Islamist, Salafi and neo-Sufi groups have long competed for their allegiance.[18] In addition, from the 1990s, it was not uncommon for British Muslims to spend time studying in the intellectual centres of the Muslim world in the Middle East and North Africa. Their search for an authentic Islam – as with American Muslims from similar backgrounds – frequently combined escapism and romanticisation of tradition with spiritual tourism. They were 'often nostalgic for a deeper history, in an Islamic east that is not an airplane ride away but an epoch away, when Islam was a global superpower, a thriving rich civilization'. These student travellers were fired by 'the hope of recovering their tradition's lost knowledge [its] lost dignity'.[19] On their return, they too have begun to establish their own independent centres.[20]

If the traditional madrasas are to maintain their share of the educational market they are faced with difficult decisions. In a majority Muslim context, they might turn to the government to limit and regulate such ever increasing diversity of Islamic expression, the role of Muslim empires and governments in the past.[21] This, of course, is not possible in Britain. Further, their historic claim to be 'heirs of the Prophet' – custodians and interpreters, *par excellence*, of the Islamic tradition – is increasingly being challenged. Not least by Muslim academics who teach Islamic Studies in Western universities. They are often the authorities with whom government prefers to consult in making policy or as spokespersons sought out by the media and civil society. Increasingly, these are women, as we will see in subsequent chapters.

So we are back with several troubling questions: do the madrasas have the confidence and intellectual capacity to develop a vision for Muslim communities living in Britain and the West? Is there any appetite to engage critically with modern academic disciplines? What role, if any, do they envisage for Muslims who are not trained in their specific knowledge traditions but have a range of other specialisms and expertise? Is it assumed that they will simply accept their religious guidance or will they be seen as active participants in a shared quest for solutions to pressing contemporary problems? In short, is there the desire and capacity to contextualise Islam in Britain?

The world of a traditional scholar (1): Mufti Saiful Islam

To understand how the Deobandi school of thought has been translated into Britain, we will consider the teaching of a young scholar who is among the first to be qualified as a legal specialist – a mufti – at their principal madrasa in Bury. We encountered Mufti Saiful Islam (b. 1974) in an earlier chapter delivering a legal decision – *fatwa* – on the contentious issue as to whether it was legally permitted for a young woman to travel alone to a distant city for the purpose of study or employment without a chaperone. His answer was a resounding negative.

His fatwa repeated, almost word for word, that on the same topic by probably the most celebrated contemporary Deobandi scholar in Pakistan, Justice Mufti Taqi Usmani.[22] This reminds us that the madrasa world does not value novelty and originality; indeed, legal innovation – *bid'a* – is to be avoided. What matters is continuity and precedent. 'Most Muslims believed that the best generation had been the Prophet's, and each successive generation had gone downhill from there.'[23] For the young mufti to repeat the word of a respected, older scholar from South Asia is not so different to the Salafis whose UK conferences invariably include a 'telelink' with a scholar from Saudi Arabia.[24] It is a sign of humility not plagiarism.

We will now turn to further fatwas given in Saiful Islam's book *Your Questions Answered* on a range of subjects, including family planning, attitude to modern science and how Muslims should conduct themselves with regard to wider society. The tone of this work and its urgency is captured by the comment on the back of the book:

> As time is passing by and we are drawing closer to the Last Day, we are witnessing our *ummah* ['community' of Muslims world-wide] in a state of crisis. Ignorance has prevailed, misguided 'so-called scholars' have emerged in great numbers issuing incorrect verdicts (fatwas) and misleading people, therefore *fitnah* (corruption) is spreading at an alarming rate.

The Deobandi tradition, to which the mufti belongs, emerged after the failure of the Indian mutiny in India in 1857. It was from the first 'oppositional in character, defining itself against the popular customs of the Sufi shrines, other ulama, and non-Muslims, Hindu and British . . . part of a sectarian environment often embroiled in what has been dubbed a fatwa-war.'[25] The ethos and teaching of many of the mufti's fatwas continue to carry the unmistakeable stamp of Deoband's historic origins.

Central to the Deobandi ethos is the necessity of *taqleed*, 'following' the legal tradition to which they adhere. Saiful Islam defines *taqleed* as 'to follow and accept an opinion and a legal verdict of a particular [scholar] without demanding proof and evidence from him who has attained the highest calibre and proficiency in the four sources [of Islamic law].'[26] The role of the enquirer, then, is to formulate the question and to accept the authority of the scholar. He or she is not envisaged as a participant in an ongoing conversation.

In response to the questions: 'Can you explain what Evolution is and how wrong Charles Darwin's theory is regarding man? What does the Holy Qur'an say about the beginning of life?' Saiful Islam's answer is unmistakeably creationist. The mufti asks rhetorically: 'Did a one-celled being evolve into an ape-like creature and man evolved from him or was man as he is now, from the beginning?' and concludes triumphantly with a quotation for the Quran (15:26–9) to support his contention that 'who else would know about the origin of man if not the Creator who was there at the time and created man with His Hands?'[27]

The mufti is here drawing on the writings of the Turkish writer Adnan Oktar, known by his pen name, Harun Yahya, a creationist hugely influential across the Muslim world. Through a foundation Oktar set up in 1991, he has more than '150 books published under his name in over a dozen languages, well-produced but cheaply sold magazines [and] audio-visual material . . . often distributed free'.[28] Saiful Islam's bookshop includes many such titles. The mufti's stance is not eccentric. A Muslim specialist points to the 'calamitous state of science' in the Muslim world today, where fifty-seven Muslim countries in the Organisation of Islamic Conference (OIC) contribute a mere 1 per cent of articles to mainstream scientific journals. The central reason he advances for this state of affairs is the absence of 'a culture that appreciates learning and inquiry and encourages curiosity and criticism'. This he explains is the result, in part, of being embedded in a contemporary religious culture awash with spurious ideas about 'scientific miracles'. When Muslim theologians 'talk about science at all it is all about how everything from electricity to relativity can be "discovered" in the Qur'an'.[29]

Saiful Islam in another answer, this time to the query whether family planning is allowed, is equally uncompromising:

> poverty or fear of poverty is not a valid reason for contraception, nor is it permissible to practice contraception on account of not being able to provide for a large family. According to the Holy Qur'an, 'There is not a living creature, but its provision is the responsibility of Allah . . .' (11:6) . . . [Nor is contraception] permitted on the basis that it is fashionable to have small families. The fashion to have small families is the practice of other nations. The Holy Prophet said, 'Whosoever imitates a group

becomes one of them.' In addition, a small family is in direct conflict with the instruction of the Holy Prophet who said, 'Marry those women who are affectionate and reproduce in abundance ... verily, I will compete with you (your large numbers) over the other nations on the Day of Judgement.[30]

This is a somewhat coded way of saying that to copy non-Muslim Britons and have small families is to become like them, hell-bound unbelievers. The second comment makes sense when we recall that, in a pre-modern world, large numbers equate to power. The mufti seems totally unaware of how such comments might be construed by non-Muslims. The mufti also has a section on the pros and cons of polygamy: he is clear that taking a second wife is not to be undertaken lightly and must be conditional on justice. To illuminate what this might entail, he cites a Quranic verse: 'You will never be able to maintain perfect justice (i.e. in terms of natural affection) between wives however much you desire to do so, so do not incline too much to one of them (by giving her more of your time and provision) ...' (4:129).[31] The mufti seems unconcerned that in Britain polygamy is illegal. Such insouciance is not confined to this tradition – amongst Salafis in the UK polygamy is 'not uncommon'.[32] The mufti also recycles intra-Muslim sectarianism. The opening chapter on 'belief' locates the work firmly within the bitter Deobandi-Barelwi sectarian environment of South Asia. It challenges views shared by most Barelwi Sunnis, for example, that the Prophet has knowledge of 'the unseen', reflects God's light and is omnipresent.[33]

Throughout the book, the impression given is that Islam is a self-contained world. Typical is the following comment:

Islamic lifestyle has no parallel. Islam provides moral guidance to every aspect of human life and gives the solution to our daily problematic issues. The Holy Prophet is an exemplary role model for the whole of mankind. *So the question arises, why is there any need for Muslims to emulate the conduct of others?*[34]

The answer to this rhetorical question is clear. In contrast, wider, non-Muslim society assumes the appearance of an assault course with trip wires everywhere to embarrass the devout: at school or in offices the unsuspecting male might be expected to shake hands with the opposite sex; socialising with Muslims – not to speak of non-Muslims – is best avoided because of doubts over whether the food is properly halal, as well as the possibility that alcohol might be available. In a society where interest is everywhere, Muslims must avoid any interest-bearing account and avoid working in most financial institutions. 'One must decide between temporary worldly gains and the curse and anger of Allah . . .'[35]

There is also little warrant here for relating to people of other faiths. Indeed, the mufti seems worried about the inroads of religious and cultural practices associated with Christianity. In a booklet entitled *The Prophet Jesus* unbelievers condemned to eternal hellfire include those who 'say Jesus is Son of God'. Buying or accepting Christmas presents, putting up Christmas decorations and sending Christmas cards are all alike 'forbidden'.[36] The overall logic of the book, as with many Salafis, is to create a parallel world – as far as this is possible – minimising interaction with non-Muslims. A worldview obsessed with maintaining theological purity and social boundaries.

The world of a traditional scholar (2): Shaykh Shams Ad Duha Muhammad

Mufti Saiful Islam – whose heritage is Sylheti Bengali – lives and works within a relatively closed, ethno-Muslim community in Bradford. Shaykh Shams Ad Duha (b. 1976), from the same ethnic and Deobandi background, has had to develop his teaching in the radically different context of hyper-diverse London. Another difference is that where Saiful Islam pursued advanced studies at the Bury madrasa to become a mufti, Shams Ad Duha chose to pursue an MA in Islamic Studies at Birkbeck College, University of London.

After spending more than eight years in Deobandi seminaries in Dewsbury, Nottingham and Bangladesh, he returned to East London in 1998 where he taught in a local mosque, then at a secondary school in 2001. Aware of a serious shortage of scholars who understood the British context, he and a number of friends established Ebrahim College in 2003 to develop a madrasa programme which contextualised Islam in Britain. The college also began to offer part-time courses for busy professionals on different aspects of Islam; its online courses now reach some three thousand students. As director of the college, Shams is responsible for developing its courses, contributes to teaching, writes for their magazine – *Islamique* – and preaches, with many of his sermons and talks uploaded to YouTube.

In adapting curriculum materials to address the 'cultural dissonance' with the world of British Muslims, the shaykh labours under no illusions as to the challenges ahead and speaks of it as a 'work-in-progress'.[37] He has had to rein in his impatience to keep traditional Muslims on board. His rationale for many of the changes introduced at the college was that even on their own terms the madrasas were not delivering. For example, in the three Deobandi madrasas he attended, he was aware that few of his teachers could speak Arabic well, whether Quranic or modern; the work of translation was also deeply flawed since most of the students did not have an adequate grasp of Urdu or English. So Ebrahim College privileges learning of Arabic, the precondition to access texts directly rather than through Urdu translations.

Located within a global city, Shams realised the college could no longer limit itself to studying the Sunni, Hanafi legal tradition preferred in South Asia. Similarly, traditional methods of teaching principles of jurisprudence though learning precedents without understanding by what criteria such precedents were selected would no longer do. For example, most madrasas taught a famous twelfth century Hanafi legal text – *Hidaya* (Guidance) – without locating it within a developing historical tradition. This pointed to a fundamental weakness in the madrasa education, to which we will return, namely, a lack of serious historical study. Too often revered texts floated free of history and context, effectively sacralised and studied though a self-referential tradition of commentary and super commentary.

A number of radical departures from madrasa practice have been introduced. English has replaced Urdu as the medium of instruction. This is for a number of reasons. English is the language of most British-born Muslims in London, irrespective of their ethnicity; Urdu carries with it historical and cultural baggage specific to South Asia that can isolate British Muslims from an engagement with wider society, exemplified, for example, in the 'strong repugnance toward Western Learning' which Pakistan's Deobandi luminary, Justice Mufti Taqi Usmani exhibits.[38] In all, Urdu's continued use would limit the appeal of the college.

A second departure is in the attitude to the outside world. Historically, this has been marked by suspicion. Muslim researchers, male and female alike, have commented on the difficulty of gaining access to madrasas.[39] Few journalists or academics manage to circumvent the control of the gatekeepers.[40] Ebrahim College embodies a very different ethos, both open to outsiders and prepared to partner with the Oxford-based Centre for Christian-Muslim Studies in running summer schools to provide an opportunity for clergy and imams in training to study together.

The third major departure from madrasa practice was that all courses, over time, have become co-educational. This latter meant negotiating a number of sensitivities, for example, ultra-conservative women were not enamoured of the prospect of being taught by men and vice versa. The result has been a blend of principle and pragmatism. Women attend lectures in a variety of dress codes from face-veil (niqab), to scarf (hijab), to those who choose not to wear any head covering. Occasionally, lectures have had to be done via video links. The shaykh wanted women to have the same opportunity to study as men – too often, women-only provision in madrasas represents a thinned-out male curriculum studied in less depth and with less intellectual rigour.[41] At Ebrahim College, some 60 per cent of madrasa students are now women, and the male teachers have been won over by their sheer quality. Co-education, of course, remains anathema to traditional, South Asian scholars such as Judge Mufti Taqi Usmani.[42]

While Saiful Islam seems willing to recycle an imported, intra-Muslim sectarianism, for Shams Ad Duha such sectarianism is to be vigorously combated. This is the focus of two articles in the college magazine, *Islamique* – 'Let's agree to disagree'. He insists that in such cities as London, characterised by diversity

'unprecedented in most Muslim countries', it is critical for the
health and future well-being of Muslim communities that they
learn to live well with such diversity. However, he regrets the
fact that the 'principles and etiquette' for dealing with such differences, although present in the Islamic tradition, are not an
'integral part' of madrasa training.[43] These he seeks to retrieve
and exemplify.

Such a task is urgent given the 'chaos' at street level, where
'fights break out . . . hatred brews below the surface [and] Muslims
look at each other in bewilderment each considering the other to
be either ignorant or arrogant'. Such intolerance is predicated on
'the idea that there is a single, true Islam',[44] a position increasingly
common in Pakistan and many Muslim countries where appeals
to coercion to impose this true Islam can increasingly be heard.[45]

Shams Ad Duha displays a similar candour and courage in two
sermons – both on YouTube – where he addresses other taboo
subjects: *Young Muslims Leaving Islam – Causes and Solutions* and
the related topic *How to Deal with Doubt*. These topics entered
the public domain with an article in *The Observer* – 'Losing their
religion: the hidden crisis of faith among Britain's young Muslims'
and a follow up television programme.

The Observer article quoted from a criminologist's study to the
effect that 'In the Western context, the biggest risk ex-Muslims
face is not the baying mob, but the loneliness and isolation of
ostracism from loved ones. It is stigma and rejection that causes
so many ex-Muslims to conceal their apostasy.' The author of the
article commented that: 'Like the gay liberation movement of a
previous generation, Muslim apostates have to fight for the right
to be recognized while knowing that recognition brings shame,
rejection, and intimidation and, very often, family expulsion.'
Shams Ad Duha stressed that 'apostasy' was a real problem that has
to be named. He mentioned his own experience of attending an
inter-faith gathering, at which a young Muslim declared he was
leaving Islam because of the problem of evil which he could not
square with the existence of God. Shams continued that for such
Muslims the formulaic repetition of a Quranic verse – 'there is no
compulsion in Islam' – was belied by the fact that their lives were
'made hell to force them to come back'.

In the related talk, he spoke of the need to take seriously expressions of doubt. Most young Muslims, after all, were looking for answers and did not want to leave.[46] He gave the example of another young man, who told him that there are lots of young people like him looking for answers but there seemed to be 'no places to go to ask questions in private, safely and with security'. Too often, he said, the community response was to attempt to silence him with 'fear of hellfire'. This would hardly do, the shaykh insisted, given that they were struggling with the question of God's existence! A second response was to put an arm around the individual and suppose that such affection would win over his doubts. However, such a well-intentioned but patronising response simply side-stepped the questions. In all, Shams Ad Duha, instead of blaming those who had left Islam, lambasted the community for its multiple failures – not least the lack of safe spaces where matters of doubt could be addressed with the seriousness they deserved.

Where Mufti Saiful Islam continues to look to South Asian scholars for inspiration, Shams Ad Duha, through the medium of English, is able to draw on a wide range of visiting Muslim scholars. Recent speakers include American professors Jonathan Brown and Ebrahim Moosa. Shams commends Brown's new study – *Misquoting Muhammad: the Challenge and Choices of Interpreting the Prophet's Legacy* – which, along with his website, addresses the multiple interpretive dilemmas for contemporary Muslims who seek to be faithful to the teaching of Quran and Prophetic Sunna; namely, what to do about child marriage, wife beating, draconian apostasy laws and slavery, whose proponents appeal to such sources, not least as expanded and embedded in Islamic law.

Exhortations to follow – *taqleed* – the traditional teaching of the historic schools of law increasingly lack conviction. The situation requires renewed, intellectual effort (*ijtihad*) to develop and popularise the interpretive skills necessary to make sense of such difficult texts in the modern world.[47] This is also the burden of an important study by the other visiting lecturer, Professor Ebrahim Moosa, *What is a Madrasa?* Moosa has long argued that early texts reflect an expansive imperial mind-set which frequently trumps Quranic ethical imperatives.[48] Such texts, however revered, have to be contextualised to detect and correct such biases, whether imperial, sectarian or patriarchal.

In all, the director of Ebrahim College stresses the importance of both the disciplines of history and philosophy for students of Islam. He consistently argues for engagement with wider society to develop the resilience needed to respond confidently to the many challenges British Muslims face rather than succumb to a sense of grievance and despair – a psychological precondition for the appeal of ISIS's end time narrative.[49] He is also keenly aware of a huge deficit in Islamic literacy among British Muslims and acknowledges the responsibility of the *ulama* in colluding with such ignorance. The traditional expectation that educated Muslims will simply defer to them will no longer do. However, he is also aware of the huge pressure created by government, the media and wider society that a renewed Islamic literacy should converge with the norms of liberal society. In reality, he insists, Muslims and policymakers cannot second guess the outcome of such re-thinking.

Mufti Saiful Islam and Shaykh Shams Ad Duha exemplify two discrete emphases which have emerged from within the Deobandi tradition transplanted into Britain. One we might characterise as 'conservative traditionalist', the other 'critical traditionalist'. The former is largely content to rehearse and re-enact the teachings of revered scholars from South Asia and, to this end, privilege Urdu as the language of instruction. The latter, though the medium of English, is able to access new Islamic thinking developed in the West, drawing on the full range of academic disciplines. As will become clear, despite the emergence of a critical traditionalist stream, conservative traditionalism continues to dominate the madrasa landscape.

Inside a British madrasa: curriculum, ethos and impact

Hamid Mahmood completed his training at a Deobandi madrasa in Dewsbury, West Yorkshire in 2005. Returning to London, he set about earning a living to support his family. This entailed holding down four poorly paid, part-time teaching jobs in a variety of

Muslim institutions.[50] Aware that he could not sustain this style of work indefinitely, he convinced Heythrop College, University of London to allow him to access the undergraduate degree course in Abrahamic Studies. Doing well in his first degree, he went on to complete an MA in Islamic History at another University of London college, Queen Mary's.

Mahmood's MA thesis provides a unique insight into the history, curriculum, ethos and impact on graduates of Deobandi madrasas in the UK. At its heart are interviews with twelve graduates who, like him, had completed their graduation some six to seven years earlier. He wanted to establish what career paths they subsequently pursued, the extent to which the curriculum helped them face the challenges of contemporary life and what reforms, if any, they considered necessary.

Seven of the twelve had found employment in mosques, five had gone on to get additional qualifications, mostly degrees. One had become a telecoms analyst, another a health-care chaplain who had attended the Olympics in this capacity, the rest were teachers. Only one of the twelve thought reforms were unnecessary. Predictably, those who had moved out of the mosque culture were most searching in their criticisms of the curriculum for not equipping them to understand, still less engage, wider society. With one exception, all valued the extent to which the madrasa had rooted them in the Islamic tradition.

One graduate stated that 'the lack of career opportunities and lack of recognised qualification' left him feeling 'helpless and paralysed', unable to support his family. As with Hamid, he was not the only graduate who worried about supporting his family. Because those working in mosques were poorly paid, many had to find 'part time jobs such as working as retailers, B&Q, Asda, and taxi drivers' to eke out a living. This was poor recompense for eight or nine years intense study, and unsurprisingly generated some bewilderment and resentment.

Another graduate had started an organisation to provide mosque personnel with basic practical knowledge as to how British bureaucracy worked, such as accessing 'tax credits, filling in forms, paying the bills'. A majority wanted what amounted to an exclusive study of texts to be complemented with practical skills, especially teaching, communication and management competences; the languages of instruction to be English and Arabic, rather than Urdu; and a balance between religious and secular subjects. The telecoms analyst, in retrospect, was critical of the 'very narrow world-view' inculcated by teachers with little exposure to wider society outside 'their ideological comfort zones'. He was not alone in pressing for a greater focus on academic excellence, an educational culture of appraisals and 'written independent research', as well as recruiting on the basis of merit rather than the personal contacts.

The teacher of religious education and Arabic at secondary school offered the most detailed series of reforms which included the study of Western philosophy, history and culture; compulsory A levels in Maths, English, Sciences and Arabic, as well as a 'deep study of world religions'. Moreover, the madrasa, instead of pushing its graduates into becoming imams and mosque teachers, should encourage them into 'teaching professions, counseling, journalism, law, social enterprise [and] chaplaincy' which would also 'encourage integration'. Most tellingly, he complained the madrasa 'totally lacks' the capacity to enable its students to 'critically analyse theories and concepts from an Islamic perspective'.

For another graduate, students exhibit 'no independent analysis' but are encouraged to 'regurgitate ideas given to them via archaic books that they have memorized without question'. In short, the educational culture generates conformism allowing no place for 'dissent and originality'. This, in part, is rooted in a tradition where the relationship of teacher and student is more akin to 'master and follower'. In such a culture, independent study of the Quran is tantamount to having 'committed a sin'.[51]

This last comment takes us to the heart of the matter. The style of teaching and curriculum has a quite distinctive ethos, however uncongenial to some of its graduates. This is clear in the wording of Hamid's certificate awarded on completion of his studies where he is reminded to follow in 'the steps of the pious predecessors . . . to avoid religious innovations, and to hold on to Islam as it was for centuries'. This continuity with a revered past is embodied in the personal style of teaching where the student is authorised (*ijaza*) to teach a particular text having sat at the feet of a scholar who, in turn, traces his own authority to teach that text back to accredited teachers in an unbroken chain (*isnad*) often reaching back across the centuries to the Prophet and his companions.

Hamid provides an invaluable window into the etiquette of study which he characterises as 'textual piety'. The student reads the section of the prescribed text prior to his lesson with his teacher. The latter then checks that he has read the text correctly, provides a commentary on the lines read, which the student memorises or writes down. In the evening, in groups of about four, a student repeats the teacher's interpretation and the others listen attentively, occasionally adding something from their notes. Such repetition is thought to embed the lesson in the heart. Once they have mastered the text, which is to say, are able to repeat the teacher's interpretation, they will move on to a more difficult text.

Now, of course, this emphasis on memorisation and face-to-face education is deeply rooted in an oral culture which has persisted well into the modern era. As late as 1800, 'literacy rates' in the Middle East were between 1 and 2 per cent of the population and even lower in most of the Asian and sub-Saharan regions.[52] Before the impact of printing on the Muslim world in the nineteenth century, manuscripts remained expensive and out of reach of most students. Such works had to be carefully checked by someone with authoritative knowledge of the text. Even today, especially in Pakistan, orality rather than literacy remains the norm for the majority.[53]

Hamid highlights a number of further weaknesses: the students continue to study individual books without locating them within a developing historical tradition. This 'style of learning is one which follows on from the atomistic style of interpreting the Qur'an verse by verse . . . a recognisable feature of medieval exegetes'.[54] The student's task is to reproduce the wisdom of the past rather than to question it. This was already a problem for Ebrahim Moosa, thirty years earlier, when studying at a Deobandi madrasa in India. He found that to challenge sharia practices 'involving gruesome amputations and floggings' would be to invite 'denunciation and charges of anathema' since they were supported by the consensus of the past scholars.[55]

Other weaknesses concern the topics covered and the limited range of texts chosen to illustrate them. Deoband traces its syllabus back to that of a famous eighteenth-century Indian scholar, Mullah Nizamuddin (d. 1748), hence its name the *Dars-i Nizami* (the Nizami curriculum). However, Nizamuddin operated within the context of the Mughal Empire and selected 'classical texts for an educational syllabus that produced highly skilled and literate scholars, bureaucrats, writers and intellectuals' to staff the empire.[56] Deoband's context was different: India was now part of the British Empire and Muslim elites looked for education in the new colleges founded or supported by the British. As a result Deoband retrenched and shed much of this more expansive curriculum to focus on the Hadith, following the reformist scholar Shah Wali Ullah (d. 1762). 'Ptolemaic astronomy, Galen medicine, and Aristotelian physics', however, were still taught.[57]

Hamid, in his analysis of the curriculum of a sample of four British Deobandi madrasas, points out that most time is spent on mastering the Arabic language. After which, pride of place goes to the study of the Hadith to which the entire last year is devoted. In addition, substantial time is spent on Hanafi law and jurisprudence. The key legal text is the twelfth-century *Hidaya* (Guidance), which takes for granted that in a range of legal cases, 'the evidence required is of two men or of one man and two women'. The formula that one man equals two women has been extrapolated from a Quranic verse dealing with a particular issue and generalised to encompass all legal cases.[58]

By contrast, there is hardly any study of Islamic history and minimal study of Quranic commentary. The chosen text was written by two fifteenth-century scholars in Egypt and known as *The Interpretation of the Two Jalals* – both shared the same first name.[59] It has been characterised as a short, 'no-frills' accessible text, 'avoiding controversial material that might be slanted to a mystical or philosophical interpretation'.[60]

Hamid was also frustrated with the lack of any study of modern disciplines. He quotes from a lecture on 'Islam and the International Monetary System' delivered by an Islamic economist at a Deobandi madrasa in South Africa. Its author bewails the fact that 'the Muftis are giving fatwas without knowledge of international monetary economics.'[61] Hamid drily comments, in light of his own experience, that it is 'difficult to understand how a close and focused reading of texts explaining medieval transactions and business laws help the student in an ever-changing economy of the 21st century.'[62] Hamid's experience is far from idiosyncratic. The doyen of 'Islamic Economics', Professor Muhammad Nejatullah Siddiqui, distilling a lifetime of research and lecturing in Islamic universities and madrasas across the Muslim world observes that:

> Our current methods of teaching crush all independent thinking, extinguish any flicker of curiosity and kill all creativity. The absence of empirical work makes our researches hollow. We are entirely focused on texts to the total neglect of observing ground realities and learning lessons history can teach.[63]

Hamid partly roots the emergence of such a fossilised tradition in the trauma of colonisation. This generated a defensive mind-set with the madrasa re-imagined as an 'ideological fortress . . . [with] defensive, impenetrable walls that would allow no ideological explosives to breach its fortifications . . . [Its] pedagogy was devised to protect Islam as opposed to allow its natural evolution.' Within its defensive walls, the *ulama* saw change not as a legitimate, evolving historical process, which must be understood and faced, but of 'conspiracies' to be resisted.[64] Professor Moosa also noted that amongst the madrasa circles he studied in in Indo-Pakistan many 'believe that real-world events are shrouded in complex conspiracies . . . anyone who does not see the world through this distorted glass of conspiracies is either a stooge of American propaganda or worse, a sell out.'[65] Hamid is committed to challenging such a mind-set. He supported young British Muslims going on pro-Gaza demonstrations to protest Israeli policy as a safety-valve for legitimate anger in the community. However, he was saddened when a leading imam opposed their participation at the rally since it involved gender-mixing. For the imam, correct gender relations trumped the importance of allowing a democratic channel for pent-up frustrations and the peaceful expression of political dissent.

As a result of his own experience, Hamid has established his own after-school madrasa, since none of the many in his area of

London, Walthamstow, embodied the ethos and curriculum he wanted for his own daughter. He named it 'Fatima Elisabeth' after one of the earliest English Muslim women. This signals his aspiration to embody the best of English and Islamic cultures. To this end, the medium of instruction is English, and among its many activities is a literary club to familiarise children with English literature. It is unapologetically non-sectarian and seeks to allow plenty of space for curiosity and questioning.

Measuring the impact of Islamic education: a space for experience and exploration?

In 2010, Dr Abdullah Sahin developed the first MEd in Islamic Education in Britain. His pioneering work, which addresses deficits in madrasa religious formation, is informed by his studies as an Islamic educator in three different contexts. Turkish by nationality, he studied Islamic theology for five years at the Divinity School of the University of Ankara – a 'highly modernized urban, secular context'.[66] For his PhD in the School of Education at the University of Birmingham he researched how Muslim sixth-form students – mainly with roots in South Asia – developed their religious identities within a secular and plural context. After completing his doctorate, he went on to research the same issue of religious identity formation in a wealthy Arab country, Kuwait.

These very different contexts made him aware of a shared crisis in religious formation in Islamic institutions across the Muslim world which impacted the nature of Islamic identity and religiosity nurtured in young Muslims. He concluded bleakly that 'a rigid Islamic identity has come to engulf the worldwide Muslim society . . . (rendering it) *incapable of conducting proper dialogue either with its past or its surrounding reality.*'[67] At the heart of the problem was a style of Islamic education he characterised as 'an instruction-centered and rigid inculcation process that largely ignores the personal agency of the learner'.[68] Hamid's research exemplifies the limitations of such a model of education.

It is helpful to review the main findings of Dr Sahin's case study of British Muslims in three majority Muslim inner-city schools in

Birmingham. His aim was to attend to 'the actual experience of Muslim youth by investigating their ways of interpreting, finding meaning in and living out their religion.'[69] He then rehearses the reasons for the initial resistance to aspects of the MEd programme among some of the *ulama* and how he addressed such opposition. His Birmingham research demonstrated that religious identity was constructed along two axes of commitment and exploration which yielded a number of religious subjectivities: 'a *diffused* mode, where neither commitment nor exploration is present; a *foreclosed* mode, where there is a strong commitment that is not informed by the exploration process; and an *exploratory* mode, where there is strong exploration but no real commitment.'[70] One significant conclusion was that 'male participants reflected a predominantly foreclosed mode of religious subjectivity, while female participants fell largely under the exploratory mode. There was also a significant number of young people in the diffused mode, who were losing interest in religious issues...'.[71] In the Kuwait study, as in Birmingham, most of the exploratory type of religiosity was observed among the female participants.[72]

Dr Sahin exemplifies each of the three categories. 'Arif' embodies the *diffused* mode. An eighteen-year-old student, he chafed at the restrictions his devout parents imposed on him with regard to going out and mixing with non-Muslim friends. He was more relaxed about gender interaction at college than some of his Muslim friends. He struggled academically at college, hinting that there was inadequate support as he tried to juggle two learning cultures: 'an authoritarian mode at home and being left to learn on his own at school'. Arif had a strong emotional attachment to basic Islamic teaching, but, lacking personal commitment, did not practice. God was perceived 'to be a punishing figure who did not act either rationally or compassionately in His relationship with humans ... a fearsome judge'. This led to alienation and guilt. When asked whether he would consider consulting an imam to help him navigate the many different demands on him, Arif replied: 'Definitely not ... I used to go to the mosque. Everybody used to get beaten ... for not pronouncing Arabic words correctly ... They do not understand what is happening to us ... they would not listen to us at all.' Arif, like many in this category,

wanted to preserve Islam as a cultural marker that enabled them
to resist being assimilated into what was dubbed 'white culture'.[73]

'Hasan' exemplified a *foreclosed* identity. His Islamic understanding was an extension of that of his parents shaped by the
revivalist Deobandi movement, *Tablighi Jamaat*.[74] He exhibited no
real effort to 'interpret [the tradition] differently or in personal
ways'. Although living in a diverse society, he spent most of his
time within his own community and did not have experience
with or interest in exploring other cultures. 'He made an effort
to keep a certain distance from other cultures, and religion was
used as the key element justifying this isolationist policy.' Hasan
explained that he was not encouraged to question or think deeply
about complex topics. 'Only with such an unquestioning mode . . .
could he gain Allah's blessing.'

Given their 'conception of a punishing God', the foreclosed
spent 'most of their time calculating good and bad points . . . gained
in daily life in a nearly obsessive-compulsive manner'. Accumulat-
ing such religious merit was seen as essential in influencing one's
destiny in the Hereafter. A religiosity aptly described as a 'calcula-
tor mentality'.[75] For the foreclosed, 'there was no place for ambi-
guity and uncertainty in religion.' This stance went along with
a passionate conviction of 'the superiority of Islam against other
religious traditions and the secular liberalism of modernity.'[76] It
also assumed an unbridgeable chasm between them.

'Aisha' embodies the *exploratory* identity. She has studied other
religions at college which has acted as a trigger to learn more
about Islam, as well as recognising common elements enabling
co-operation around 'social justice and human rights'. Confronted
with Muslim diversity where she lived, she did not understand
why her family could not pray in other mosques: 'I know that they
accuse each other [of] being Wahhabi, Sufi, Salafi, as if the word
Muslim is not enough.'[77] As a young woman she felt her parents
did not understand the challenges of living well with the cultural
diversity to which she was daily confronted. Her parents wanted
her to wear the headscarf. However, she balked at wearing it at
school: 'It just felt weird and did not go with what I was doing
with my friends; I wear it at home but rarely outside when I am
with my friends.'

Like the young people Shaykh Shams Ad Duha spoke about in the previous section, Aisha simply wanted the 'space and time' to think through issues. She was troubled by aspects of Islam that appeared to suggest a culture of gender inequality where a man 'can marry four women ... from different religions ... but a Muslim girl cannot marry a non-Muslim man. I wanted to discuss these teachings, but I could not get any explanation from [my parents] ... They just said, "This is religion, you cannot question ...".' Aisha was aware that her parents frequently confused religion with culture. She longed for a 'faith ... that could accommodate discussion, argumentation and, above all else, her psychosocial and gendered reality'.[78]

Dr Sahin was prompted to develop his MEd for Islamic educators as he became aware that most *ulama* were themselves foreclosed, exposed to an authoritarian and rigid process of knowledge transmission. He worried that if the *ulama* could not engage and encourage the exploratory aspiration of some of the students, they – along with those within the diffused category – could 'easily regress back into a foreclosed Islamic subjectivity ... that blocks their personal development and hinders them from relating meaningfully to wider society.'[79] His case study in Birmingham was completed before 9/11. Developments since 9/11, 7/7 and now ISIS have deepened his conviction that the diffused and foreclosed types of religiosity are a necessary – if not sufficient – predisposition which explains why some young people are attracted to the siren voices of religious extremism. A cursory acquaintance with the relevant literature indicates how some young people can flip very quickly from diffused or foreclosed identities to endorsing violent extremism.[80]

Sahin worries that without the intellectual tools to engage and reason with the Islamic tradition in the light of contemporary conditions, young people will assume the growing default position of Muslims across the world: namely, seeking 'to replicate certain historical constructions of Islam without giving any consideration to the radically different conditions of contemporary life.'[81] This is an approach to Islamic learning exemplified by many Salafis for whom correct religious teaching is regarded as the transmission of authentic information drawn from the original sources which cannot be questioned; 'it can only be retrieved, read out, explained, memorized, and applied.'[82] This understanding of Islam as standing outside history obliterates 'the distinction between *interpretation* and *revelation*'.[83]

In reality, sacred texts and their reception across the generations is never a passive process, presupposing a fixed content to be implemented in any socio-historical context. The danger of pretending to operate with an unchanging tradition is to conflate and identify a particular construction of the past with the way things have always been. This results in the world view and practices of Al-Shabab in Somalia, Boko Haram in Nigeria, the Taliban in Afghanistan and Pakistan, as well as Al-Qaeda and ISIS. A Muslim legal specialist observes with regard to such practices:

> In enslaving non-Muslims and executing and immolating captured Muslims and non-Muslims, the Islamic State, claims to be applying the norms followed by the early Muslim community in its wars in the 7th century; but even granting that the early Muslim communities did enslave some of its captives and execute others, their practice *at that time* was in accord with prevailing customary standards of war that applied to both sides in any conflict, and thus are more accurately understood to be reflections of the customary law of war in the 7th century rather than reflection of the permanent Islamic rules of warfare.[84]

Dr Sahin was aware that if Muslims are to avoid such dangers, the MEd must provide an Islamic educator in mosque, school or madrasa with the historical and contextual skills to make sense of revered texts, as well as quarrying the rich archive of Islamic scholarship to discover new insights relevant for the modern world; all this in dialogue with the best of contemporary scholarship. This is what Sahin attempts in his MEd with modules grounded in an expansive engagement with the peaks of Islamic scholarship, past and present, an imaginative and critical re-reading of the Quran and Sunna, in a sustained engagement with the best of contemporary educational thinking. His model of 'Islamic education' is compelling and multi-faceted. He defines it as a lifelong critical and dialogical process of personal and social transformation. The educational process aims to facilitate growth into an intelligent and mature faithfulness, whereby recognition of the Creator fulfils the art of being human and brings about a just and balanced faithful society, where human dignity and difference are respected and protected.[85]

His monograph, drawing on his study diary, includes fascinating material which identifies the challenges he had to overcome in the first years of teaching the MEd. For many of the young, British-trained *ulama* Islamic education was routinely associated 'with an uncritical study framework where the reverence attached to the subject, literally prevents enquiry and analysis.' A South Asian student on the course comments: 'Islamic education . . . always meant listening carefully to the lectures, memorising lots of information . . . I have never thought as a Muslim teacher, I would be expected to prepare students to question and think for themselves . . .' In such traditional religious formation they were

> not encouraged to examine the [Islamic] sources or put the diverse Islamic sciences into their historical context . . . Moreover, there was no recognition that people could receive and make sense of the same timeless faith content differently [and discern new meanings for today]. Religious knowledge, due to its sacred character was sent directly by the Creator and assumed to have been received unmediated through successive generations of Muslims . . .

In all, there was a deep psychological resistance and insecurity among the young Muslim faith leaders in conducting inquiries into the original texts and in engaging with the foundational sources. They exhibited 'a pious reverence towards the texts and their authors rather than actual exploration of ideas and meanings within texts.' Indeed, students had to be reassured that such questioning had an honoured place in the Islamic tradition itself.

Over time, they began to imbibe Sahin's well worked out Quranic educational hermeneutics. This demanded an 'open, listening and

guiding attitude' to teaching young people who are 'naturally curious and full of questions'. His method, rooted in Quranic material,
was one of 'critical faithfulness'. Over time, his students began to
value the new insights and skills he was generating. Furnished with a
new self-confidence, they have become his ambassadors. It is no surprise that Shaykh Shams Ad Duha has sent two of his key educators
to complete the MEd programme.[86]

Contextualising Muslim leadership: Islamic chaplaincy

Chaplaincy to institutions, whether hospitals, prisons, the armed
forces or educational institutions, has deep roots in British society.
Initially, this service was provided by different Christian denomi-
nations, then progressively extended to incorporate practitioners
of other religions settled in the UK, first the Jewish community
and latterly Muslims. However, the very notion of chaplaincy
presupposes a distinctive, Christian concept of pastoral care. This
means that Muslim chaplains have to adjust to a radically new
institutional culture.

This is clear from an excellent study of Muslim chaplaincy by
two Muslim academics who identify the challenges. They point
out that there is 'no formal tradition of institutionalized pastoral
care in Islamic societies'.[87] Further, the public ethos of the institution means that they are expected to work with people of all faiths
– not least as colleagues – and co-operate with Muslim chaplains
from other legal traditions. To function in such an environment
requires 'an ability to think and act in new ways'.[88] In short, they
are enacting, however provisionally, new legal thinking (*ijtihad*).

This they illustrate with many telling examples. Most schools
of Islamic law deem physical contact between unrelated men and
women as forbidden. A newly appointed chaplain, acting according to this norm, refuses eye contact or to shake hands with female,
non-Muslim colleagues. This is interpreted 'as discriminatory and
misogynist, and formal disciplinary action was taken against him'.
The senior chaplain advises him to allow the avoidance of a collective sin – colluding in a portrayal of 'a negative and bigoted
picture of Islam' – to trump the personal sin entailed by such an

action. The authors observe that 'those who feel unable to make such compromises rarely stay in chaplaincy'.

Differences between legal schools can also impact institutional behaviour. So what to do about dogs checking visitors to prison for drugs? For the Hanafi legal school, a dog's saliva is deemed impure, not so for the Maliki tradition. In such a situation, 'certain prisons are investing in disposable aprons that they put on visitors so that the dog does not touch their clothing'. What is to happen when one legal tradition disallows a person to say funeral prayers for the deceased in the absence of a body? The chaplain, according to the Hanafi tradition, should not allow a prisoner to say such prayers in prison. However, the Maliki tradition does allow it. The chaplain in question, faced with the grief of the prisoner unable to attend the funeral, proves willing to endorse the more permissive stance.

A final example of new thinking among Muslim chaplains turns on their co-operation with the Jewish community. Both religious traditions object to the legal requirement to carry out post-mortem examinations. Such procedures both delay burial and involve the dissection of body parts to establish the cause. According to Islamic law bodies should be buried within twenty-four hours and the body untouched allowing 'the right of the deceased to return to the earth intact, in readiness for the day of Judgment'.[89] Both communities have co-operated with coroner-led projects in Bolton and Salford, and in Rochdale, to examine 'the feasibility of non-invasive magnetic resonance imaging (MRI) of the deceased body, instead of invasive pathological post-mortems'. Using the scanners at night, when less likely to be in use for the living, 'means that the cause of death can be ascertained quickly, and in some cases this can enable the burial within the prescribed time'. Muslims across the country are becoming aware of what has become known as the 'Bolton Protocol'. Its use might be extended to other grieving families.

The authors are right to conclude that 'some of the largely unrecorded and pioneering work of Muslim chaplains, underpinned by good relations with Jewish faith leaders, coroners and senior health service managers, is enabling the development of new initiatives that have wider public significance'.[90] The irony is that 'it is hard to find evidence of sustained day-to-day "interpretive legal effort" [*ijtihad*] taking place *outside* chaplaincy settings to any significant degree'.[91] In all, a theology of pastoral care with a distinctive Islamic inflexion is emerging within such institutions. In mosques, imams are taught to be distant: 'You ask [the] imam for [a] *fatwa*, he gives you a *fatwa* and then he leaves. [By contrast in] prisons you've got a Life Unit, you build relationships ...' Inevitably, such professionalism will, over time, make an impact on the wider Muslim community, especially where such chaplains rejoin mosque communities as imams.[92]

On letting the genie out of the bottle: the Cambridge Muslim College

In 2009 the Cambridge Muslim College (CMC) opened its doors to the first cohort of madrasa graduates to study its Diploma in Contextual Islamic Studies and Leadership. Its rationale is clear from an address by the Dean of CMC, Dr Tim Winter (aka Shaykh Abdal Hakim Murad) – a lecturer of Islamic Studies in the Faculty of Divinity at Cambridge – delivered at a conference in Hounslow entitled 'Our mosques, our future' in the autumn of 2008.[93]

Winter muses that none of the UK's madrasas has produced an individual capable of holding their own on *Newsnight*, able to command a crowd in Trafalgar Square or galvanise Muslim youth towards a 'mainstream, normative and convivial Islam'. No one enjoys a following among intellectuals and the grassroots, such as Shaykh Hamza Yusuf does in America. The absence of 'a positive, outwardly oriented 21st century' Islamic formation, he ascribes, in large measure, to the 'entrenched' sectarianism of such institutions shaped by the mother houses in South Asia which continue to 'control the syllabus and which are *effectively unreachable*'.[94]

Winter argues that many British Muslims react against this religiosity either by adopting a secular lifestyle or embracing a Saudi-funded, Salafi Islam. For Dr Winter, the ready accessibility of Saudi literature compounds the marginalisation of many women already embedded in a rural, patriarchal culture, imported from South Asia. Because the Saudis seek 'to excise Sufism from Islamic history', they remove an 'extraordinary constellation of women saints' as female role models. Winter insists that it was the Sufi lodge, rather than the mosque, which provided an institutional space for women, a place for healing and inter-faith encounter. He suggests Muslims should generate alternative spaces to the mosques, not least where the young can explore Islam. Indeed, this suggestion has been taken up by the 'isylabus' network, which reflects the CMC ethos.[95]

Winter's response to the inability of madrasa graduates to connect their textual training with contemporary realities is to 'cherry pick from the most able 10 per cent' and give them an intense exposure to the history, institutions and intellectual life of British society. This is the logic of the diploma course and a precondition is a command of English. This enables them to benefit from a suite of stimulating public lectures and educational visits, *inter alia*, to the House of Commons and Canterbury Cathedral.

Merely to list the topics to be covered in the diploma provides an insight into the extent of the gaps Winter envisages in traditional madrasa formation: the first term, modules on British Islam and a series of introductions to the social sciences, the UK state, world history, world religions, Islamic counselling; the second term, effective community leadership, modern British political history, Islam and religious pluralism, as well as introductions to astronomy, Western intellectual history and science; the third term, Islam and gender, modern British intellectual history, modern Muslim history, modern religious leaders – 'examining the role of a public theologian' – religious ethics in the modern world, sacred art and architecture.

The diploma, intended as part of a four year BA in Contextualising Islamic Studies the CMC is developing, reflects Winter's own priorities. He, along with Hamza Yusuf and Nuh Keller – an American Muslim scholar based in Jordan – are pioneers of an influential neo-Sufi movement often referred to as 'Traditional Islam' (TI). This aspires to be 'an intellectual, activist form of classical Sufism', a scholarly alternative to Salafi and Islamist expressions of Islam, emphasising respect for traditional scholarship represented in the four juristic legal traditions and recognising 'tassawuf (Sufism) as being a valid part of the Islamic tradition'.[96]

Winter seeks to commend a more expansive understanding of classical Islam to attract British Muslims perplexed by the cacophony of Islamic voices each claiming to embody authentic Islam. Winter is helped at CMC by Dr Atif Imtiaz, its academic director. If Winter is a theologian, Imtiaz is a social scientist. His PhD in Social Psychology from LSE focused on a case study of identity and the politics of representation among Muslim youth. He has worked as an Equality and Diversity manager in the NHS and advised the British government on deradicalisation. His own spiritual odyssey has taken him for Islamism to TI. Imtiaz's journey reflects many of his generation growing up in the 1990s, when the only choice seemed to be between a fossilised Islam transmitted through Urdu or that of the smart, young English-speaking Islamists belonging to Young Muslims (YM). In 1995 he penned the YM 'manifesto' document, *Striving for Revival*, with its claim that 'Islam is a complete and comprehensive way of life (*deen*) and it offers guidance for all spheres of life: personal, interpersonal, spiritual, physical, communal, penal, judicial, economic, political etc.'.

This reflects the tendency of Islamist movements 'to be totalizing, closed ideological entities which believe they can address all of life's complexities and ambiguities'.[97] However, Imtiaz, as president of YM, was having doubts and expressed disquiet about 'YM's "pick and mix" approach to the four schools of Islamic law; a lack of intellectual depth, shallow understanding of modernity, absence of spirituality, failure to offer a coherent strategy for the UK and frustration with his previous teachers.' This triggered a personal crisis and he resigned as president in 1997. In the midst of his PhD studies, he began 'to seriously consider the neo-Sufi discourses of American TI scholars ... [Nuh] Keller and Hamza Yusuf, went to study Arabic in Jordan and became a *murid* (spiritual disciple) of Keller before returning to the UK'.[98] Joining the CMC was in line with this changing trajectory. Imtiaz was one of a growing number of student travellers following in the footsteps of the likes of Keller and Yusuf. The experience of these young people has been vividly captured and evaluated by an American Muslim anthropologist, Zareena Grewal, who accompanied a number of them on their travels.

Dr Grewal distinguishes the experience of Keller, who stayed in Jordan, from Yusuf, who returned to the USA. Both started life as anti-establishment. Grewal writes of Keller's depictions of the US as 'a dystopic, spiritual toxic-waste dump and his expectations for his students to relinquish their attachments ... to politics, basketball, and fast food'. Some were persuaded by his austere piety and erudition, others became disillusioned with his 'social conservatism', 'rigid gender segregation' and opposition to a liberal arts model of a 'marketplace of ideas'. For Keller, certain thoughts are bad for you, so the answer is 'don't read the paper, don't watch TV'.[99]

Dr Grewal blames such teachers for not equipping student travellers with the confidence and debating skills to be able to argue their corner amidst the conflicting Islamic voices back home. She also argues they are disingenuous in presenting themselves as mere carriers of an unchanging tradition when, in fact, they mediate and change it. This, she claims, was what Keller was doing in omitting the chapter on slavery and the sexual use of slaves in his translation of the classical, medieval legal text, *Reliance of the Traveler*.[100]

The impulse to excise references to slavery from a revered, legal text fails to encourage a forthright acknowledgement of the pervasive nature of the phenomenon across Muslim history.[101] The West, over time, has acknowledged its own 'horrible histories', less so the Muslim world.[102] Such selective amnesia ill serves contemporary Muslims. For example, it obscures, the long shadow cast by concubinage in shaping formative attitudes to marriage and gender in Islamic law.[103] This 'culture of forgetting' can also damage inter-religious relations.[104]

Hamza Yusuf pursued a different trajectory to Keller. Initially, he too would contrast the dystopia of America with an imagined utopia – in his case, Mauritania where he studied. He returned to America in 1988, where Grewal comments, most Muslim Americans were susceptible to his 'mythmaking' about Mauritania because they knew

little of the history or politics of this fabled country; many might be surprised to learn it is the poorest in the Arab League or that it has been ruled primarily by a series of brutal military juntas since independence from France.[105]

It was also one of the last bastions of slavery.[106]

In 1996 Yusuf established the Zaytuna Institute in California, named after the ancient centre of Islamic scholarship in Tunisia. The institute offered a range of short, intensive courses both in California and in historic Islamic centres across the Muslim world. Yusuf's lectures would emphasise the glories of Islamic history and the importance of the preservation of classical Islamic sciences. After 9/11, he signalled a dramatic change, repudiating his earlier anti-American stance as contributing, unwittingly, to the anger which lay behind violent extremism. He gave up his turban and flowing robes for suit and tie and found himself a guest at the White House. In 2004 Zaytuna developed into a college by launching a pilot seminary programme. In 2012 it purchased a permanent campus in Berkeley at the Graduate Theological Union (GTU), one of the foremost centres for theological study in America. The first Muslim institution of higher learning within the GTU, Zaytuna aims to grant graduate degrees within a decade. Yusuf even began pursuing a PhD at the GTU 'after years of discrediting the Western academic study of Islam and the "illiberal" education offered by the modern university'.[107]

The CMC seems to be closer to Yusuf than Keller. This renders it less vulnerable to criticisms levelled at TI as little more than 'a flight to the past'[108] – characterised by a 'cult-like relationship between the Shaykh and *murids*', an uncritical romanticisation of tradition which closes down enquiry into problematic elements of Islamic law such as 'the patriarchal construction of religious authority'.[109]

Dr Winter, as an academic teaching Islamic studies, carries the additional responsibility of being a Sufi shaykh wishing to make space for Sufism in any retrieval of 'the old religious wisdom' enshrined in madrasa and Sufi lodge.[110] This explains a certain tension implicit in CMC's plans to develop a four-year degree programme of contextualising Islam where the first year is spent in Jordan learning Arabic, presumably within Keller's spiritual orbit. Then, studying in an institute in Damascus which offers the Al-Azhar traditional curriculum, which is not so different from the traditional, South Asian madrasa curriculum.

However, what is clear is that the CMC has launched on an unpredictable path: once the language of instruction becomes English and the institution located in a British academic environment, it cannot avoid the multiple challenges of engaging constructively and critically with the best that is currently thinkable in the humanities, social sciences and the full array of modern sciences, not least as they engage Islamic Studies. Only time will tell whether CMC can successfully marry the confessional and the academic.

No discipline is more challenging to classical Islam than history. It can be emancipatory, as well as a solvent of tradition. In one of his essays, Dr Winter, looks critically at how the legal notion of *dhimma* − Christians and Jews as 'protected' minorities − needs to be understood contextually. He acknowledges that the status was 'hedged around with a set of legal disabilities' which made sense in early Islam where 'non-Muslims were identified with combatants or ex-combatant nations'. However, in the modern context of the nation-state, 'minorities can no longer be considered members of conquered peoples'. So any attempt to reimpose such legal disabilities 'cannot be viewed as a faithful recreation of the practice of the early Muslims'.[111]

But, of course, such contextualising of a legal tradition is controversial. We have noticed, in passing, that Deobandi and Salafi alike accept polygamy as a given in Islamic law. This, indeed, is also the position of many globally influential scholars, such as the Islamist Yusuf al-Qaradawi (b. 1926).[112] However, as we have observed, Muslim women form the majority of those with an exploratory identity. Many are more likely to be attracted to compelling, contextual arguments for regarding

> the permission of polygamy [as] erroneous, not only because it ignored the Qur'an's moral *élan* and its fundamental goal of establishing an ethical and egalitarian society, but also because it failed to assess properly the context of the verses that discuss polygamy in terms of how they were revealed, whom they referred to, and to whom they were addressed.[113]

Over time, the CMC will have to address such fraught issues.

In this chapter, we have identified the many drivers in the UK for a shift from 'textualism' to 'contextualism'. This is unlikely to be a painless process. Modern technology allows views of traditional scholars in Saudi Arabia or South Asia to be transmitted across Britain. Such scholars are seldom aware of the historical specificities of British society, intellectual, institutional, cultural or religious. However, the contextual imperative is unlikely to be arrested. An encouraging feature of the British situation is the small but growing number of *ulama* who are also graduates from British universities. Over time, this should enable a more robust conversation across different intellectual traditions. A lot turns on its success. The absence of a credible traditionalism 'opens the door for rank scripturalism and toxic do-it-yourself Islam'.[114]

Notes

1. The word simply means people of 'knowledge' (*'ilm*).
2. See Manuela Marin, 'The 'ulama', in Maribel Fierro (ed.), *The New Cambridge History of Islam, vol. 2, The Western Islamic World, Eleventh to Eighteenth Centuries* (Cambridge: Cambridge University Press, 2010), pp. 679–704; 682.
3. We follow the convention used by Ebrahim Moosa in his book – *What is a Madrasa?* (Chapel Hill: University of North Carolina Press, 2015) – where he uses the term 'madrasa' (literally 'place of study') as a hold-all term for such institutions. In academic literature they are also referred to as *Dar al 'uloom* (House of (religious) sciences).
4. See J. Birt and P. Lewis, 'The pattern of Islamic reform in Britain: the Deobandis between intra-Muslim sectarianism and engagement with wider society', in M. van Bruinessen and S. Allievi (eds.), *Producing Islamic Knowledge: Transmission and Dissemination in Western Europe* (Abingdon: Routledge, 2011), pp. 91–120. Based on a 2003 survey, they noted that: 'One was established in the 1970s [1975], three in the 1980s, eighteen in the 1990s and three in the first few years of the new century' (p. 93).
5. Innes Bowen, *Medina in Birmingham, Najaf in Brent: Inside British Islam* (London: Hurst & Co., 2014), cites one informed insider who has calculated that the Deobandis now have some twenty-two madrasas. The next group – the Barelwis – have no more than five.

6. This characterisation of Deobandi Islam is given by probably the finest modernist scholar of the last century, Fazlur Rahman, in his seminal work, *Islam and Modernity: Transformation of an Intellectual Tradition* (Chicago: University of Chicago Press, 1982), p. 115.

7. A Danish political scientist, Jytte Klausen, in her 2005 study of emerging Muslim elites in Europe – parliamentarians, city councillors, community activists and professionals involved in civic and self-consciously Muslim organisations – noted that in five of the countries she studied between 10 and 22 per cent could be described as 'neo-orthodox', i.e. those who consider Western norms to be incompatible with Islam, which means Muslims should attempt to live separately while remaining loyal citizens. The exception was Britain, where the percentage was over 70 per cent. See Klausen, *The Islamic Challenge: Politics and Religion in Western Europe* (Oxford: Oxford University Press, 2005), p. 95.

8. For a readable and detailed overview of eight of the most significant expressions of Islam imported into the UK from South Asia and the Arab world, see Bowen, *Medina in Birmingham*.

9. The contentious *hadith* includes the words: 'And this *Ummah* will split into seventy-three sects, all of them in Hellfire except one . . .'; Annabel Inge, *The Making of a Salafi Muslim Woman: Paths to Conversion* (Oxford: Oxford University Press, 2017), p. 92. Also see the section 'Boundary maintenance in a competitive market', pp. 119–26. The term Wahhabi is not a self-designation but applied to the movement by its critics to point up the influence of the preacher and thinker Muhammad Ibn Abd al-Wahhab (1703–92).

10. This data is drawn from an invaluable website produced by an independent Muslim statistician, Mehmood Naqshbandi and published 23 September 2016. It can be downloaded at www.muslimsinbritain.org/resources/masjid_report.pdf.

11. This data, based on an initial analysis of some thousand plus mosques, was sent in an email to members of the Muslims in Britain academic network. Naqshbandi speculated that the remaining 600–700 mosques not yet analysed would 'probably reveal that the actual make-ups are even more narrowly defined – exclusively Mirpuri [Pakistan], Sylheti [Bangladesh], Surati [Indian] . . .' (email sent 23 September 2016). The point he is making is that within each of the national categories, one regional community dominates.

12. See Muhammad Qasim Zaman, *Modern Islamic Thought in a Radical Age: Religious Authority and Internal Criticism* (Cambridge: Cambridge

University Press, 2012), p. 159. This outstanding work is unusual in covering both South Asia and the Arab world.

13. Ibid. pp. 161–2.

14. Ibid. p. 311. Zaman identifies the strategies utilised to marginalise them including assertions that they were eccentrics, if not unhinged, and far from the mainstream.

15. See S. A. Khan, 'The phenomenon of serial nihilism among British Muslim youth of Bradford, England', in F. Ahmed and M. Seddon (eds), *Muslim Youth: Challenges, Opportunities and Expectations* (London: Continuum, 2012), pp. 24–8. A study of young, working-class Bangladeshi men in Tower Hamlets also points to the 'spectacular failure' of mosques to connect to such young men which leaves a 'gaping void' where religious guidance should be. See J. Gest, *Apart: Alienated and Engaged Muslims in the West* (London: Hurst & Co., 2012), pp. 120–1.

16. W. I. U. Ahmad, 'Creating a society of sheep? British Muslim elite on mosques and imams', in W. I. U. Ahmad and Ziauddin Sardar (eds), *Muslims in Britain: Making Social and Political Space* (Abingdon: Routledge, 2012), p. 173.

17. See Dietrich Reetz, 'From Madrasa to University – the challenge and formats of Islamic education', in Akbar Ahmed and Tamara Son (eds), *The Sage Handbook of Islamic Studies* (London: Sage, 2010), p. 117. Pakistan and Bangladesh are once again outliers in the Muslim world with regard to the provision of primary and secondary education which are shockingly low: see Robert Heffner (ed.), *The New Cambridge History of Islam*, vol. 6, *Muslims and Modernity: Culture and Society since 1800* (Cambridge: Cambridge University Press, 2010), p. 513.

18. For more detail, see Sadek Hamid's *Sufis, Salafis and Islamists: the Contested Ground of British Islamic Activism* (London: I. B. Tauris, 2016). The resurgence of Sufi groups is unsurprising since a Pew report indicated that more than three quarters of South Asian Muslims consider Sufis Muslim, while the figure was less than a quarter for Southeast Asia, and less than one in five of Muslims in Central Asia (see *The World's Muslims: Unity and Diversity*, Pew Research Center, 9 August 2012, http://www.pewforum.org/2012/08/09/the-worlds-muslims-unity-and-diversity-executive-summary/.

19. See Zareena Grewal's *Islam is a Foreign Country: American Muslims and the Global Crisis of Authority* (New York: New York University Press, 2014), pp. 32, 34.

20. For example, look at the website http://isyllabus.org.uk for such a network and the history of its teachers.

21. See Shahab Ahmed, *What is Islam: The Importance of Being Islamic* (Princeton: Princeton University Press, 2016), p. 461.

22. See Justice Mufti Taqi Usmani, *Contemporary Fatawa* (Lahore: Idara-e-Islamiat, 2001) which also begins with a *hadith* which cites the Prophet saying: 'Let no woman travel for more than three days (being the equivalent of 48 miles ...) unless her husband or her mahram is with her ...' (p. 293). Saiful Islam's bookshop in Bradford sells a number of Taqi Usmani's books, including this one.

23. Carla Power, *If the Oceans were Ink: an Unlikely Friendship and a Journey to the Heart of the Quran* (New York: Holt, 2015), p. 103.

24. See Inge, *The Making of a Salafi Muslim Woman*, p. 109.

25. Birt and Lewis, 'The pattern of Islamic reform in Britain', p. 92.

26. Saiful Islam, *Your Questions Answered* (Bradford: JKN publications, 2010), p. 69 – the four sources of law are listed as the Quran, *hadith*, *ijma* ('consensus' of scholars) and *qiyas* ('analogy').

27. Ibid. pp. 79, 81.

28. See Nidhal Guessoum, *Islam's Quantum Question: Reconciling Muslim Tradition and Modern Science* (London: I. B. Tauris, 2011), p. 315.

29. See Moneef R. Zou'bi, 'What about Science?', *Critical Muslim*, 15 (July–September 2015), pp. 135–42; 136.

30. Saiful Islam, *Your Questions Answered*, pp. 208–9.

31. Ibid. p. 221.

32. See Inge, *The Making of a Salafi Woman*, p. 180.

33. Saiful Islam, *Your Questions Answered*, pp. 34, 39, 44.

34. Ibid. p. 283 – italics ours.

35. Ibid. p. 265.

36. See Birt and Lewis, 'The pattern of Islamic reform in Britain', p. 104.

37. The material here is taken from a lengthy interview with Shams Ad Duha on 7 December 2015.

38. See Moosa, *What is a Madrasa?*, p. 223. Moosa continues: '"It is no secret," 'Usmani confidently claims, that "at present all the intellectual misguidance found among Muslims can be traced to its source, the West." Without being specific, 'Usmani claims Western thought corrupted the "social mindset" of Muslims ...'

39. See S. Gilliat-Ray, 'Closed Worlds: (Not) accessing Deobandi dar-ul-uloom in Britain', in *Fieldwork in Religion*, 1 (2005), pp. 7–33, and Alison Scott-Baumann and Sariya Cheruvallil-Contractor, *Islamic Education in Britain: New Pluralist Paradigms* (London: Bloomsbury Academic, 2015), p. 115.

40. See Bowen, *Medina in Birmingham*, pp. 25–6. An amusing and inform-
    ative insight into the influence of the gatekeepers is provided in the
    first of two programmes on BBC Radio 4, *The Deobandis* in 2016.
    These are still available on the BBC iPlayer, along with two further
    programmes broadcast on the BBC World Service on Deobandis
    in India and Pakistan, respectively. All were fronted by the veteran
    correspondent who has covered South Asia for twenty years, Owen
    Bennett-Jones.
41. Scott-Baumann and Cheruvallil-Contractor, *Islamic Education in
    Britain*, p. 121.
42. See Moosa, *What is a Madrasa?*, where he speaks of Justice Mufti
    Taqi Usmani's 'incomprehension, dismay and sadness' when visiting
    a madrasa in Jakarta to discover the *hadith* class is co-educational.
    'Gender mixing causes emotional turmoil' to the South Asian scholar
    but not to the scholar from Indonesia – home of the biggest Muslim
    community in the world (p. 146).
43. One of Islam's most famous medieval scholars – al-Ghazali (d. 1111)
    – often regarded as Islam's Thomas Aquinas, devoted a short book
    to this issue. One of America's leading Muslim scholars has recently
    translated it with an excellent introduction, both locating it within its
    own specific context of sectarianism and teasing out its continuing
    relevance for Muslims today. See Sherman Jackson, *On the Bounda-
    ries of Theological Tolerance in Islam: Abu Hamid al-Ghazali's* Faysal al-
    Tafriqa (New York: Oxford University Press, 2002). More recently
    a young British Muslim academic, Dr Tajul Islam, who lectures on
    contemporary Islam at Leeds University, has written a splendid PhD
    on the topic of managing contemporary sectarianism in Britain.
44. See Zaman, *Modern Islamic Thought in a Radical Age*, p. 171. The
    dismal world of the Islamic Studies curriculum – *Islamiyyat* – in
    Pakistan's school and college textbooks is illuminated in the fol-
    lowing comment: 'Typically [they] do not mention the existence
    of the four legal school or the complex and tentative way in which
    Islamic law is actually deduced. Instead, they portray a legal system
    that sprang full-grown and uniform from the brows of the Prophet.
    To students taught from such textbooks, *disagreement about matters of
    Islamic law can appear only to be motivated by perversity*. Likewise, the
    Islamiyat books are generally legalistic and Sunni in orientation . . .
    ignoring Shi'ism . . . [and] even Sufism, the dominant spiritual tra-
    dition in Pakistan' (italics ours). See John Walbridge, *God and Logic
    in Islam: The Caliphate of Reason* (Cambridge: Cambridge University
    Press, 2010), p. 171.

45. We have cited from the two articles in issues 4 and 6. All the back numbers of *Islamique* are accessible on the Ebrahim College website.

46. This point is well made by Simon Cottee, *The Apostates: When Muslims Leave Islam* (London: Hurst & Co., 2015), pp. 38–45. He poignantly remarks that most respondents in his research not only felt Muslim but 'aspired to be *devoutly* Muslim'. Most had attended mosque school where they learned to recite the Quran in Arabic without understanding it. 'In an effort to become better Muslims they took it on themselves to properly understand the meaning and history of Islam.' But as they began to read revered texts themselves they ran up against violent texts which they found difficult to square with their liberal ideals. So began their reluctant journey out of Islam.

47. A model of its sort has just been produced by Dr Mustapha Sheikh, a young Muslim academic at Leeds University who offers an accessible and readable study entitled *A Treasury of Ibn Taymiyyah: Timeless Wisdom of His Words* (Markfield: Kube Publishing, 2017).

48. See P. Lewis, *Young, British and Muslim* (London: Continuum, 2007), p. 6.

49. A female scholar, Khola Hasan offers an insightful, short analysis of how the grievance narrative is developed and trades off the Islamic 'end of times' genre of texts and is used by ISIS. See 'Ustadh Khola Hasan analyses the psyche of British Muslims going to Syria', on the Barelwi-Sufi website organised by Qari Asim, imamasonline, dated April 2015.

50. The material in this section draws on three lengthy interviews with Hamid on 29 June 2013, 30 September 2014 and 20 October 2015 during which he gave permission for his MA thesis to be cited.

51. Hamid Mahmood, *The Dars-e-Nizami and Transnational Madaris in Britain*, MA thesis, Queen's College, University of London, September 2012, pp. 59–65. Available on his website, http://hamidmahmood.co.uk.

52. See Heffner (ed.), *The New Cambridge History of Islam*, vol. 6, pp. 512–13.

53. In 1990, levels of female participation at primary school were almost 100 per cent in Indonesia, Iran and Turkey, 90 per cent in Egypt, 72 per cent in Saudi Arabia, 68 per cent in Bangladesh and 26 per cent in Pakistan. See Heffner, *The New Cambridge History of Islam*, vol. 6, p. 513.

54. Mahmood, *The Dars-e-Nizami*, p. 36. A splendid way in to such exegesis is offered by Jane McAuliffe (ed.), *The Qur'an* (New York:

W. W. Norton & Company, 2017) both in her introduction and translated excerpts from revered and influential Quran commentaries across the centuries.

55. Moosa, *What is a Madrasa?*, p. 22.

56. Ibid. p. 84. Chapter four of Moosa's book is an excellent overview of the changing contexts within which madrasas had to function in the last three centuries in India – or Indo-Pakistan as we would now describe it – and how this impacted their syllabus.

57. See Walbridge, *God and Logic in Islam*, p. 163.

58. See P. Lewis, *Young, British and Muslim* (London: Continuum, 2007), p. 98.

59. Written by Jalal al-Din al-Mahalli (d. 1449) and Jalal al-Din al-Suyuti (d. 1505). There is a translation by Aisha Bewley, *Tafsir al-Jalalayn* (London: Dar Al Taqwa Ltd, 2007).

60. Moosa, *What is a Madrasa?*, p. 120.

61. Mahmood, *The Dars-e-Nizami*, p. 36.

62. Ibid. p. 37.

63. See Muhammad Nejatullah Siddiqui, 'My life in Islamic economics', *Critical Muslim*, 15 (July–September 2015), p. 151.

64. Mahmood, *The Dars-e-Nizami*, p. 43.

65. Moosa, *What is a Madrasa?*, p. 247.

66. Abdullah Sahin, *New Directions in Islamic Education, Pedagogy & Identity Formation* (Markfield: Kube Publishing, 2013), p. 23.

67. Ibid. p. 15. The inability of contemporary Muslims to connect with their own multi-layered and sophisticated past is exemplified in the brilliant study by the late Shahab Ahmed, *What Is Islam*.

68. Sahin, *New Directions in Islamic Education*, p. 3.

69. Ibid. p. 23.

70. Ibid. p. 5. Sahin adds a fourth religiosity mode – *achieved* – where commitment goes hand in hand with exploration, the product of age, experience and reflexivity; a category relevant to adults rather than the young people in his research.

71. Ibid. p. 6.

72. Ibid. p. 162. Sahin makes clear that women were questioning, *inter alia*, the reasons for gender segregation at Kuwait's universities and why women were not encouraged to participate actively in politics.

73. Ibid. pp. 122–8. Sahin points out that 'white culture' is largely understood as negative and mediated through Hollywood movies and pop culture, e.g. 'anti-religious . . . a culture centred around consumption, leisure and pleasure . . . [and] disrespectful of morality and traditional family values' (p. 136).

74. See Bowen, *Medina in Birmingham*, chapter two for *Tablighi Jamaat*.
75. Moosa, *What is a Madrasa?*, p. 19.
76. Sahin, *New Directions in Islamic Education*; these comments represent a summary of his argumentation, pp. 129–34.
77. Ibid. pp. 137–8. We have conflated comments from a couple of people within the 'exploratory' category.
78. Ibid. pp. 141–2.
79. Ibid. p. 145. Sahin's threefold categorisation and broad conclusions find echoes in another study by a social psychologist, Dr Atif Imtiaz, who uses different terms: 'coconut' (for Sahin's 'exploratory'), 'rude boy' ('diffuse') and 'extremist' ('foreclosed'). 'The "rude boys" mix between three cultures: African-American hip hop, Northern Pakistani and Northern Industrial.' He comments that the extremists are exposed to the 'dual risk of ghettoization and assimilation . . . the result of a *total incomprehension* about how to integrate into wider society without losing one's integrity' – S. M. Atif Imtiaz, *Wandering Lonely in a Crowd: Reflections on Muslim Conditions in the West* (Markfield: Kube Publishing, 2011), pp. 85, 88 – italics ours.
80. See Shadi Hamid, *Islamic Exceptionalism: How the Struggle over Islam is Reshaping the World* (New York: St Martin's Press, 2016), p. 223.
81. Sahin, *New Directions in Islamic Education*, p. 30.
82. See Inge, *The Making of a Salafi Woman*, p. 115.
83. Jackson, *On the Boundaries of Theological Tolerance*, p. 6.
84. Mohammad Fadel cited in Hamid, *Islamic Exceptionalism*, p. 234 – italics ours.
85. Sahin, *New Directions in Islamic Education*, p. 212.
86. The material quoted is drawn from chapter 8 of Sahin, *New Directions in Islamic Education*.
87. M. Mansur Ali and Sophie Gilliat-Ray, 'Muslim chaplains: working at the interface of "public" and "private"', in Waqar U. Ahmad and Ziuddin Sardar (eds), *Muslims in Britain: Making Social and Political Space* (London: Routledge, 2012), p. 86.
88. Ibid. p. 89.
89. Ibid. p. 91.
90. Ibid. pp. 96–7.
91. Ibid. p. 92.
92. For an example of the positive impact a chaplain can have on the wider Muslim community when he rejoins a mosque community, see Lewis, *Young, British and Muslim*, pp. 107–9.

93. The information in what follows is taken from the YouTube video of that name. We are indebted to Hamid Mahmood's thesis in drawing attention to this video.

94. Emphasis ours.

95. See their website, http://isylabus.org.uk – a network of teaching outside the mosque which reflects the ethos of the CMC as engaged Sufism, with its teachers combining degrees in a variety of disciplines and training overseas usually the Arab world or Turkey. They have centres in Leeds, Aberdeen, Manchester, Glasgow and Birmingham.

96. See Hamid, *Sufis, Salafis and Islamists*, pp. 66, 76.

97. Ibid. p. 24.

98. Ibid. pp. 27–8.

99. Grewal, *Islam is a Foreign Country*, pp. 270, 207–9.

100. Ibid. pp. 209, 267–8. Another Muslim scholar accuses Keller of 'well meaning but deceitful manipulation' of the same text in his translation and expansion of materials on female circumcision; see Kecia Ali, *Sexual Ethics and Islam: Feminist Reflections on Qur'an, Hadith, and Jurisprudence*, 2nd edn (Oxford: Oneworld, 2016), p. 139.

101. One example will suffice: 'Modern historians . . . produce reliable estimates that Islamic raiders enslaved around a million western Christian Europeans between 1530 and 1640; this dwarfs the contemporary slave trade in the other direction, and is about equivalent to the numbers of west Africans taken by Christian Europeans across the Atlantic at the same time'; Diarmaid MacCullock, *Reformation: Europe's House Divided 1490–1700* (London: Allen Lane, 2003), p. 57.

102. We have borrowed the term 'horrible histories' and the larger point about a reluctance of Muslims to engage in the Islamic equivalent, from a fine public lecture given by Dr Tajul Islam, entitled 'Teaching Medieval Texts: methodological concerns, practical solutions' on 14 September 2016 . We are grateful to Dr Islam who lectures in contemporary Islam at Leeds University for providing a copy of this lecture.

103. This is the burden of Kecai Ali's pioneering monograph, *Marriage and Slavery in Early Islam* (Cambridge, MA: Harvard University Press, 2010). She points out that three of the four founders of the Sunni 'schools of law' owned concubines with concubinage considered 'a normal part of the sociosexual patterns of life in this era'. Unsurprisingly, attitudes to female slavery/concubinage seeped into and shaped how marriage and gender were understood

within Islamic law: 'Early Muslim jurists adhered to a bottom-line view of marriage as a transaction that conveyed to the husband, in exchange for a pecuniary consideration paid to the wife, a type of control, power, or dominion ... analogous to (but more limited than) a master's power over his female slave. It is this dominion over her that makes intercourse between them lawful' (pp. 22, 12). The rest of her study unpacks the continuing negative impact of such thinking on contemporary attitudes which she seeks to challenge and subvert – a task rendered urgent by the activities of ISIS (see the pertinent comments in Ali, *Sexual Ethics and Islam*, pp. 67–71).

104. This useful phrase is taken from an important new study by Dario Fernandez Morera, *The Myth of the Andalusian Paradise: Muslims, Christians and Jews under Muslim Rule in Medieval Spain* (New York: ISI Books, 2016), which concludes that inter-religious relations were characterised by a precarious co-existence rather than an imagined tolerant conviviality (*convivencia*; p. 236). Such a conclusion is a better basis for honest encounter than well-intentioned mythmaking since it posits the need to develop new rationales for such relations rather than supposing the hard intellectual work has already been done and has only to be retrieved from history. For inter-faith relations in Africa, see John Alembillah Azumah, *The Legacy of Arab-Islam in Africa* (Oxford: Oneworld, 2001), where he writes: 'Within the African context, the memory of eighteenth- and nineteenth-century Muslim slave raids and massive enslavement of traditional African communities most of whom are now overwhelmingly Christian, is still alive and vivid in affected communities' (p. 15).

105. Grewal, *Islam is a Foreign Country*, p. 167.

106. We owe this information to Dr Tajul Islam who, inspired by Hmaza Yusuf, also went off to study classical disciplines in Mauritania. As a British Asian, he found local Sufi shaykhs and scholars less ready to open their doors to him than to a privileged, white, American convert.

107. Grewal, *Islam is a Foreign Country*, pp. 164–5, 312.

108. We have borrowed this haunting and suggestive phrase from Tajul Islam's public lecture.

109. Hamid, *Sufis, Salafis and Islamists*, pp. 142–5.

110. In a recent article Winter acknowledges that the Quran is 'the authentic root of two disciplines whose mutual relations are controversial: formal systematic theology (*kalam*) and Sufism (*tasawwuf*)' while he makes clear his own preference when he states: 'The ascent

to the One ... is not through the logic-chopping powers [of reason] ... but through acquiring a true and loving ear that can properly hear this [divine] music' (pp. 30–1) – Tim Winter, 'Education as "drawing-out" the forms of Islamic reason', in M. Zaman and N. Memon (eds), *Philosophies of Islamic Education: Historical Perspectives and Emerging Discourse* (London: Routledge, 2016), pp. 26–42.

111. Abdal Hakim Murad, *Qur'anic Truth and the Meaning of 'Dhimma'* (Burr Ridge: The Nawawi Foundation, 2010), p. 17.

112. Zaman, *Modern Islamic Thought in a Radical Age*, p. 203.

113. See Abdullah Saeed, *Reading the Qur'an in the Twenty-First Century: a Contextualist Approach* (Abingdon: Routledge, 2014), p. 102.

114. Moosa, *What is a Madrasa?*, p. 253.

3

Engaging Democracy and Debating Islam

A road less travelled

In survey after survey, Muslim countries show large majorities in favour of democracy. An exception is Pakistan where a recent poll gave a figure of 42 per cent. This fell to 31 per cent when asked for their preference as between a democracy and a strong leader. The same survey indicated that Pakistan was the only country where a majority (59 per cent) thought that the family should choose a woman's husband.[1]

At the same time, large majorities across South Asia, Southeast Asia, MENA (the Middle East and North Africa) and sub-Saharan Africa support making sharia the law of the land. Most Muslims seem to want 'neither a theocracy nor a secular democracy and would opt for a third model in which religious principles and democratic values coexist'.[2] However, when it comes to the implementation of aspects of Islamic law there were deep, regional variations. Once again, South Asia stood apart with regards to those who favoured severe criminal punishments for infractions of Islamic law. For example, more than three quarters supported the execution of those who left Islam.[3] Such bald statistics suggest that a polity which would honour both aspirations will have to give great thought to how the sharia is to be interpreted and by whom.

The issue of religious freedom is especially sensitive because it often goes hand-in-hand with democratisation. A startling example was the impact on the Catholic world of the Vatican 2 *Decree on Religious Liberty* (1962–5) which declared unequivocally that the human being had a right to religious freedom – a fundamental part of human dignity – which must be enshrined in the constitution of society as a human right. In this revolutionary departure from tradition, the Catholic Church was itself burying Christendom.[4] This, in part, enabled a third wave of democratisation in the modern world between 1974 and 1989 whereby thirty countries in Europe, Asia and Latin America made the shift from authoritarianism to democracy, three quarters of which were Catholic.[5]

A growing number of Muslim scholars teaching in the West have sought to address different aspects of the challenge to bring Islamic law into alignment with fundamental principles of democracy. We will briefly mention two such contributors. Abdullah An-Naim, an American law professor of Sudanese ancestry, has persuasively argued that constitutionalism, human rights and citizenship – the stuff of democracy – risk being compromised until and unless three principles explicit in traditional interpretations of sharia are re-interpreted, namely, 'male guardianship of women (*qawama*), sovereignty of Muslims over non-Muslims (*dhimma*), and violently aggressive *jihad*'.[6] Professor An-Naim illustrates how a Quranic verse taken to establish this general principle of male guardianship has been used to deny women the right to hold any public office which entails the exercise of authority over men. In addition, other verses have been used 'to restrict the right of women to appear and speak in public or to associate with men, which thereby limits their ability to participate in government . . .'[7]

Professor An-Naim is clear that given the social and moral authority the sharia enjoys among Muslims it is not enough for government officials to intervene to stop discrimination against women and non-Muslims through the coercive and disciplinary power of the state, without enabling serious re-thinking to take place and to win popular support.[8] If this does not happen, the likelihood is that such progressive legislation and policy will be resisted and subverted. The task of re-thinking, of course, presupposes the existence of intellectual freedom, as well as appropriate institutional spaces and a willingness by interested parties to debate contentious issues.

The reasons for the absence of such freedom, especially in the Arab world, are identified in a recent monograph by another distinguished American legal scholar – this time of Egyptian heritage – Professor Khaled Abou El Fadl. As well as outlining his own detailed and imaginative proposals to retrieve and reclaim the ethical and humanist dimensions of the sharia, the work is enlivened by many personal anecdotes. El Fadl blames the omnipresence of repressive, authoritarian regimes and the dehumanising and reductionist impact of Islamist and Wahhabi/Salafi movements for the intellectual impasse in which much of the Muslim world finds itself.[9]

Educated as a young man in Kuwait and Egypt, to complement his secular education, El Fadl recounts how he searched out scholarly, Islamic study circles, where he was taught to think rather than engage in rote learning. Such circles had been created as a challenge to government controlled and certified institutions. Suddenly, he drops into the text the following aside:

> Tragically, several of the students I studied with earlier were chased out of the country or perished in the unlawful detention centers that function as slaughterhouses for the most dedicated and courageous members of society. The government seemed . . . determined to suppress . . . any autonomous expression of religious learning.[10]

This reminds us that modern Muslim nation-states have themselves politicised Islam by seeking to capture and monopolise the use of Muslim symbols to legitimise the nation-state, frequently nationalising Islamic institutions, providing an Islamic rationale for nationalism in civic education, privileging certain understandings of sharia and thus opening a Pandora's box of competition over the control and definition of such 'hegemonic Islam'.[11]

Professor El Fadl mentions a fatal rupture in his friendship with a former mufti of Egypt and the current shaykh and rector of Azhar – the venerable centre of traditional Islam in Cairo – because both supported the military coup in 2013 against an elected civilian government comprising a majority of the Muslim Brotherhood. For El Fadl this renders imperative the need 'to reclaim and restate our Islamic tradition so that it can no longer harbor despots and tyrants' – the challenge, par excellence, for political reflection within Islamic legal jurisprudence (*fiqh*).[12]

Professor El Fadl is also scathing about the intellectual failures over half a century of Islamist and Salafi/Wahhabi alike. He documents how Islamists became 'addictive' to a self-congratulatory apologetics – anachronistic claims that Islam pioneered democracy, gender equality and human rights – which undercut the need to engage in intellectually rigorous and self-critical scholarship. At the same time, with traditional scholarship thinned out through government control, space was created for Wahhabism. He proceeds to offer reasons for the spread of Wahhabi Islam – not least Saudi petrol dollars – and an analysis of its character: its supremacist and insular mind-set, its literalism, rank intolerance of rationalism, Sufism and Shi'ite Islam, along with its antagonism to the non-Muslim, routinely derided and demeaned. Further, El Fadl blames their teaching and practice for what he describes as 'the social death' of Muslim women.[13]

By neglecting the messy realities of actual Islamic history, Wahhabis can postulate a golden age of early Islam – the first three generations (the *salaf*) – a historical utopia ripe for retrieval and reproduction in contemporary society. The Islamists, for their part, faced with feelings of powerlessness, allowed political interests to dominate and reinvented Islam as an ideology of nationalist defiance to the Western other. 'Therefore, instead of Islam being a moral vision given to humanity, it becomes constructed into a nationalistic cause ... often the antithesis to the West.'[14] In all, freedom of thought is exiled from much of the Muslim world. As a footnote to El Fadl's discussion, we might note that where violent Islamist meets Wahhabi theology, the fruit of the resulting hybrid is less Islamic utopia than ISIS dystopia.

With these background observations, we can begin to understand both the opportunities and pitfalls facing British Muslims. They do not have to craft a democracy but rather learn the skills to engage political and civic life. We will consider the changing shape of Muslim public and civic engagement and the extent to which it has been successful in winning legal, institutional and policy changes to accommodate their distinctive needs.

A related issue we will explore is the increasing salience in public and civic life of Muslim women. Unsurprisingly, their increased participation has met with opposition from within Muslim communities. An earlier chapter considered the controversy ignited when the Muslim Women's Council in Bradford committed to developing a women's only managed mosque and centre of intellectual excellence for Muslim women. We will foreground some of the complementary campaigns of the Birmingham-based Muslim Women's Network for the UK (MWNUK) and the growing body of emancipatory Islamic scholarship it draws upon. As elsewhere across the Muslim world ' a great transformation of women's roles is under way, and it is creating realities on the ground at variance with classical sharia's patriarchal guardianship'.[15]

In Britain, Muslims do not have to struggle to create spaces where intellectual freedom is a given. One of the positive themes of this book is the growing number of Muslim academics teaching in British universities. In the next section we will look at how they are contributing to a particularly important debate about whether the sharia mandates a particular form of governance – an Islamic state/caliphate – or guidance. This debate, often heated, includes Islamists and ex-Islamists. It also makes clear that in the exchange of ideas between the majority Muslim world and Muslims as minorities in the West, the latter are increasingly demanding a hearing.

Just as we were able to discern a new debate emerging within the world of the traditional Deobandi *ulama* in the previous chapter – not least through an engagement with new, scholarly disciplines accessible in English – so in this chapter and the next, we will identify Islamists and Salafis also beginning to participate in public and civic life. By virtue of participating in democracy – as the majority do – they, of course, render traditional notions of Muslim sovereignty over non-Muslims (*dhimma*) increasingly redundant. In a democracy, the stance of the state and other institutions is crucial in enabling intra-Muslim debate across deepening sectarian divides, as well as welcoming as wide a range of Muslim voices to participate in public and civic life. Here we will discover a more troubling picture.

An Islamic state: sharia imperative or captive to ideology?

The very notion of an Islamic state is both product and reaction to the creation of nation-states in the Muslim world. More particularly, it is a response to the abolition of the caliphate in 1924 by the leader of the newly formed Turkish Republic. Its abolition created fear for the future of the Muslim community worldwide – the *ummah* – buffeted by Western colonialism and imported ideologies, whether nationalism, capitalism, communism or liberalism.

Although the caliphate had not enjoyed real power and influence for centuries – the Ottoman sultans only reclaimed the title in the eighteenth century – it symbolised the existence of institutional continuity reaching right back to the Prophet's death, a theory of political power and religious legitimacy. Many Muslims now felt orphans in an unfamiliar geopolitical landscape where leadership was captured by 'secular' elites in the military, judiciary and bureaucracy, with Islamic law increasingly reduced to personal status and family law such as marriage, divorce and inheritance. Whether in Turkey, or later with the post-colonial creation of nation-states such as Egypt and Pakistan, Western models of political and economic development were in the ascendancy.

State funding shifted from Islamic educational institutions to the establishment of Westernised institutions of learning which saw the emergence of the familiar products of modernity: journalists, school teachers, lawyers, engineers, doctors and so on. Drawn from village backgrounds into the burgeoning towns, many remained profoundly attached to Islam but increasingly disillusioned with the *ulama* – frequently dismissed as bearers of a fossilised tradition, incapable of responding to the intellectual and political challenges of modernity. It was from their ranks that Islamism emerged.

Hasan al Banna (1906–49), the founder of *al-Ikhwan al-Muslimun*/the Muslim Brotherhood in Egypt in 1928 was a state-trained teacher, while the founder of Jama'at-i Islami in India in 1941 was Abu'l A'la Mawdudi (1903–79), a scholar and journalist. Islamism, past and present, is a diverse phenomenon, with its proponents at different times and places embracing now political gradualism, now militant revolution; with regard to other expressions of Islam such as Sufism, al-Banna was sympathetic, Mawdudi, was antagonistic; the Muslim Brotherhood became a mass movement, Jama'at-i Islami remained an elitist vanguard movement seeking to influence and infiltrate elites.[16]

However, Islamism shared family resemblances. First, hostility to Western elites as carriers of godless, 'secular' ideologies – indeed, the terms used to translate 'secular' across South Asia meant 'godless'.[17] Secondly, a commitment to God's sovereignty (*hakimi-yya*) which translates into the ambition to create an Islamic state embodying God's law.[18] Thirdly, Islamism was not just a political ideology but a movement, par excellence, of religious and moral reform which offered a range of overlapping attractions in a world of strong states and weak civil society.

For example, some joined the Muslim Brotherhood (MB) because it provided moral purpose and guidance to help them 'get into heaven'; for others, it offered a sense of belonging; 'for the charity-minded', it provided health care, youth activities, educational and self-help courses, even assistance to find work. Others were drawn to MB's explicit political work, whether 'street protest, parliamentary advocacy, running for office, or (in the 1940s) sending volunteers to fight against an incipient Israeli state'.[19] Islamism also sought to restore pride to the wounded psyche of colonised peoples. Al-Banna could, on occasion, call for the restoration of the early Islamic empire and speak of 'sacred conquests'. Empires based on conquest, it seemed, were fine, as long as the right sort. After all,

> the Muslim conqueror was a teacher endowed with the light, guidance, mercy and compassion with which the teacher must be graced, and the Islamic conquest ... brought civilization, culture, guidance and education. How can this be compared with what Western imperialism is doing at the present time?[20]

Islamists aspired to re-establish historic continuity by factoring in a role for a renewed caliphate. For al-Banna, the caliphate was the end point of a reformed and united *ummah* but otherwise peripheral to its actual political revival. For Sheikh Taqiuddin al-Nabhani (1909–77), the Palestinian Islamist who founded Hizb ut-Tahrir (the Party of Liberation) in Jerusalem in 1953, the caliphate was interpreted as both a sharia obligation and the necessary structure to reform and unite the community. 'The public call for the caliphate became their primary identifier.'[21] For al-Qaeda, an appeal to the caliphate was little more than part of their Islamic symbolic repertoire to mobilise support.

The caliphate also featured in the programme of the *Murabitun*, a Sufi network, established by Ian Dallas (b. 1930) – a convert to the Moroccan Darqawi order – who took the name Shaykh Abdalqadir. He created his first community in Norwich in 1976. The movement today claims some twenty establishments across the world. They have minted their own gold dinar currency, as a harbinger, they hope, 'to the destruction of the global capitalist banking system and the re-establishment of the caliphate'.[22]

Islamism, gradualist and revolutionary alike, is anathema to many traditional *ulama*. Typical are the views of Judge Mufti Taqi Usmani – the influential contemporary Deobandi scholar in Pakistan mentioned in an earlier chapter – who fulminates against the likes of Mawdudi who 'in their zeal to refute secularism ... characterize politics and government as the true objective of Islam ... [with] other Islamic commandments ... [e.g.] worship ... mere means for political ends, just a way of training people [towards political mobilisation]'.[23] Usmani, while not rejecting democracy, regarded it with considerable ambivalence with 'ignorant, willful masses' – no match for the pious rulers of yesteryear – embodying a popular sovereignty which could threaten to overrule God's commandments. Usmani embraced the traditional role for the *ulama* with regard to politics, which was not assuming a political role for himself but to offer religious guidance to people and political elites alike. He was 'adamant that on matters concerning the sharia the work of the legislative assembly is only credible to the extent that it is guided by the 'ulama'.[24]

In Britain and the West, the whole project of Islamism has not just been questioned by the *ulama* but its every dimension – interpretation of Islamic texts and history, basic concepts, organisation, ideology and ethos – scrutinised and found wanting by

Muslim thinkers. Few critiques have been more sustained and searching than that developed by the British Sudanese scholar Dr Abdelwahab El-Affendi. For more than four decades, Dr El-Affendi has been researching and interacting with leading Islamists, not least in London, which offered 'a breathing space and an arena for reflection, rethinking and re-organization' to political exiles.[25] His first book, *Who Needs an Islamic State?* (1991), sought to enable Islamist thinkers to critically engage the best insights of political science and Islamic history.

Appointed in 1998 the first co-ordinator of the Democracy and Islam Programme at the Centre for the Study of Democracy (CSD) at the University of Westminster, he has travelled extensively in the West and the Arab world holding conferences and workshops on political violence, democracy and Islamism. With the Arab Spring, many of his friends and students found themselves in positions of influence, especially in Tunisia. In 2008, he brought out a second edition of his book, *Who Needs an Islamic State?* If this work has a hero it is probably Rachid al-Ghanoushi, leader of the Tunisian Islamist party and one of the few serious intellectuals the Islamist movement can boast. While other Islamists regard themselves as guardians of Islamic morality, a role they arrogated to themselves with the demise of the caliphate, Ghanoushi has little patience with such presumption. For him, the Islamic movement is just another actor on the democratic stage, seeking through persuasion and not coercion to win votes. It has 'neither a monopoly in the interpretation of Islam, nor in dictating morality'.[26]

Dr El-Affendi's confidence in Ghanoushi was subsequently vindicated. With the Arab Spring turning prematurely into winter, Tunisia kept hope alive. Ghanoushi's 'vision and charisma' persuaded the Islamist party, Ennahda, to share power with secularists and endorse 'a relatively liberal constitution . . . passed with broad consensus in January 2014'.[27] While the Tunisian experiment presented an Islamist party playing a central role in the transition from authoritarian to democratic politics, this contrasted with the Egyptian Freedom and Justice Party (FJP), the political front for the Muslim Brotherhood. El-Affendi is scathing about the failure of Mohamed Morsi (FJP), who won the presidency in 2012, to create a broad-based coalition to consolidate democracy. Instead, he aligned himself with the more hardline Salafis, controversially rushed through an unpopular constitution and, although enjoying full executive and legislative powers, sought to pass a constitutional decree blocking any judicial challenge to his powers.

Such decisions confirmed fears about the secretive style of the Brotherhood, with real power over the FJP exercised by the Supreme Guide and MB leaders. Reviewing this catalogue of mistakes, Dr El-Affendi wearily concludes that the dominant Islamists in much of the Arab world and South Asia have 'no notion of self-criticism, and utterly fail to accept sympathetic criticism'.[28] This is intimately connected to Islamist self-understanding as God's elect, married to a very modern notion of the leader and party being a revolutionary vanguard committed to capturing state power, so as to enact God's law.

We will consider contemporary criticisms of each of these assumptions – God's elect, Islam as ideology, the state as an appropriate vehicle to enforce sharia. Dr El-Affendi has a very sharp criticism of Islamist self-understanding as being the religious and political elite. He argues that such a combination is only possible because they can appeal to an idealised and sanitised version of Islamic history, especially that of the Rightly Guided Caliphs who immediately succeeded the Prophet on his death. In so doing, they bypass the actual history of the four Rightly Guided Caliphs. This saw a dreadful civil war (*fitna*) from 656 to 661 following the murder of the third and fourth caliphs, Uthman and 'Ali, with Muslim fighting Muslim, resulting in a divided caliphate.

The civil war gave birth, in embryo, to Islam's main schism, later formalised as Sunni and Shi'i (the partisans of 'Ali), as well as a minority movement of religious zealots known as *Khawarij*. Where the Sunnis saw the caliphate as properly belonging to the Prophet's family – the Quraysh – the Shi'is privileged the family of 'Ali, while the *Khawarij* were egalitarian, pitting their understanding of religious merit against kinship. Dr El-Affendi argues that, instead of reflecting on this as a cautionary tale for contemporary Muslims, Islamists retreat to an idealised political theory of the caliphate articulated three centuries later. According to this, the establishment of the caliph is mandatory, resides in one person rather than a collective and that individual has to be 'the best, most virtuous and most competent male Muslim from Qurashite lineage . . . designated by the influential leaders of the community'.[29] He insists that Islamists draw on such a theory to foreground piety and virtue in both leader and movement. In ignoring the need for constitutional checks and balances, the stuff of modern democracy, they reenact the failure of the Islamic political theory to address what to do when caliphs fall short of such ideals and topple over into oppression and tyranny. Moreover, scarred by the early civil wars, the default position of Sunnis became political quietism – better to support an oppressive leader than risk fragmenting the *ummah* and imploding into civil war.

For Muslims to create a movement to both embody and commend religious and moral reform is neither surprising nor sinister. The problem is when this is allied to very modern notions of revolutionary politics, the state and God's law. One of the many ironies that critics of Islamism have pointed out is that on the one hand it sees itself as resisting and confronting alien Western ideologies, yet at the same time it radically reconfigures Islam by recourse to modern, Western notions. For example, *Hizb ut Tahrir* disavows democracy yet as with other Islamist movements has few reservations about assuming the role of revolutionary vanguard – borrowed from the communist lexicon – and 'the use of thoroughly modern terms such as *mabda* (ideology), *dawla* (state) and *dustor* (constitution)'.[30]

The Islamists represent a double rupture with the past: first, through their radical re-interpretation of the sharia as ideology and their choice of the modern state to impose such an ideology. In short, they exaggerate the role law can play in reforming society, while relying exclusively on an institution, the state, which has always existed in an uneasy relationship with Islamic jurists. We will start by reflecting on the massive shift in the range and reach of power represented by the modern state when compared to power exercised in the pre-modern Islamic world, the environment in which the sharia developed, then consider how Islamic vocabulary is given radically new meanings within the Islamist lexicon.

Historians remind us that the term which best captures the relationship in pre-modern empires between the power holders, the sultan and Islam is 'indifference':

> the nature of ritual practice, codes of law, spiritual orientation ... has been irrelevant to the state. The religious leadership lent legitimacy to those [Muslim] polities that maintain a framework of institutions within which Muslims can lead their religious life; they expect patronage to mosques, schools and shrines but not control of what goes on.[31]

After all, in the pre-modern period, Muslim empires lacked the capacity and intrusive reach of the modern state and depended on local notables, including the *ulama*. Intra-Muslim political changes had little impact on trade or the community of the learned. 'Both tend to continue their activities within their own networks where towns, trade routes and centers of learning are crucial, but the identity of the ruler of the borders between the states matter relatively little.'[32]

Muslim rulers, of course, appointed judges but also made laws embodying a measure of legal pluralism. For example, in criminal matters, because sharia provisions demanded a heavy burden of proof that made conviction difficult, the rulers' courts applied more flexible standards of evidence. In short,

> much of the day-to-day business of trying criminals, regulating commerce, raising taxes, and conducting military campaigns was left to legislation not directly elaborated in the shari'a or its associated jurisprudence – even if ... all parties agreed that the sultan's actions were in accord with the spirit of the shari'a ...[33]

The Muslim jurists, for their part, as producers and purveyors of Islamic law, 'typically had a close and symbiotic relationship with the masses and a subtly antagonistic relationship with the ruler ... [often deemed] a source of corruption that undermined Islamic principles and law, either because of *Realpolitik* or because of the ruler's personal failings'.[34] Islamic beliefs and practices were properly the preserve of the community not the state.

> The meaning of Islam was explicated by the societies in which the jurists lived and developed their views. And because it was a societal and collective enterprise, it was open to a multiplicity of views and to a degree of tolerance for difference.[35]

Now such legal indeterminacy is anathema to the modern state. This is why many newly established Muslim nation-states codified and centralised law drawing on continental European models. Islamists such as Mawdudi were outraged by such developments but in awe of the range and reach of the modern state, colonial and post-colonial. Aware of its all-encompassing ambition, he would write in 1938: 'Now [the state] also decides what to wear ... what to teach your kids ... what language and script to adopt ... the state is beginning to acquire the same status that God has in religion.' Mawdudi's reaction was to equate Islam with the state and re-interpret key Quranic terms accordingly. God is understood as master of metaphysical and political realms: 'Ruler, Dictator ... and Legislator' of the political realm. Rituals like prayer were equated to military training: 'prayer, fasting ... provide preparation and training for the assumption of just power'. In sum, 'the word *deen* [religion] approximately has the same meaning which the word state has in the contemporary age'.[36] One term, in particular, represented the capstone of Mawdudi's ideology. This was his elaboration of the Quranic term *hukm* which in its original Quranic context meant 'judgement' – specifically divine judgement of humans in the next life. Mawdudi, instead, drew on its politicised meaning of 'rule', developed by traditionalist scholars drawing on post-classical sources. He then 'coined the term *al-hakimiyya* or divine sovereignty' which he juxtaposed to popular sovereignty deemed illegitimate, thereby delegitimising democracy. The term was adopted by Sayyid Qutb and 'became entrenched in many Islamist circles'.[37]

Such a dramatic reinvention of tradition has met with considerable opposition. As El-Affendi remarks, the Muslim majority does not take kindly to the 'condescending and arrogant attitude of the Islamist groups' to being the virtuous, religious vanguard, par excellence, of a renewed society. Further, Mawdudi's belief that the state has the ultimate responsibility to promote virtue and combat vice meant that it must be 'totalitarian ... interfering in the private affairs of individuals'.[38]

A recent study of the escalating denial of religious freedom worldwide makes bleak reading. While it makes clear that all religions, as well as communist and ex-communist regimes, are implicated either by state or societal pressures or both, the data makes clear that there is a particular problem in the Muslim world. Of fourteen countries where strong political and societal pressures exist, which translate into systematic persecution of minority Muslim groups and sects, as well as religious minorities, only one country is non-Muslim. To explain this, the authors suggest a correlation with state-led attempts to impose sharia. This generates conflict with other Muslim groups who contest how the sharia is being interpreted and applied.[39]

Engaging public and civic life: from Muslims in Britain to British Muslims

The majority of the first generation of Muslim migrants from South Asia came from Muslim majority countries – Pakistan and Bangladesh – and rural areas where religious community and society were co-terminous. Moving into Western, industrial cities, they formed ethno-religious enclaves in an indifferent or hostile society. Such enclaves also saw the consolidation of imported kinship networks and a hierarchy of clan solidarities. Further, Islamic jurisprudence (fiqh) did not envisage minority Muslim communities formed by voluntary economic migration from Muslim lands to non-Muslim lands. In all, Muslims had few religious guidelines to help orient them as a minority in this new and bewildering context.[40]

Inevitably, the journey from the periphery to accessing mainstream political and civic life involved much experimentation and many false starts. It meant addressing tensions between ethnic and religious identity, isolation versus engagement, managing sectarian differences and making institutional space for a British-born 'Islamically conscious and technological – MTV, iPhone and Facebook – generation'.[41] The latter did not see themselves as part of an ethno-Muslim enclave. Many are successful, suburbanised professionals.

The distance the Muslim communities have travelled can be gauged by comparing two high profile movements in which Muslims were involved. The first was in May 1989, when some 70,000 Muslim protestors from across the country demonstrated in London against the publication of *The Satanic Verses* novel by Salman Rushdie. The second was when tens of thousands of Muslims took part on 15 February 2003 in the demonstration in London to oppose the invasion of Iraq, which attracted an estimated 2 million people, organised by the Stop the War Coalition (SWC) – one of many such events across the world.

The first was a 'PR disaster' with demonstrators photographed burning the British flag and effigies of Rushdie. The style of protest seemed 'directly imported from the Indian sub-continent' by its first-generation, migrant organisers.[42] Such images, along with earlier book burnings, did irreparable damage to the perception of British Muslims in wider society. They were perceived as an illiberal minority, attacking freedom of expression, unaware of the dark associations of book burning in the European imagination.

This contrasts with the involvement in the SWC in 2001 – before the invasion of Afghanistan – and its anti-Iraq war demonstrations, of two small Muslim networks outside the Muslim mainstream organisations, *Just Peace* and the Muslim Association of Britain (MAB). The former drew on second-generation Muslim professionals active in the City Circle established in London in 1999; the latter was established in 1997 to give voice to the concerns of a network of educated Arabs, marginalised in Muslim communities dominated by South Asians. Here was a new generation of British Muslims catalysing an alliance across sectarian and ethnic differences within the Muslim communities, as well as with non-Muslims, on a common anti-war platform, involving a huge array of organisations and activists. The difference between the two demonstrations in 1989 and 2003 could not have been greater.

This is not to say that such an alliance was without its challenges. The Socialist Worker Party and other groups involved in
SWC from the radical left were uneasy with the participation of
groups such as MAB deemed reactionary and a threat to working-class solidarity. Muslim groups, such as Hizb ut Tahrir and
some Muslim traditionalists, also opposed such alliances. What
is significant is that MAB was loosely aligned with the Muslim
Brotherhood – here we see them taking the Tunisian path of co-
operation with a diversity of groups, secular and non-Muslim.
This reminds us that across all Muslim traditions a transition
is taking place as a new generation begins to make their presence felt, often as carriers of a reformist agenda. Too often critics
of Islamic movements make no allowances for such debate and
evolution. It is no exaggeration to claim that Muslim involvement in such a mass movement was 'a springboard' for the development of Muslim civil society and 'created opportunities for a
new generation of Muslim leaders to emerge from the shadows
of the first generation' and engage British politics.[43]

The shape and contours of Muslim political participation
have also changed in the last thirty years so that we might now
speak of its normalisation across the full range of positions and
parties, encompassing cabinet ministers and lord mayors. This has
been enabled by a number of factors. First, unlike the situation
in many other European countries, Commonwealth migrants to
Britain automatically enjoy the right to citizenship, including
political rights. Second, the ethnic clustering of Muslims in certain towns and cities at ward level translated into the election of
Muslim councillors.[44] The first Muslim mayor was appointed in
Brent in 1981 and Bradford in 1985. Today there are more than
300 Muslim local councillors.

With more than half of British Muslims today settled in just
fifty parliamentary seats – in ten of which the Muslim population was over 20 per cent, and in two some 40 per cent (Bethnal
Green and Bow in East London and Bradford West) – it was only
a matter of time before the first MP was returned.[45] This hap-
pened in 1997 when Mohammed Sarwar was elected in Glasgow
Govan for Labour. The following year Labour appointed the first
Muslim Life Peers in the House of Lords. Other landmarks were

the appointment of the first minister in 2007 (Shahid Malik), the first to attend a meeting of the Cabinet in 2009 (Sadiq Khan) and the first woman to serve the Cabinet in 2010 (Baroness Warsi); 2010 also saw the first female Muslim MPs and Conservative Muslim MPs returned.

The third factor enabling the election of Muslim MPs was the point at which this becomes a priority for national parties. This turns on the shift in perception to looking at minorities through a religious rather than an ethnic lens. This shift was well advanced by 1997 when the Muslim Council of Britain (MCB) was established to represent Muslim concerns and lobby the government. The new Labour government formed in that year welcomed the MCB as its interlocutor. This was consistent with New Labour's communitarian turn, whereby religious congregations were seen as 'reservoirs of under-tapped and responsible voluntarism that could be channeled into the government's initiatives for civil renewal'.[46]

For the British state, to engage representative religious bodies has a long history. In 1992 a Conservative government established the Inner City Religious Council (ICRC), located within the Department of the Environment, as part of a shared response to the Church of England's critical *Faith in the City* report, which drew attention to the extent of poverty in Britain's urban areas. The ICRC began an ever-expanding circle of 'government initiatives linking religion, community, urban neighbourhood and social cohesion'.[47] Religious communities were seen as having people, networks, organisations and buildings to engage hard-to-reach areas in programmes of urban regeneration.

The period from 1997 to 2005 was in many ways the high point of MCB engagement with government and government departments. With MCB's stated aims including 'better community relations and work for the common good of society as a whole', they were knocking at an open door.[48] Their leaders were often invited to receptions at the Home Office and Foreign and Commonwealth Office, occasionally representing the latter in delegations to Muslim-majority countries. Their lobbying, often in partnership with other faiths and civil society groups, yielded significant gains, 'including: strengthening legislation on religious

discrimination and incitement to religious hatred ... state funding
for Islamic schools; and the introduction of a question about faith
identification in the decennial national census'.[49]

This period of close collaboration ended with the shock of
7/7 and the growing divergence between government and MCB,
whether over the invasion of Iraq or the shift in government policy
away from cohesion to security. Post-7/7, the Home Office initiated a wide-ranging process – Preventing Extremism Together
(PET) – with working parties involving more than a hundred Muslim participants drawn from politics, media, business, education and
the third sector. Among its many recommendations, the government chose to foreground three: a Mosques and Imams Advisory
Board (MINAB), the Radical Middle Way – which offered road
shows against extremism involving leading Muslim scholars from
across the world – and community forums on Islamophobia and
extremism.

Thus began a process of recognising diversity within the
Muslim communities, establishing and funding the Young Muslims Advisory Group (YMAG) and National Muslim Women's
Advisory Group (NMWAG) to circumvent the entrenched
influence in Muslim organisations of first-generation, male gatekeepers. The MCB was now but one voice among many making
claims to represent different sections of the Muslim communities, for example, the devotionalist, Barelwi-oriented British
Muslim Forum (BMF), or embodying specific expertise, such as
Quilliam, a counter-extremism think tank, comprising ex-Hizb
ut Tahrir activists – poachers turned gamekeepers – and the collective of liberal British Muslims for Secular Democracy.

Large sums of money were made available. From 2006 to 2008,
£13.8 million was spent on the 'Faith Communities Capacity
Building Fund' with another £7.5 million on the 'Face to Face and
Side by Side' strategy to enable meeting and shared projects across
the country's different religions. The government also appointed
a Prime Minister's Faith Envoy, the MP John Battle – popularly
referred to as the God Czar! But even these sums were dwarfed
by the £60 million allocated to the Prevent Strategy (2007–10).
Since the main beneficiaries were Muslim third sector organisations, it has been described without exaggeration as 'a watershed

for Muslim representation ... easily the largest single investment ever made in British Muslim civil society'.[50]

While criticisms continue of aspects of British government policy, not least Prevent – which we address in the next chapter – for many Muslims, the move away from dependence on one organisation towards a more complex democratic constellation of representation, including women and young people, was broadly welcomed. The government funded initiatives which brought together different Muslim schools of thought with little history of collaboration around a common theme. So MINAB, comprising four organisations reflecting the main sectarian traditions in the UK, was charged with a variety of tasks, including how to upgrade the training of imams to enable them to better connect to a growing young, British-born generation.[51]

A second welcome project was the 2009 Department of Communities and Local Government (DCLG) commissioned report *Contextualising Islam in Britain*. This was led by a team from Cambridge and Exeter Universities and involved Muslim academics, religious scholars and activists from most of the distinct Muslim schools of thought. The report addressed a wide variety of topics, including the appeal of Islamist politics. Its authors pointed out that:

> Most Muslims are still brought up with the story of Islamic political success, where the ideal is to combine temporal and spiritual authority. However, there is a need to re-read the story of manifest destiny ... and to differentiate between the prophetic and the temporal ... It is important to distinguish between the sovereignty of God and the sovereignty of human beings. Some young Muslims do not make this distinction, which is the fundamental basis of democracy.[52]

The major injection of money to fund new Muslim networks, nationally and locally, the exposure of increasing numbers of British Muslims to civil servants, politicians and policymakers, has generated a new sophistication and confidence. This translates at city level into Muslims increasingly involved in religious and secular partnerships to promote equality and economic sustainability, for example, 'the "Fairness Commission" in Tower Hamlets ... [fronted] by an Anglican priest ... [or] the "Social Inclusion Process" in Birmingham ... headed by the Anglican Bishop ...'[53]

What has been dubbed the 'Christian turn' saw the Coalition government (2010–15) acknowledging and supporting the central role in inter-faith relations, for forty years, of the Church of England.[54] This was exemplified by £5 million pounds allocated in 2011 to fund programmes such as Near Neighbours (NN) which promote mutual learning and social action across faith and non-faith groups in four urban areas, Birmingham, Bradford, Leicester and parts of East London. Its novelty lay in being administered by the Church Urban Fund with applicants requiring the counter-signature of the vicar in whose parish the project was to take place.

NN was supported by Baroness Warsi for whom 'Christianity and its extensive UK-wide networks can ... be the glue in a fractious country that *locally* holds communities together' with the Church of England, in particular, 'the faith hub around which other faiths can coalesce'.[55] As the Coalition's God Czarina – as minister at the Foreign Office and for 'Faith and Communities' at the DCLG 2012–14 – she was able to develop an unrivalled overview of the different religious traditions in Britain. If she valued the organisational range and reach of the Church of England, as well as its inclusive ethos, she also enabled government match funding for Muslim and Christian charities. This reflects the new professionalism of the Muslim charities sector – especially Islamic Relief – which had a history of collaboration with the likes of CAFOD and Christian Aid.[56]

If Warsi was sympathetic to some aspects of the Coalition's policy with regard to Muslim communities, she worried that the goodwill generated by the previous Labour government's resourcing of many new Muslim networks was being dissipated by relying on an ever decreasing pool of Muslim organisations somewhat arbitrarily deemed 'mainstream' or 'moderate'. This made nonsense of what was happening on the ground. For example, in Tower Hamlets, the East London Mosque (ELM) was deeply embedded in local governance networks and forums for the delivery of local priorities including the Nafas Drugs Project and a

Muslim Women's Collective. It was also a member of Citizens UK, which enables co-operation across London of hundreds of civil society organisations working for progressive social change. In short, although pejoratively labelled 'Islamist', it was 'the largest local non-governmental provider of local services and education as well as cultural and political activity'.[57]

Such crude labelling does not allow for inter-generational transitions within such a broad grouping. Just as we saw the MAB moving towards a Tunisian style of post-Islamism, so, many Muslim groups – Salafi and Islamist alike – fractured and reconfigured under intense media and government scrutiny post 9/11 and 7/7.[58] One example is instructive. Dr Ghayasuddin Siddiqui was a member of the self-styled 'Muslim Parliament' created by Kalim Siddiqui. The latter boldly declared at its inauguration in January 1992 that 'Western civilization . . . is the modern world's sick man . . . destined for oblivion . . . [with Islam] the antidote to a morally bankrupt world'. The hand-picked members were urged to draw inspiration from the Prophet who 'showed us how to generate the political power of Islam in a minority situation and how to nurse . . . it until the creation of an Islamic state and the victory of Islam over all its opponents'.[59] Dr Ghayasuddin Siddiqui is now a trustee of British Muslims for Secular Democracy (BMSD) and campaigns against forced marriage, domestic violence and murder in the name of honour.

> The Muslim Institute, which he helped to form back in 1973 – at one time acting as a front for the Iranian Embassy in London – was re-founded in 2010 and now has a more progressive outlook publishing the quarterly magazine *Critical Muslim*.[60]

In an earlier chapter we saw an ex-president of another Islamist organisation – Young Muslims – resign and join a neo-traditionalist group. Others like Dr Siddiqui become post-Islamists. What matters is less the genealogy of groups but what they say and do.

Dr Siddiqui's example reminds us of another conceptual shift that is slowly having an effect. Namely, Muslim thinkers revisiting the term 'secular' and realising that in a Western, intellectual and historical context, it does not necessarily entail hostility to religion. A British Deobandi scholar has recently reflected on this issue drawing on historic debates amongst Indian scholars who opted to remain in India rather than leave for Pakistan at partition, as well as a recent discussion by Rowan Williams. He concludes that where the nation-state embodies a 'soft' secularism – or what Williams describes as 'programmatic' secularism – which 'recognises the religious voice and allows it public space for debate in order to influence policy' this is acceptable to Muslims as a minority.[61]

Where the state opts for a 'hard' secularism – Williams 'procedural' secularism – which excludes or penalises religious voices in public life, this illiberal turn can hollow out public life. These issues have been dealt with in an illuminating manner in a book of essays – *British Secularism and Religion, Islam, Society and the State* – which draws on contributions from two leading thinkers, a Muslim theologian and a political scientist, with rejoinders from Christian, Jewish and secular thinkers. In all, it offers a model of courteous and constructive debate.[62]

What is most surprising is that this work has been produced by a publishing house associated with the Islamic Foundation based at Markfield in Leicester – which was inspired by the Jama'at-i Islami movement. For the founder of this Islamist movement – Mawdudi – secularism, democracy, partnership with other Muslim groups and non-Muslims, along with the involvement of women in leadership were anathema and the creation of an Islamic state indispensable. Yet here we have a publication whose afterword is by a distinguished female Muslim scholar – Maleiha Malik – a professor of Law at King's College, London University, and where every Mawdudian assumption is negated or significantly nuanced.

In Britain and India, where Muslims are a minority, it is not uncommon to find Mawdudi's views challenged or quietly set aside by many within the movement.[63] Tensions, of course, remain. Recently, the Islamic Foundation debated the wisdom of publishing some of Mawdudi's works, which are little more than anti-Western diatribes.[64] Where a new generation feels the pace of reform is too slow, they simply drift away. Indeed, some of the key personalities involved in the book have moved on, including Dilwar Hussain, whom we met at the beginning of this study. He went on to establish the liberal reformist New Horizons initiative which seeks to reclaim and foreground in policy the ethical imperatives of the sharia.[65]

This dynamic of a new generation challenging and re-thinking the legacy of its founding fathers is also evident in the Sufi network mentioned earlier, which in the late 1970s championed jihad. It has since dropped the name Murabitun with its militant associations and now focuses on education: its lasting legacy in the West has not been jihad but rather 'the growth of enthusiasm for, and competence in, the classical scholarship of Islam'.[66] This example of a Sufi movement prepared to embrace politics and, in certain contexts, jihad, gives the lie to some supposed binary of apolitical 'good Muslim', invariably Sufi, and politicised 'bad Muslim', invariably Islamist. A specialist on Sufism has recently exposed the embrace of this binary by American and British governments as premised on multiple misunderstandings.[67]

A quiet revolution: Muslim women accessing public and civic life

We turn now to educated, British Muslim women who are increasingly a visible presence, finding their voice and beginning to make an impact on public and civic life. At the same time, they are also the most unsparing critics of the patriarchy and misogyny still embedded in the political and religious leadership of many Muslim communities. The existence of deep-seated resistance to Muslim women's empowerment qualifies any premature congratulation that the struggle has been won.

However, the battle has been well and truly joined. If the first Muslim women MPs were elected in 2010, five of the six new MPs elected in 2015 were women, including the first Conservative MP, Nusrat Ghani. With the 2017 election, a majority of Muslim MPs – eight of the fifteen – are women. This is, in part, because the Labour Party has since 2007 sought to bypass the hold of male gatekeepers by identifying all-women short lists for certain constituencies.

Another welcome and related expression of female empowerment is the increasing number of female Muslim academics. In the previous chapter, we mentioned the excellent MCB document – *British Muslims in Numbers* – where the lead analyst was a young female social scientist, lecturing at Oxford. The standard introduction to Islam in Britain is authored by another female, Professor Sophie Gilliat-Ray; of six Muslim contributions in the recent book of essays – *Muslims and Political Participation in Britain* – five are by females.[68] And, of course, amongst the small pool of Muslim public intellectuals, pride of place probably goes to another woman, Professor Mona Siddiqui, a specialist in Islamic Law and Inter-Religious Relations at Edinburgh University.

A key milestone on the long road to Muslim women accessing power was the high profile of Salma Yaqoob, the first woman to lead the small Respect Party from 2003 to 2012. Respect was founded in January 2003 on the back of the Stop the War Coalition (SWC), by the environmentalist George Monbiot and Salma Yaqoob, who chaired the Birmingham chapter of SWC, with support from the Socialist Workers Party (SWP).[69] Buoyed up by the success of the SWC and disillusion with the Labour Party, the time seemed propitious for such a new party.

The party did well in local and national elections in three areas which were very active in the SWC: East London, Birmingham and Bradford – all with large Muslim communities, sympathetic to its anti-imperialist and pro-Palestinian stance. In 2005, the maverick politician, George Galloway – expelled from the Labour Party – stood for Respect in Bethnal Green and Bow and became its MP. Salma Yaqoob came second in the Birmingham Small Heath and Sparkbrook constituency. Standing for the same constituency in 2010, she was narrowly defeated. By this time, the SWP had withdrawn from the Respect Party which, by default, became known as a Muslim party. Galloway lost in 2010 but then went on to win a by-election in 2012 in Bradford.

Our focus here is less with the electoral fortunes of the Respect Party – they declined markedly with Salma Yaqoob's resignation in 2014 and the loss of its one MP in 2015 – than with the significance of such a high profile Muslim woman running for political office and the opposition this provoked from within the Muslim communities. In an earlier chapter, we mentioned that in Tower Hamlets, Bangladeshis from Sylhet had imported a style of politics dependent on patronage and kinship ties, where ethnic politics tended to be a proxy for Muslim politics. In Birmingham and Bradford, the largest communities are from Mirpur in Pakistan-administered Kashmir. They too have imported an exclusionary, patriarchal, clan politics – *biraderi* (lit. 'brotherhood') – hierarchically organised with landowners at the top and artisans at the bottom.

In Birmingham and Bradford, a new generation of British Mirpuris – especially women and men excluded from such politics – was attracted to Salma Yaqoob's politics. In 2004, in the Birmingham postal vote scandal, three Muslim Labour councillors were banned by an election commissioner who found them guilty of corrupt practices. Salma Yaqoob and George Galloway used the Respect Party platform to campaign against such vote rigging, postal voting and resisted pressure of clan elders to select on the basis of such loyalties. As Salma Yaqoob explained:

> Women in particular have been disenfranchised. Postal votes are filled out in the 'privacy' of one's own home. But it is not private when family members, candidates or supporters can influence – subtly or otherwise – the way you complete your vote.[70]

Respect with Salma Yaqoob as its leader was also able to put forward female candidates as local councillors who, in turn, were well placed to garner a female vote for the party. In a wide ranging *Guardian* interview in 2010, she made clear that her stance had provoked threats and denunciations from within the Muslim communities:

> I've had death threats and criticism that I support gays – because I have a clear anti-discrimination position – and there have been claims that it is haram [forbidden in Islam] to vote for women. People say to me, 'Have you no shame?' and they accuse me of immodesty and ask my husband why he lets me speak in public. It's been an uphill struggle.

However, she also speaks of winning some of her critics around and had even had invitations from some mosques to give the Friday sermon. As a graduate and practitioner of psychotherapy, she has shown the same patience to win round non-Muslim voters initially put off by a hijab-wearing candidate. With five appearances on *Question Time*, she was, for a time, the most prominent Muslim woman in British public life.

Galloway's shock victory in 2012 in Bradford West, where he overturned a 6,000 Labour majority in one of its safest seats, was a replay of many of the same dynamics operating in Birmingham. We might characterise his victory as a result of an inter-generational civil war within the Mirpuri community, with the young, both male and female, rallying around Galloway, seen as an eloquent champion of Palestine and other Muslim causes and a critic of the stranglehold exercised by the two dominant Mirpuri land-owning clans. The Respect Party was able to mobilise students and young professionals, who used social media and family networks to get people to vote. Not only did they win the parliamentary constituency but also five local council seats.

The dynamics of the Respect Party victory are detailed in an exemplary study, *The Bradford Earthquake*. Its author states unequivocally, that 'without years of neglect, stemming from an accommodation with power brokers to exploit clan voting solidarity of biraderi . . . there would not have been fertile ground for Galloway in Bradford'. The study carefully lays bare the baneful consequences of such exclusionary politics as practised by the two dominant clans, in cahoots with Labour bosses, which between them accounted for fourteen of the twenty Black and Minority Ethnic councillors returned on a Labour ticket before the 2012 elections.[71] Whatever the failings of the Respect Party in general, and of Galloway in particular, Salma Yaqoob proved to be a pioneer in creating space for a new generation of young British Muslims, especially women, to participate in the political process as candidates and campaigners.

At the other end of the political spectrum, another Muslim woman – daughter of an immigrant father from rural Punjab in Pakistan – was making her presence felt in the Conservative Party. Sayeeda Warsi, too, during her initial foray into electoral politics

in 2005, fell foul of such tribal politics. Standing as a parliamentary candidate in her home town, Dewsbury in West Yorkshire,
religiously conservative men from traditional clans sought to de-
legitimise her candidacy and openly celebrated her defeat: in the
full glare of the media, on completion of the count, she was met
with 'jeers and boos' outside the town hall, 'a moment that in its
own way will always stay with me'.[72]

As the first Conservative cabinet minister, Baroness Warsi
would have the last laugh. She remains a very visible and activist
role model embodying the claim to gender equality for a new
generation of Muslim women.[73] She has also sought to strike at
the religious roots of such patriarchy, by urging Muslims to stop
giving their daughters an influential manual of correct behaviour,
entitled *Bahishti Zewar* – 'Heavenly Ornaments' – the contents
of which, if taken seriously, cannot but inhibit the emergence
of a confident, outward looking, generation of British Muslim
women.[74]

An abridged and annotated translation of this work makes
it clear that it takes for granted that women are subordinate to
men. Such religious knowledge for women enables men to better
'manage' them. After all, the ideal is for the woman to remain at
home, secluded from all but family and selected female friends.
Its male author

> lists women among men's possessions . . . identifies dominant
> women as a sign of the Last Day . . . [with women] the great-
> est number in hell . . . A woman is to follow her husband's
> will and whims in all things, to seek his permission on all
> issues . . . Never think of him as your equal, never let him do
> any work for you . . . [Women] are dependent even for their
> salvation on their husbands' happiness.[75]

An infamous *hadith* suggesting that women are congenitally
crooked is cited and men urged to exhibit patience with such
waywardness. Authored by a leading Deobandi scholar of an earlier generation – the Indian Ashraf 'Ali Thanawi (1863–1943) –
it remains 'one of the most influential Islamic books of modern
South Asia and, in several English translations, in the South Asian

diaspora'.[76] Warsi might hope to gain a hearing from those we characterised in the previous chapter as 'critical' traditionalists but not the 'conservative' majority.

If women's activism is to have any chance of gaining a hearing from such conservatives, it will have to be grounded in an Islamic scholarship which tackles head on the principle of male guardianship of women, which underpins much of the patriarchy and authoritarianism in Muslim communities. Such scholarship is now becoming available through the work of the international Muslim women's movement – *Musawah* ('Equality'). *Musawah* has enlisted the services of some of the finest Muslim scholars, male and female, to tackle this issue.

A three-fold approach has been adopted. First, scholars have recovered a hidden history of Islamic scholarship whereby, in early Islamic history, women were producers of religious knowledge as transmitters of *hadith*. This they contrast with the later period which sees the development of the schools of law which reduces women to sexual beings, placed under male authority. 'Their voice in the production of religious knowledge is silenced, their presence in public space curtailed – their critical faculties . . . denigrated.'[77]

Secondly, there has been close textual study of two legal concepts which in classical legal jurisprudence place women under male guardianship: '*Qiwama* [which] is understood as a husband's authority over and responsibility to provide for his wife. *Wilaya* denotes the guardianship rights of a father (or, in his absence, another male member of the family) . . . over his daughters until they are married.' In an intellectual tour de force, a female scholar has documented the historic stages whereby a key Quranic verse – 4:34 – and with it the concept of *qiwama*, has been re-interpreted to support and consolidate the principle of male guardianship.[78]

Finally, contemporary case studies of women's actual experiences of the outworking of such gendered concepts and traditional Muslim family laws across the Muslim world were commissioned. Such empirical study exposes the hollowness of the apologetic defence of such guardianship as 'protection' not 'discrimination'.[79] In all, *Musawah* has provided a rich resource of scholarship to dismantle the notion of male guardianship, support Muslim activism for equality by arguing within the tradition, retrieved and critically evaluated. The fruit of this international and collaborative scholarship is now available in the work they commissioned, *Men in Charge? Rethinking Authority in Muslim Legal Tradition.*

In Britain, an initiative which has done most to self-consciously embody such insights as they support women's activism is the Muslim Women's Network for the UK (MWNUK). MWNUK, Birmingham-based but with a national reach, began work in 2003 committed to gender equality and human rights underwritten by such pioneering Islamic scholarship. The network sought, through advocacy and research, to provide independent advice to government departments on issues touching Muslim women and public policy. In short, they wanted their expertise to enable Muslim women's voices to be heard: voices traditionally rendered inaudible through government dependency on male-dominated Muslim organisations.

By 2016 MWNUK had 700 members, individuals and organisations, encompassing academics, students, voluntary sector employees, health professionals, experts in women's rights and migration issues, businesswomen, local government employees, police officers and housewives. Eighty per cent of the membership was Muslim, with a majority between twenty-two and forty-five years old.[80] Their activities range from a travelling exhibition showcasing successful Muslim women for educational and community groups; a five day training course for women – *Gender, Islam and Advocacy* – to study classical Muslim jurisprudence, Quranic interpretation and contemporary Muslim scholarship which supports their local initiatives; easy-to-read factsheets, for example on how to combat religious discrimination in the workplace or sexual grooming of young Asian women; to a helpline which began in 2015 which largely deals with marriage, divorce, mental health issues, forced marriage and domestic violence.

Their reputation as a trusted and reliable interlocutor for policymakers turns on their independence and research which accesses hard-to-reach Muslim women. Shaista Gohir MBE and chair of MWMUK has also demonstrated her outspokenness and courage. In 2010 she resigned from the Muslim Women's National Advisory Group (MWNAG) set up two years earlier.

She complained that the NMWAG was meant to empower Muslim women but had become little more than 'a tick-box' exercise with little government consultation.[81] Later, she intervened in the Trojan Horse affair in Birmingham. While critical of the government's conflation of religious conservatism with religious extremism, she had provided evidence to those investigating Islamist entryism in a small number of Birmingham state schools. Such evidence, taken from women in the network as well as her own direct experience as a Birmingham mother, exposed them to 'bullying and harassment'.

Consistent with their advocacy for women and girls, they objected that in some of these Birmingham schools girls were effectively pressurised to wear the hijab and self-segregate on the basis of gender. They were shocked that 'marital rape was condoned as some boys were taught that a wife is not allowed to refuse sex'.[82] Posters were put up declaring that whoever did not pray was a non-believer. There was a narrow arts curriculum, anti-Western rhetoric with intimidation of non-Muslim and Muslim staff who stood up to them. In all, this bespoke the influence of unreformed Islamists.

The MWNUK has always been adept at using contacts in the media, local and national, to publicise their campaigns. In January 2016, they wrote to the trustees of Birmingham Central mosque formally complaining about the behaviour of the mosque's chairman, a local councillor, later selected as the city's Lord Mayor. The meeting with him had been intended to formalise a joint project on forced marriage since data from their helpline indicated a high numbers within the Pakistani community of women and girls being pressured into forced marriage. In all, this was part of their outreach programme to mosques to invite them to engage issues of concern to women.

Faced with the evidence, the chairman flatly denied that educated women could be 'pressured, emotionally blackmailed or threatened into marriage' and asserted that government figures were also exaggerated. Shaista Gohir and her colleague were outraged at his summary dismissal of their data drawn from grass roots research. In their letter, they warned the mosque that they would be lodging a formal complaint with the Charity

Commission to investigate why none of the mosque's thirty-nine trustees were female and raising concerns about why the mosque seemed to be promoting a caste hierarchy. The letter concluded with a citation from the Quran which mandated that justice should trump kin loyalties![83]

This was followed with letters to the then Prime Minister, David Cameron and the Labour leader, Jeremy Corbyn, headed 'Main barriers to Muslim women's participation in Britain'. Here the contents of their complaint to the mosque was rehearsed and the conclusion drawn was that if Muslim women's public and civic participation was to be enhanced the 'systematic misogyny' in mosque and political party – given the overlap in membership of both institutions – would have to be addressed. At the moment, they insisted, 'highly credible' women candidates are 'routinely blocked in favour of men with lesser CVs'. They made a number of recommendations including an independent inquiry to investigate how 'postal voting, candidate selection and local membership are controlled [by *biraderi*/clans] to block independent candidates' especially women. They also wanted charity law amended to prevent the exclusion of women from governance structures in mosques.

The story snowballed and was picked up by a BBC *Newsnight* episode under the heading: 'Are Muslim men stopping Muslim women becoming Labour councillors'. Shaista Gohir was one of those interviewed, along with other women who complained of the use of 'sabotage, smear campaigns and slander' to frustrate their political ambitions. For example, it was claimed that a thirty-one-year-old married woman with children and long standing Labour party activist was first choice to stand for a seat in Peterborough until her father objected and the local branch upheld his objection. *Newsnight* subsequently revisited this story when the Bradford MP Naz Shah added her voice to the campaign, pointing to attempts by clan politicians entrenched in the local party to blacken her reputation and intimidate her into silence. She made clear in an article in the *Huffington Post* – where she commended the 'excellent work' of the MWNUK – that without an all-woman shortlist she 'wouldn't have stood a chance' of election.[84]

MWNUK has another influential advocate, the conservative politician Baroness Warsi. In the context of outlining some of the dilemmas Muslim women face in seeking a religious divorce, she singled out their comprehensive report – *Information and Guidance on Muslim Marriage and Divorce in Britain* (2016) – arguing that 'Muslims and government would be well advised to engage with its recommendations'.[85] The report is striking. It quotes from *Men in Charge?* (Mir-Hosseini (ed.), 2015) to undercut men's authority over women; it includes an appendix to argue a Muslim woman does not need a guardian's consent to marry; it offers a model Muslim marriage contract which urges women to include a condition that does not allow the husband to commit polygamy and a provision to delegate to the wife the right to divorce; it is critical of the practice in sharia councils where an abused woman is expected to give intimate details to a panel of men. Most striking is a section entitled 'Religious blackmail by religious authorities', where they question the use and reliability of certain *hadith* frequently cited on sharia council websites to make women feel guilty about pursuing a divorce at all.

Clearly, if democracy and equality before the law is to be inclusive of Muslim women, the question of who can legitimately claim to articulate the ethical values and norms of the sharia becomes a political issue. In the recent past, the spokespersons have invariably been male. This is now changing with institutional space being extended to incorporate women's claims to represent significant Muslim constituencies, as delegates of Muslim women's networks or as experts – not least with an expertise in Islamic law.

We will conclude with two examples that illustrate this shift. In setting up an independent review in May 2016 to map the number and evaluate the practices of sharia councils to discern whether they discriminate against women, the Home Secretary chose as its chair an academic and specialist in Islamic law, Professor Mona Siddiqui.[86] Similarly, it is illuminating to look at those invited as witnesses to give evidence at the first session in October 2016 of the parallel parliamentary Home Affairs Committee inquiry into sharia councils. Of ten witnesses attending its three sessions, eight were women. The only men were chairman and vice chairman of the UK Board of Sharia Councils set up by Regent's Park mosque in London.

The women invitees comprised the chief executive of a Muslim woman's organisation in Rochdale, the chair of MWNUK (Birmingham), a spokesperson for 'One Law for All' (London) – an umbrella group including the British Muslims for Secular Democracy – a senior fellow of the European Foundation for Democracy, the president of the Association of Muslim lawyers and two members of different sharia councils. The senior fellow was Dr Elham Manea, a political scientist of Yemeni background who recently completed a four-year study of sharia councils in Britain.[87] When mentioning the women involved, we must not forget the two Muslim MPs who are members of the committee, Nusrat Ghani (Conservative) and Naz Shah (Labour), both of whom attended the inquiry. The book still given to some British Muslim women at their marriage – 'Heavenly Ornaments' – presupposes that public life is an exclusively male space, seclusion at home the ideal for women, who defer to male scholars and would not presume to challenge sharia norms. Yet here we have women active in public and presuming to adjudicate on what is or is not to count as Islamic law and its conformity to democratic norms. A quiet revolution.

Notes

1. Figures taken from the Pew Research Center survey 10 July 2012 'Most Muslims want democracy, personal freedoms, and Islam in political life'. The six countries surveyed were: Lebanon (84), Turkey (71), Egypt (67), Tunisia (63), Jordan (61) and Pakistan (42) – figures in brackets give percentages in favour of democracy. The survey also indicated that while 88 per cent of women in Pakistan supported women's employment only 46 per cent of men did.

2. John L. Esposito and Dalia Mogahed, *Who Speaks for Islam: What a Billion Muslims Really Think* (New York: Gallup Press, 2007), p. 63.

3. See Pew Research Center, 30 April 2013, 'The world's Muslims: religion, politics and society' which surveyed 38,000 people in face-to-face interviews in eighty-plus languages, covering thirty-nine

countries. Here Turkey and Lebanon were among the minority which did not support sharia, with 12 per cent and 29 per cent respectively. While 76 per cent in South Asia supported the death penalty for apostasy, this compared with 27 per cent in Southeast Asia, 56 per cent in MENA and 16 per cent in Central Asia.

4. As the Catholic historian Eamon Duffy noted in his *Saints & Sinners: A History of the Popes* (London: Yale University Press, 1997): 'This was truly revolutionary teaching, for the persecution of heresy and enforcement of Catholicism had been a reality since the days of Constantine, and since the French Revolution pope after pope had repeatedly and explicitly denounced the notion that non-Catholics had a right to religious freedom. On the older view, error has no rights, and the Church was bound to proclaim the truth and, wherever, it could, to see that society enforced the truth by secular sanctions. Heretics and unbelievers might in certain circumstances be granted *toleration*, but not *liberty*' (p. 274). Needless to say, this radical change did not happen upon a whim but was grounded in the preparatory, intellectual re-thinking done by a leading Jesuit thinker, John Courtney Murray.

5. See Samuel P. Huntington's seminal article in the *National Interest*, 24 (summer 1991), 'Religion and the third wave'. Here Huntington observes that there were three waves of democratisation in modern history: the first from the 1820s to the 1920s which was rooted in the American and French Revolutions, inspired by Protestant and Enlightenment thought. The second, from the end of World War II to the mid-1960s, was promoted by the Allied victory in the war – this latter included some which resulted from de-colonisation. The third wave, in its Catholic expression, was a product, *inter alia*, of the Vatican 2 Decree on Religious Liberty and Pope John Paul II's struggle against authoritarianism.

6. Abdullah Ahmed An-Naim, *Islam and the Secular State: Negotiating the Future of Shari'a* (Cambridge, MA: Harvard University Press, 2008), p. 283. Asma Afsaruddin, in her *Contemporary Issues in Islam* (Edinburgh: Edinburgh University Press, 2015), devotes chapters three to five to illustrate the sort of re-thinking now being done with regard to these three issues, as well as making clear the pioneering methodologies developed to enable such re-reading of revered texts – however subversive of aspects of traditional interpretation.

7. The verse in question is 4:34; An Naim, *Islam and the Secular State*, p. 109. The Quranic texts cited are: 24:31, 33:33, 53, 59.

8. A recent article points out how the respected Pakistani modernist scholar, Fazlur Rahman (d. 1988), was tainted by his close association with an authoritarian government; for example, he justified a 'notorious' Press and Publications Ordinance which 'drastically' curtailed freedom of speech; supported a statist vision whereby the state sought to regulate and train imams; and legitimised a strong man at the helm of government by arguing that in the Quran 'God's concept is functional, i.e. God is needed not for what He is or may be but for what he does. It is exactly in this spirit that Aristotle compares God to a general in the army. For the general (in Aristotle's concept) is not a soldier among other soldiers – just as God is not an extra-fact among facts – but represents "order", i.e. the fundamental function of holding the army together.' See Muhammad Qasim Zaman, 'Islamic modernism, ethics, and shari'a in Pakistan', in Robert Heffner (ed.), *Shari'a Law and Modern Muslim Ethics* (Bloomington: Indiana University Press, 2016), pp. 177–200; 184.

9. Salafism is the movement's self-description but its critics use the term Wahhabism, recalling the puritanical reformer, Muhammad ibn 'Abd al-Wahhabi (d. 1792), whose alliance in 1744 with the tribal leader Muhammad ibn Sa'ud contributed to the creation of the first Saudi state.

10. Khaled Abou El Fadl, *Reasoning with God: Reclaiming Shari'ah in the Modern Age* (Lanham: Rowman & Littlefield, 2014), pp. 23–4. There is an accessible and appreciative review of this landmark study in *Critical Muslim*, 14 (April–June 2014), pp. 213–21.

11. The term has been coined by Jocelyne Cesari in her important monograph, *The Awakening of Muslim Democracy: Religion, Modernity and the State* (Cambridge: Cambridge University Press, 2014) in which she foregrounds the role of the modern Muslim nation-state – even when notionally 'secular', as in the case of Turkey, Tunisia and Iraq – as largely responsible for the politicising of Islam.

12. El Fadl, *Reasoning with God*, p. 271. Egypt's grand mufti at the time, Ali Gomaa, in sermons and promotional videos proffered religious justifications for the military coup against the Muslim Brotherhood and the necessity of draconian methods. He would declare: 'When someone tries to divide you, then kill them … [indeed] Blessed are those who kill them. . .': see Shadi Hamid, *Islamic Exceptionalism: How the Struggle over Islam is Reshaping the World* (New York: St Martin's Press, 2016), p. 118.

13. El Fadl, *Reasoning with God*, pp. 271–82.

14. Ibid. p. 204.
15. See Robert W. Hefner (ed.), *Shari'a Politics, Islamic Law and Society in the Modern World* (Bloomington: Indiana University Press, 2011), p. 46.
16. See Roxanne L. Euben and Muhammad Qasim Zaman (eds), *Princeton Readings in Islamist Thought: Texts and Contexts from al-Banna to Bin Laden* (Princeton: Princeton University Press, 2009), pp. 53, 81. This excellent anthology clearly identifies both commonalities and differences. Already by the 1940s the Muslim Brotherhood could claim half a million members – preparing the ground for the Muslim Brotherhood's Mohamed Morsi to become the 'first democratically elected president' of Egypt in 2012 (see Hamid, *Islamic Exceptionalism*, pp. 81, 101). In his exemplary paper included in the House of Commons Affair Committee, 'Political Islam and the Muslim Brotherhood Review', published 1 November 2016 – *Political Islam: Beyond the Muslim Brotherhood* – Dr Matthew J. Nelson of SOAS considers the very different political trajectory of Islamism in South Asia, where 'the terrain of political Islam is not dominated by a single "Islamist" party focused on the capture of state power, as it is in much of the Middle East. It is defined by sectarian and especially, intra-Sunni rivalries . . . Deobandis and Jama'atis have political parties each known for securing roughly 2–4% of the popular vote.'
17. The Urdu terms used are *la-dini* and *ghairmazhabi*.
18. See Shiraz Maher, *Salafi-Jihadism: The History of an Idea* (London: Hurst & Co., 2016), chapter 10 – 'The dawn of modern political Islam' – for a clear exposition of the centrality and importance of this idea as developed by Mawdudi and influencing Arab Islamists through the works of translation by the Indian scholar Abul Hasan 'Ali Nadwi (1914–99).
19. Hamid, *Islamic Exceptionalism*, p. 85.
20. Gudrun Kramer, *Hasan al-Banna* (Oxford: Oneworld, 2009), p. 101. Alas, as so often is the case, the conquered did not share this perception. Historians have recently recovered their voice. For example, see Robert G. Hoyland, *Seeing Islam as Others Saw it: a Survey and Evaluation of Christian, Jewish and Zoroastian Writings on Early Islam* (Princeton: Darwin Press, 1997).
21. See Reza Pankhurst, *The Inevitable Caliphate? A History of the Struggle for Global Islamic Union, post 1924 to the Present* (London: Hurst & Co., 2014), p. 99. Pankhurst is a member of Hizb ut-Tahrir and was imprisoned in Egypt before being released through the good

offices of Amnesty International who adopted him as a prisoner of conscience.

22. Ibid. p. 182.

23. Muhammad Qasim Zaman, *Ashraf 'Ali Thanawi: Islam in Modern South Asia* (Oxford: Oneworld, 2008), pp. 117–18.

24. Ibid. p. 118.

25. See Abdelwahab El-Affendi, 'Londonistan's other big bang', *Critical Muslim*, 13 (January–March 2015), pp. 119–37; 121. This excellent article documents his experience and shares his insights as co-ordinator of the CSD Democracy and Islam Programme.

26. Abdelwahab El-Affendi, *Who Needs an Islamic State?*, 2nd edn (Peterborough: Upfront Publishing, 2008), p. 95.

27. Hamid, *Islamic Exceptionalism*, pp. 180, 187.

28. Abdelwahab El-Affendi, 'On the Muslim Brotherhood', *Critical Muslim*, 14 (April–June 2015), pp. 237–44; 243.

29. El-Affendi, *Who Needs an Islamic State?*, p. 69. Early Islamic history is full of irony: it is the zealotry of the Khawarij which approximates to something rare in Islamic political thought, namely 'a conditional and contractual version of monarchy'; while revered Sunni scholars such as al-Ghazali (d. 1111) allowed for no public participation in the election of a caliph, and 'opts instead for having a single elector'. Moreover, while there were a number of reasons for Uthman's murder, a significant factor was his inability to run an expanding Islamic empire with the same tribal mechanisms fit for a small Medinan city-state with which he was familiar. It is only after the second *fitna* – 678–85 – that the Umayyad Caliph Abd al Malik (d. 705) consolidates the shift from tribal levies to a paid standing army and develops 'the more autocratic, top-down caliphate' with Arabic as the new language of the emerging bureaucracy, the minting of coins, and standardised system of taxation with which to pay for the army. See Hugh Kennedy, *The Caliphate* (London: Penguin, 2016), pp. 40, 64–5, 228.

30. Pankhurst, *The Inevitable Caliphate?*, p. 115.

31. Barbara D. Metcalf, *Islamic Contestations: Essays on Muslims in India and Pakistan* (New Delhi: Oxford University Press, 2004), pp. 199–200.

32. Knut Vikor, *Between God and the Sultan: A History of Islamic Law* (Oxford: Oxford University Press, 2005), pp. 186–7, cited in Hamid, *Islamic Exceptionalism*, p. 26.

33. Hefner, *Shari'a Politics*, p. 18.

34. Bernard Haykel, 'The political failure of Islamic law' (The Dallah Albaraka Lactures on Islamic Law and Civilization, 24 September 2013), *Occasional Papers*, 12 (2014), p. 21.

35. Ibid. p. 22.

36. Irfan Ahmad, 'The State in Islamist thought', *ISIM Review*, 18 (autumn 2006), pp. 12–13. Professor Ahmad has expanded his treatment of such terms in chapter two of his ground-breaking monograph, *Islamism and Democracy in India: the Transformation of Jamaat-e-Islami* (Princeton: Princeton University Press, 2009).

37. Afsaruddin, *Contemporary Issues in Islam*, pp. 72–3.

38. El-Affendi, *Who Needs an Islamic State?*, p. 93.

39. See Brian J. Grim and Roger Finke, *The Price of Freedom Denied: Religious Persecution and Conflict in the Twenty-First Century* (Cambridge: Cambridge University Press, 2011). They also point out that Muslim-majority countries in sub-Saharan Africa have the lowest levels of religious persecution vis-à-vis other Muslim areas, as well as Christian-majority countries in the same region. This they attribute to the prevalence of Sufism.

40. See P. Lewis, *Young, British and Muslim* (London: Continuum, 2007), pp. 5–11 for an expanded treatment of such issues. Of course, Muslim migrants from East Africa and India had already learned the skills and competences of being a minority.

41. Aminul Hoque, *British-Islamic Identity: Third-Generation Bangladeshis from East London* (London: Institute of Education Press, London University, 2015), p. 108. Their creation of a British Islamic identity was 'accelerated' by their ability to 'read and speak English, allowing them to research via textbooks, conferences and the internet in the dominant language' (p. 158).

42. Timothy Peace, 'British Muslims in the anti-war movement', in Timothy Peace (ed.), *Muslims and Political Participation in Britain* (London: Routledge, 2015), pp. 124–37; 126. This is a pioneering collection, showcasing current research into Muslim participation both in terms of electoral politics and civil society initiatives.

43. Ibid. p. 125.

44. For example, in Bradford, the Muslim communities grew from circa 3,000 in 1961 to 130,000 in 2011. This translated into three Muslim councillors in 1961 to twenty-four in 2011 out of a total of ninety councillors from across the Bradford Metropolitan district. The majority represent nine inner-city wards where Muslim communities are clustered.

45. Timothy Peace, 'Muslims and the electoral politics in Britain: the case of the Respect Party', in Jørgen S. Nielsen (ed.), *Muslim Political Participation in Europe* (Edinburgh: Edinburgh University Press, 2013), pp. 299–321; 299.

46. Therese O'Toole, Daniel Nilsson DeHanas, Tariq Modood, Nasar Meer and Stephen Jones (eds), *Taking Part: Muslim Participation in Contemporary Governance* (Bristol: Bristol University, 2013), p. 41. This seminal study breaks much new ground, empirically and conceptually. It not only looks at the changing shape of Muslim engagement nationally but also in three cities/towns: Birmingham, Leicester and Tower Hamlets; as well as identifying three distinct policy domains in which Muslims are active: equalities and diversity, partnership with faith and inter-faith bodies for the purposes of welfare and service delivery, and security and counter-terrorism.

47. Ralph Grillo, 'From "Race" to "Faith"', in Steven Vertovec and Susanne Wesendorff (eds), *The Multiculturalism Backlash: European Discourses, Policies and Practices* (London: Routledge, 2009), pp. 50–71; 58.

48. Sean McLoughlin, 'The State, new Muslim leaderships and Islam as a resource for public engagement in Britain', in J. Cesari and S. McLoughlin (eds), *European Muslims and the Secular State* (Aldershot: Routledge, 2005), pp. 55–69; 60.

49. O'Toole *et al.*, *Taking Part*, p. 19.

50. Ibid. p. 20.

51. MINAB comprises MAB – Sunni Arabs close to the Muslim Brotherhood; MCB, whose leadership comprises mainly Deobandi and reformist Islamists; BMF, a Barelwi-dominated network; and Al-Khoei Foundation, a small body of Iraqi Shi'a.

52. Yasir Suleiman, *Contextualising Islam in Britain* (Cambridge: Centre of Islamic Studies, 2009), pp. 32–3.

53. O'Toole *et al.*, *Taking Part*, p. 13, footnote 18.

54. See P. Lewis, 'Muslims and Christians in Britain today: living together, respecting difference?', in David Thomas (ed.), *The Routledge Handbook on Christian-Muslim Relations* (London: Routledge, 2018), pp. 367–75.

55. Sayeeda Warsi, *The Enemy Within: A Tale of Muslim Britain* (London: Allen Lane, 2017), pp. 341–2, footnote 30, italics ours.

56. Ibid. p. 342.

57. O'Toole *et al.*, *Taking Part*, p. 62.

58. See Hamid, *Sufis, Salafis and Islamists*, chapter 6, 'Fragmentation and adaptation: the impact of social change' and chapter 7, 'Contemporary British Islamic activism' for an exemplary overview and analysis of this process.

59. P. Lewis, *Islamic Britain: Religion, Politics and Identity among British Muslims*, 2nd edn (London: I. B. Tauris, 2002), pp. 52–3.

60. Peace, *Muslims and Political Participation in Britain*, p. 135.

61. Amjad M. Mohammed, *Muslims in Non-Muslim Lands: a Legal Study with Applications* (Cambridge: The Islamic Texts Society, 2013), p. 136. Mohammed also supports voting and participating in elections since the government discharges all its tasks 'without any prejudice due to religious, ethnic or social difference' (p. 168). The author developed a real understanding of how British government works, centrally and locally, through being involved in the year-long programme run by the charity 'Common Purpose', which operates in many cities to give the up and coming middle management in public, private and voluntary sectors exposure to all aspects of a city's life. In Bradford, where he joined the programme, there has been a real effort to involve members of minority religions in the city. Personal communication with Mr Mohammed.

62. Yahya Birt, Dilwar Hussain and Ataullah Siddiqui (eds), *British Secularism and Religion: Islam, Society and the State* (Markfield: Kube Publishing, 2011).

63. For India, see Ahmad, *Islamism and Democracy in India*, pp. 218–31.

64. See Sophie Gilliat-Ray, 'The United Kingdom', in Jocelyne Cesari (ed.), *The Oxford Handbook on European Islam* (Oxford: Oxford University Press, 2015), pp. 64–111; 89.

65. Dilwar Hussain's stance is exemplified in an excellent short article he wrote some years ago, *Are we too obsessed with 'Islamic Law'*, it can be downloaded at www.policyresearch.org.uk/publications.comment/obsessedwithislamiclaw.php.

66. Mark Sedgwick, *Western Sufism: From the Abbasids to the New Age* (Oxford: Oxford University Press, 2016), pp. 242–3.

67. Mark Sedgwick, 'Sufis as "Good Muslims": Sufism in the battle against jihadi Salafism', in Lloyd Ridgeon (ed.), *Sufis and Salafis in the Contemporary Age* (London: Bloomsbury, 2015), pp. 105–17. The 'school of thought' most closely associated with Sufism in Pakistan – the Barelvis – has not avoided the recourse to violence afflicting so many groups in contemporary Pakistan. See Mujeeb Ahmad, 'The rise of militancy among Pakistani Barelvis: the case of the Sunni Tehrik', in Roger D. Long, Gurharpal Singh, Yunas Samad and Ian

Talbot (eds), *State and Nation-Building in Pakistan: Beyond Islam and Security* (London: Routledge, 2015), pp. 166–79.

68. Professor Sophie Gilliat-Ray – Director of the Centre for the Study of Islam in the UK at Cardiff University – authored *Muslims in Britain: an Introduction* (Cambridge: Cambridge University Press, 2010).

69. RESPECT was an acronym standing for Respect, Equality, Socialism, Peace, Environmentalism, Community and Trade Unionism. The next few paragraphs depend on an excellent article by Peace, 'Muslims and the electoral politics in Britain', p. 308.

70. Madeleine Bunting, 'Respect candidate spearheads quiet revolution to get Muslim women involved in politics', *The Guardian*, 23 April 2010.

71. Lewis Baston, *The Bradford Earthquake: the Lessons from Bradford West for Election Campaigning and Political Engagement in Britain* (Liverpool: Democratic Audit, 2013), pp. 10, 53.

72. Warsi, *The Enemy Within*, pp. 116, 243. Warsi notes that a decade later the community had begun to change and had elected an Asian Muslim woman as their MP.

73. Warsi spoke at the launch of the Inclusive Mosque Initiative in Bristol in 2015; see A. Lewicki and T. O'Toole, 'Acts and practices of citizenship: Muslim women's activism in the UK', *Ethnic and Racial Studies*, 10: 1 (2016), pp. 152–71; 166.

74. Warsi was given this work as a girl studying in a mosque. She is scathing about its series of dos and don'ts; its insistence on 'blindly following a faith – to question was seen as wrong – and its teaching on women's education was deeply conflicted . . .' (p. 183).

75. B. Metcalf, *Perfecting Women: Maulana Ashraf 'Ali Thanawi's Bihishti Zewar (Heavenly Ornaments)* (London: University of California Press, 1990), pp. 23, 245.

76. Muhammad Qasim Zaman, *Ashraf 'Ali Thanawi: Islam in South Asia* (Oxford: Oneworld, 2008), pp. 69–70.

77. Ziba Mir-Hosseini, 'Moral contestations and patriarchal ethics: women challenging the justice of Muslim family laws', in Robert Heffner (ed.), *Shari'a Law and Modern Muslim Ethics* (Bloomington: Indiana University Press, 2016), pp. 65–82; 73.

78. Verse 4:34 reads: 'Men are *qawwamun* (protectors/maintainers) in relation to women, according to what God has favored some over others and according to what they spend from their wealth. Righteous women are *qanitat* (obedient) guarding the unseen according to what God has guarded. Those [women] whose *nushuz* (rebellion)

you fear, admonish them, and abandon them in bed, and *adribu-hunna* (strike them) . . .': ibid. p. 75. The meanings in the parentheses approximate to the consensus of classical jurists – each of which is being challenged or nuanced by recent scholarship: ibid. p. 77.

79. Ibid. p. 78.
80. The details about the MWNUK come from an extended interview with Faeeza Vaid, its Executive Director, on 17 May 2016, and from extensive materials on their website. Vaid is a young South African who trained as a lawyer in the UK and then did post graduate research studying Islam at Cape Town University in 2006 – learning Quranic hermeneutics from Sa'diyya Shaikh, a contributor to the important collection of essays edited by Ziba Mir-Hosseini, *Men in Charge? Re-thinking Religious Authority in the Muslim Legal Tradition* (Oxford: Oneworld, 2015).
81. See her article in *The Guardian*, 'Muslim women are not political pawns', 9 April 2010.
82. Information taken from their press release, 'Trojan Horse: those who have failed children and should be held accountable' on their web-site. The issue of marital rape remains hugely sensitive. In a recent study, the author points out that for traditional Islamic jurists such a category would be an oxymoron, since 'sexual rights were simply the most important thing a husband acquired upon marrying a woman, and so the possibility that a husband was violating or committing a crime against his wife by sexually coercing her simply did not arise'. See Hina Azam, *Sexual Violation in Islamic law: Substance, Evidence and Procedure* (Cambridge: Cambridge University Press, 2017), p. 19.
83. We are grateful to the MWNUK for providing us with this and the following letter to the then Prime Minister, David Cameron. The accusation about the promotion of a caste hierarchy turned on some of trustees having 'Ch' in front of their names. This stands for the caste of 'Chaudhary', a land-holding caste that sits at the top of the clan/caste hierarchy.
84. 'I would not tolerate mistreatment of women in any other commu-nity – I won't tolerate it in my own', *Huffington Post*, 18 March 2016.
85. Warsi, *The Enemy Within*, p. 175.
86. In an interview with the Radio 4 Sunday programme, 29 May 2016, she pointed out that some women who want a religious divorce go to sharia councils hoping to obtain a divorce from a recalcitrant hus-band but end up 'trapped in limbo' because the council cannot make it happen. She also suspects some of the councils privilege 'forced' family cohesion over the ethical spirit of Islamic law.

87. See Elham Manea, *Women and Shari'a Law: the Impact of Legal Pluralism* (London: I. B. Tauris, 2016). This provides an illuminating and disturbing insight into the practices and attitudes of some of the practitioners within sharia councils. She demonstrates how vulnerable uneducated women are to community pressures, especially those living in closed communities, making a mockery of claims to freedom of choice when attending the sharia council. For a different scholarly analysis, see Samia Bano, *Muslim Women and Shari'ah Councils: Transcending the Boundaries of Community and Law* (London: Palgrave Macmillan, 2012).

4

Radicals, Extremists and Terrorists: Contextualising the Challenge of Radicalisation

> We are at war ... I am a soldier ... our words have no impact upon you, therefore I'm going to talk to you in a language that you understand. Our words are dead until we give them life with our blood.[1]

Mohammed Siddique Khan issued this chilling threat before leading the deadly terrorist attacks that would become referred to as the '7/7' London bombings of 2005. The incident was shocking not only for the scale of its devastation but also because it was perpetrated by four British Muslims. While the UK had been subject to murderous IRA attacks for decades, there was something new and unnerving about Muslim 'home-grown' bombers. Unlike the perpetrators of the 9/11 attacks, most of the 7/7 bombers were British born.

In the posthumous video, Khan, in his unmistakably thick Yorkshire accent, taunts viewers from the grave by directly addressing those who might be unsure of the rationale for the attacks. Arrogating to himself the role of a resistance leader, he insists that his 'ethical stance' shaped by Islam compelled him to 'protect and avenge' his Muslim brothers and sisters against those who 'bombed, gassed, imprisoned and tortured' his co-religionists. Khan clearly states that his goals are political as well as religious, compressing his temporal and spiritual concerns into a succinct ultimatum – 'we will not stop bombing until you stop bombing us and leave us to practice our religion.'

Back to the future on 22 May 2013, Michael Adebolajo – after murdering Fusilier Lee Rigby in broad daylight on the streets of London – calmly explains to a passer-by

> The only reason we have killed this man today is because Muslims are dying daily by British soldiers. And this British soldier is one. It is an eye for an eye and a tooth for a tooth. By Allah, we swear by the almighty Allah we will never stop fighting you until you leave us alone.[2]

The following year, the notorious masked 'Jihadi John' Mohammed Emwazi shocked audiences all over the world with his ritual beheadings of Western hostages. These killings formed a core part of ISIS's theatrical repertoire and normalisation of barbarity. These savage acts of violence have helped create a climate of fear even though they do not amount to an existential threat to British society.

The quest to understand what motivates British Muslims to join extremist groups, take up arms against their own government and murder fellow Britons has become an enigma for experts trying to explain the causation for violent radicalisation. The sprawling body of literature on what causes someone to be 'radicalised' remains inconclusive. The issue has also become a sensitive problem for the vast majority of British Muslims who have no sympathy for violent extremists and feel constant pressure to disassociate themselves from the terrorism committed by their co-religionists. In this chapter we try to make sense of the pressing issue of violent radicalisation and locate it within a broader historical context by looking at past interactions between Muslim militant groups and the British state. This background then leads us to explore the processes by which young British Muslims became attracted to radical religious discourses and how this can lead to violence. After this, we evaluate the role of government counter-terrorism policies and the effect on Muslim communities.

The London bombings seared the public imagination just as the New York 9/11 attacks did, and have since shaped the social and political landscape of Britain in various ways. The aftermath of 7/7 raised numerous questions about the levels of integration within Muslim communities and whether the idea of multiculturalism had expired. For some influential right-wing commentators the spectre of domestic terrorism provided further evidence of a 'threat within' from fast-growing Muslim communities that appeared unwilling to integrate into the secular liberal norms of British society, maintained religio-cultural practices deemed incompatible with modernity and possessed a unique proclivity for criminality and violent extremism. Negative stereotypes of Muslims became normalised in many sections of the media, gained currency among politicians and energised long standing existential fears about Islam. The ruling Labour government was swift in its response as it initiated both 'hard' and 'soft' measures to deal with home-grown terrorism by enshrining new counter-terrorism legislation and direct engagement with Muslim advocacy groups.

Though some Muslims remain locked into denial and conspiracy theories about who perpetrated 7/7, most acknowledged that these issues needed to be addressed and became more open to introspection and dialogue. Until then very few British Muslims conceded the existence of jihadist discourses that were largely left unchallenged during much the 1980s and 1990s. To do so was thought to be 'washing dirty linen' in public and expressing disloyalty to Muslim causes abroad. Equally disturbing was the fact that the British state also played a role by allowing certain individuals and groups to operate freely in the UK – leading to the capital being given the disparaging moniker of 'Londonistan' as it became an organising hub for numerous jihadist groups. This arrangement formed part of longstanding government policies which viewed some radical religious movements as useful in maintaining geostrategic interests.

Violence in the name of Islam

In contemporary Western public discourse, the concept of jihad generates fear and the term is frequently used interchangeably for the ideologies collectively referred to as jihadism.[3] The idea of jihad, like other theological constructs in the Islamic tradition, has been variously interpreted and applied across diverse historical and political contexts. Often translated into English as 'Holy War', jihad actually literally means 'striving'. For Muslims, jihad implies not only warfare but also a range of more irenic connotations that include personal struggle, striving for social justice and peaceful resistance.

Linguistically, the Arabic term '*jihad*' is derived from the etymological root '*juhd*' which denotes 'effort,' with the related verb '*jahd*' – meaning 'doing one's utmost'. As a noun, jihad implies the act of striving or patient struggling in difficult times and its various forms appear forty-one times in the Quran.[4] Scholars have traditionally defined jihad to be against the self, Satan, sinful people or disbelievers.[5] This has been divided more simply as the 'greater' and 'lesser' jihads, that is to say the non-physical and physical realms. The so called 'greater jihad' refers to the personal struggle against immorality, the daily challenge to maintain good character and ethical action in the world. It can also include any good conduct or effort to promote goodness in society to the point that contemporary scholars have expanded this pacific dimension to include proselytisation or even 'e-jihad'. The 'lesser jihad' is used to describe the struggle to resist forces that seek to harm individuals or societies through violent means.

Muslim scholars throughout the centuries have debated the meaning of jihad, its ethical limits and rules of engagement in both its defensive and offensive forms. Professor of Islamic Studies Asma Afsaruddin, in her book *Striving in the Path of God: Jihad and Martyrdom in Islamic Thought*, demonstrates that the polyvalent nature of the concept cannot be reduced only to a combative definition. She acknowledges that the dominant discourses on jihad from the eighth century privileged the militaristic conception and became a fixed assumption within classical Islamic juridical and administrative literature.[6] However, she points out that there are no references to 'Holy War' in the Quran as the Arabic word for fighting is *qital*. An examination of the work of the early luminaries of Quranic exegesis such as al-Tabari (d. 923), al-Zamakhshari (d. 1144), Fakhr al-Din al-Razi (d. 1210), al-Qurtubi (d. 1273) and Ibn Kathir (d. 1373) reveal that the pacific dimension of jihad in Quranic discourse and its association with the ideas of peaceful forbearance was how the term was uniformly understood, from the ninth century onwards.

Critics of Islam frequently offer primordialist explanations that suggest that Muslims historically possess a war-like character which is given Quranic sanction to conquer and encourage violence. Islam is not unique as a religion for advocating types of 'just war' or for followers who have breached the ethical parameters of their faith. Hinduism has scriptural guidance that allows violence in self-defence, Judaism has its concept of all-destructive war, and even Buddhism has its violent tradition.[7] Historian of Christianity, Professor Philip Jenkins contends that verses in the Quran are actually far less bloody and less violent than those in the Bible and cites explicit instructions in the Old Testament calling for genocide while the Quran calls primarily for defensive war.[8] There are indeed passages in the Quran that appear to incite violence, but these categories of verses have been decontexualised by both Muslims and non-Muslims through deliberate omission of the beginning and ending of these verses when cited.

The most commonly referenced guidances in relation to combat are grouped into three types – those which obligate warfare under justified circumstances, abstention from and termination of hostilities, and peacemaking. The most frequently cited Quranic verse (9:5) by both jihadists and critics of Islam states 'slay the polytheists wherever you may encounter them, seize them and encircle them and lie in wait for them'. However, the first and last parts of this verse are rarely mentioned nor are the historical circumstances in which the full context of these commands are explained. In addition, other Quranic teachings about the importance of abstention and termination of hostilities are rarely given attention nor are the various passages such as 8:61, that instruct believers to 'seek peace and place their trust in God'. Despite these admonitions, there is no doubt that some Muslims in the past and present have abused these sacred parameters.

In contextualising these early historical precedents, one must also remember the Prophet Muhammad held both sacred and profane roles and the religion was envisaged as a universal faith, intended to be spread throughout the world. American Muslim political scientist Dr Shadi Hamid, author of *Islamic Exceptionalism:*

How the Struggle over Islam is Reshaping the World, points out that the Prophet of Islam:

> was a state builder, and state building has historically been a violent process, requiring, before anything else, the capture and control of territory. Naturally, then, the Quran *had* to have verses addressing and even endorsing the use of force. How could it be otherwise? The vast majority of Islamic scholars acknowledge, however, that the verses dealing with violence and the use of force were tied to a particular set of circumstances, and it was the task of clerics to consider when war was or wasn't justified and how it should be waged.[9]

This is an important point. Islam was an imperial religion. Early scholars explained the astonishing expansion of the first Islamic empires as a sign of divine favour – a 'Muslim manifest destiny' of sorts. The eminent Middle Eastern historian, Professor Hugh Kennedy notes in his book *The Great Arab Conquests: How the Spread of Islam Changed the World we Live in,* that there is an abundance of scholarly rationalistion for what he calls 'an ideology of conquest'.[10] This re-working of jihad into an ideology of conquest, like other premodern Islamic legal precedents, is part of a vast tradition that can be mined to support or deny modern realities.

The celebrated Pakistani Deobandi scholar, Mufti Taqi Usmani, frequently cited in this study because of his continuing influence in Britain, has nothing but 'contemptuous disdain for the view that the sort of expansionism aggressive jihad represented no longer had a respectable place in the modern world'.[11] While for a traditionalist scholar, such as Usmani, his defence of offensive jihad is theoretical – to safeguard Islam's timeless verities against erosion by modernists – not so for modern jihadists, who instrumentalise the past to argue that offensive jihad to gain and maintain territory is still both viable and desirable.

Violent Muslim militants in the late twentieth century have forced the topic of jihad into the public imagination through various acts of terrorism in the West and by attacking their own governments and even fellow Muslims. Today, the idea of jihad is most often associated with the violence of terrorist groups like Al-Qaeda and ISIS and is used by these groups themselves to describe their actions against Western military operations in Afghanistan, Iraq, Syria and elsewhere.

In contrast to traditional understandings of jihad which circumscribed war within a number of legal and ethical parameters, jihadist ideologues such as Abu Mus'ab al-Suri, Abu Muhammad al-Maqdisi and Ayman al-Zawahri have introduced modalities of combat that have little basis in established Islamic doctrine and practice. Unlike the jihad invoked in the context of resistance by Islamist ideologues such as Abdullah Azzam (d. 1989), who advocated classical approaches to the application of jihad in Afghanistan and restricted the use of violence to military combatants, they have attempted to stretch pre-modern consensual precedents associated with the operationalisation of jihad to the new situations created by modernity, particularly to recent American global geo-strategic hegemony. For these people the modern form of jihad must confront the 'Far Enemy' – America and its allies – rather than focusing on the 'Near Enemy' of Muslim regimes. This in effect means that jihadism has gone global.

Jihadist thinking presumes a binary division of the world into belief and non-belief. In this dichotomous perspective, the world is in a state of *jahiliyya* (ignorance), Muslim and non-Muslim states are in a permanent state of war until Islam attains global supremacy. The governments in the Middle East, particularly Saudi Arabia, are judged to be apostate, corrupt pawns of American and Western cultural and economic hegemony. In light of these conditions, jihad is interpreted as an obligation on *all* Muslims. This theo-political approach has been called 'Salafi-Jihadism' or 'Takfirism', which is a particularly modern fusion of ultra-conservative theology with political ideology. As noted anthropologist and researcher on terrorism Professor Scott Atran observes:

Takfiris (from *takfir*, 'excommunication') are rejectionists who disdain other forms of Islam, including *Wahhabism* (an evangelical creed which preaches Calvinist-like obedience to the state) and most fundamentalist, or *Salafi*, creeds (which oppose fighting between co-religionists as sowing discord, or *fitna*, in the Muslim community). Salafi Islam is the host on which this viral Takfiri movement rides, much as Christian fundamentalism is the host upon which White Supremacism rides. The host itself is not the cause of the virus and is, indeed, a primary victim.[12]

Takfiri jihadism justifies suicide bombing as a tactic of asymmetric warfare and condones the killing of innocents, including other Muslims, as collateral damage. The intellectual legitimation of acts of terrorism articulated in jihadist thought has not gone unchallenged as well-known scholars such as Abdallah bin Bayyah, Muhammad Tahir ul-Qadri and Muhammad Yaqoobi have offered scripturally grounded rebuttals to their legal justifications.[13] This belies the claim that Muslims have not spoken out against extremists and ignores these scholarly refutations of the likes of Al-Qaeda and ISIS and the numerous instances of ordinary Muslims who have condemned the violence of terrorists continuously over the last two decades.

A British jihad

To fully contextualise the emergence of jihadism in the UK we need to retrace the complex historical relationship between the British state and its engagement with its Muslim subjects during the imperial and post-colonial periods. British planners helped shape the cartography of the modern Middle East during and after the First World War, by placing rulers in newly created territories to maintain influence. In the pre-independence era, officials cultivated specific religious movements and individuals to counter emerging nationalist parties that sought liberation. Historian Mark Curtis, in his book *Secret Affairs: Britain's Collusion with Radical Islam*, documents how successive British governments colluded with militant Muslim groups during Empire as part of a policy of divide and rule to create strategic alliances that secured fundamental, long-term and short-term foreign policy outcomes. He observes that

Radical Islamic forces have been seen as useful to White-hall in five specific ways: as a global counter-force to the ideologies of secular nationalism and Soviet communism, in the cases of Saudi Arabia and Pakistan; as 'conservative muscle' within countries to undermine secular nationalists and bolster pro-Western regimes; as 'shock troops' to desta-bilise or overthrow governments; as proxy military forces to fight wars; and as 'political tools' to leverage change from governments.[14]

Following the success of independence movements in the region, this mutually beneficial relationship continued as the UK was keen to maintain its influence by proxy and supported reli-gious forces that would challenge communist and Arab nationalist leaders such as the Egyptian Gamal Abdel Nasser. America helped Britain to achieve these goals by propping up pro-Western mon-archs in Saudi Arabia and the Gulf States and forming covert rela-tionships with Islamist forces such as the Muslim Brotherhood in Egypt in the 1950s and 1960s.

The co-operation of Islamic movements was pragmatic as their strategic goals at times aligned with Western policy inter-ests. Secular Arab nationalism as a political project was all but extinguished by the 1970s and began to be supplanted by petro-dollar-funded Islamist movements. The British state has displayed no hesitation in collaborating with the Saudis who are known to have spent billions of pounds to promote their austere and often intolerant interpretation of Islam, in addition to financing radical Islamic groups around the globe. This process has been examined in extensive detail by Dr Christopher Davidson in his recent book *Shadow Wars: The Secret Struggle for The Middle East*, where he shows how Western powers have repeatedly colluded with the most powerful actors in the Gulf region to maintain their security interests and as a by-product have helped create the religious politics, sectarian wars and extremist Muslim move-ments plaguing the region today.[15]

The seeds of the contemporary jihadi movement were planted in the jails of Egypt in the 1960s and came to bitter fruition in the late 1970s, 1980s and 1990s. During these decades local militant Muslim groups confronted the 'near enemy' of their own governments or occupying forces in theatres of conflict such as Afghanistan, the Philippines and Kashmir. Politicised forms of Islam became a global phenomenon that were strategically co-opted in the 1980s as Britain and America worked with Pakistan to support the Afghan Mujahideen against the Soviet occupation of their country.

These 'Holy Warriors' were projected as freedom fighters defending themselves against a 'Godless Russian' invasion. Courted by Margaret Thatcher when she visited the Afghan-Pakistan border in 1981, they were even invited by Ronald Regan to the White House in 1983. This resulted in the supply of money, military hardware, training and diplomatic support. Even Hollywood chimed in with the closing credits of the 1988 film Rambo III: 'This film is dedicated to the brave Mujahideen of Afghanistan.' Indeed, some Muslims viewed Osama bin Laden as an Arab Rambo who was loved by the American government when he fought the Russians, but hated when he became their enemy.

The turning point in strategy corresponds with the personal trajectory of Osama bin Laden under the influence of his deputy, Ayman al–Zawahiri, after the end of the first Afghan war, and his subsequent shifting of focus to American foreign policy in the Middle East in general and Saudi Arabia specifically. Bin Laden sharply criticised Saudi Arabia's ruling elite after they rejected his offer to protect the Kingdom against Saddam Hussain during the first Gulf War and eventually left for Sudan after he was stripped of his citizenship. The US then became his primary target after it was judged to be at the root of the problems afflicting Muslim lands and held ultimately responsible for generating grievances that included supporting Israel against the Palestinians, its economic and military presence in Saudi Arabia and for propping up unpopular governments in the Middle East.

Despite the symbolic importance of Bin Laden, it would be a mistake to attribute the rise of global jihadism solely to Al-Qaeda, as jihadi ideas emerged in different contexts and were shaped by various local, regional and transnational dynamics. Jihadist discourses 'cannot be understood fully without recourse to the wider universe of ideas and social practices – both sacred and profane

– which jihadis themselves reference and inhabit'.[16] This includes
the failure of militant movements and subsequent repression of
these groups in Arab states in the 1980s and early 1990s. This,
combined with intellectual exchanges between movement ideologues, incubated the ideological foundations of the discourses on
matters of strategy, priority and wider socio-political milieu. The
result was the globalised spread of jihadism which mutated from
nationalist liberation struggles to terrorist transnationalist networks which established cells in the West.

During this period, the Soviet-Afghan war would serve as a
university that attracted fighters from all over the Muslim world.
Founding members of Pakistan's *Harkat ul-Ansar*, the Libyan
Islamic Fighting Group and the Kosovo Liberation Army graduated to lead terrorist cells after the end of the conflict and it is well
known that Al-Qaeda was birthed during this time. Starting off
as a resistance network, it went on to attack both Western interests and Muslim regimes in the 1990s. Members of these radical
groups sometimes were exiled and some sought political asylum in
Britain. These include the notorious preachers Abu Hamza, Omar
Bakri, Abdullah el-Faisal, the jihadi scholar Abu Qatada, as well
as leaders of moderate Islamist movements such as Rachid Gan-
noushi from the An-Nahda party in Tunisia. A few are alleged to
have been working as informers for M15 while implicated in terrorist activity overseas, while others were 'protected by the British
security services while being wanted by foreign governments'.[17]

Radicalising the youth

Jihadist discourses migrated to the UK with the arrival of the
exiled ideologues and nomadic former Mujahideen in the 1980s
and early 1990s. Unemployed and seeking a purpose, many had
travelled to and from various conflict hotspots looking for Muslim
causes in which they could participate. The British government
gave sanctuary to some of these men, including exiled preachers
and ideologues such as Abu Basir al-Tartusi, Muhammad al-Surur
and Abu Qatada who focused predominately on recruiting British
Arabs, while Abu Hamza, Abdullah el-Faisal and Omar Bakri promoted jihadist ideas among young British Muslims.[18] The latter

three were able to engage the South Asian Muslim youth through the combination of an aura of scholarly authority, showmanship and the ability to tap into issues that resonated with their concerns as members of the *ummah* – the global Muslim community. At the same time they competed with each other for influence, recruits and financial gain but collectively laid the groundwork for the jihadist networks that proliferated in the mid-2000s.

British Muslim commentator Yahya Birt writes that 'pre-11 September such radical discourses were mostly seen as an annoying, containable irrelevance by most British Muslims, and were the subject of a tacit "covenant of security" between such groups and the intelligence services, the police and the government'.[19] The government turned a blind eye to the young Muslims who went to fight in theatres of conflict such as Afghanistan, Bosnia and Kashmir pre 9/11. These young men were allowed to travel freely as there was an implicit understanding that they would not turn their guns on the British government. This tacit agreement was said to be a 'Covenant of Security' that implied radical preachers could operate and recruit to Muslim causes abroad as long as they did not incite or perpetrate violence in Britain. This was a huge mistake: it allowed jihadists to circulate their ideas unrestricted throughout the 1980s and 1990s. It even continued after the 9/11 attacks in America.

The pantomime villain-like appearance of Abu Hamza, with his hooked hand and loud-mouthed rhetoric, became a familiar staple on TV and newspapers during the late 1990s and early 2000s. Mustafa Kamel Mustafa (his actual name) rose to prominence after the setting up of his Supporters of Sharia (SOS) organisation in 1994, around the same time Abu Qatada started to gain a profile. Their particular messages helped to lay the ideological foundations for jihadism in Britain as Abu Hamza established himself at the Finsbury Park Mosque between 1997 and 2003.

He used the place to recruit a motley crew of supporters who eventually took over the mosque and turned it into a communications and recruitment centre for aspiring jihadis. These impressionable, often unemployed young men were recruited through their attendance at the mosque and invited to recreational events such as paintballing and camping where they would be shown gruesome jihadi videos. It became a base to finance his activities and from which to send hundreds of British Muslim men for combat training and fighting experience in diverse conflict zones such as Algeria, Afghanistan, Bosnia, Chechnya, Kashmir and Yemen. Abu Hamza is also believed to have mentored 9/11 suspect Zacharias Moussaoui and the attempted 'shoe-bomber' Richard Reid.

It is remarkable that Abu Hamza was allowed to roam across the UK speaking to young people for as long as he did. This occurrence appears to support the suspicion that he was given the leeway to do so in exchange for providing useful information to the intelligence services. He claimed to have secretly worked with the British secret service 'to keep the streets of London safe' by 'cooling hotheads'.[20] He appears to have overstepped the mark in 1999 after he spoke on behalf of the Islamic Army of Aden who had taken credit for kidnapping British and American tourists in Yemen.

This became an international incident and four of the foreigners were killed in the bungled rescue attempt by the Yemeni government. This is said to have occurred as a bargaining strategy to release a group of British Muslims that he had allegedly sent to Yemen – one of which was his son. This led to a new level of public scrutiny and calls for action to be taken against him and the activities at Finsbury Park Mosque. He was allowed to continue preaching despite calling the 9/11 attacks a 'towering day in history'. He evaded legal action until 2003, when the police raided the mosque as part of an alleged plot to produce the poison ricin. He was eventually arrested in 2004 under the Terrorism Act for various charges including encouraging murder, incitement to racial hatred and active recruitment for militant groups in places such as Yemen. After serving his sentence in the UK, the US government extradited him at the end of 2012.

The Jamaican convert Abdullah el-Faisal was an associate of Abu Hamza who arrived in the UK in the early 1990s and became the imam at Brixton Mosque until he was removed for his extremist preaching. His outrageous views and unsuccessful attempt to take over the mosque led to his departure and his subsequent trajectory helped to orientate some young people towards jihadism. He gained a following across the UK due to his fiery speeches with themes that alternated between condemnations of the Saudi Arabian monarchy, its religious establishment, non-Muslims and the necessity of jihad. In one of his sermons called the 'Rules of Jihad', he declared that 'we spread Islam by the Sword and . . . today we are going to spread by the Kalashnikov and there is nothing you can do about it'.[21] He is known to have delivered lectures in the Beeston area of Leeds, where three of the four 7/7 bombers lived. He was eventually imprisoned in 2003 for soliciting murder, inciting racial and religious hatred, and was deported to Jamaica in 2007.

Syrian born Omar Bakri secured political asylum in Britain in 1986 and went on to lead the British branch of the radical transnational movement Hizb ut-Tahrir (HT) around the time of the first Gulf War in 1991. HT, mentioned in the previous chapter, was founded in Palestine in the early 1950s with a mission to re-establish the *khilafah* – caliphate – a modern pan-Islamic superstate. The institution of *khilafah* is idealised by many Muslims as it represents a lost historical utopia where faith superseded ethnic, linguistic, cultural and political differences.[22] For the true believers of HT – a revitalised *khilafah* offers an alternative Islamic heterotopia to the West's dystopia. For them, this singular utopic order would solve all the political, economic and social problems of Muslims globally, challenge Western hegemony and carry the message of Islam to the rest of the world.

Of the three English-speaking preachers, Omar Bakri arguably had the most effective outreach and influence on British Muslims looking for more radical approaches to religion. As leader of the HT in Britain, he pioneered a successful, high-profile style of youth recruitment through 'pamphlet Islam' on college and university campuses across the UK. Towards the mid-1990s, the central leadership of HT in the Middle East blamed Bakri for a series of controversial stunts which they felt took focus away from the party message and they forced him to resign in February 1996. Omar Bakri went on to lead the extremist Al-Muhajiroun group (AM), a shortened version of Jamaat al-Muhajiroun, a front for HT which he created in 1983 while exiled in Saudi Arabia. Towards the end of the 1990s, Omar Bakri developed links with the leading jihadist terror networks that recruited British

Muslims and infamously described the perpetrators of the 9/11 terror attacks as 'the Magnificent 19'.

Pressure began to be applied on his group in 2003 after the bombing of a night club in Israel was found to be carried out by two British Muslims who had prior connections with AM. Anticipating proscription in 2004, he disbanded AM and in 2005 informed his followers that the 'covenant of security' had been violated by new anti-terrorism legislation and that Britain had become *Dar al-Harb* (Land of War) in which the *kafir* (non-believers) have no sanctity for their own life and property. After the 7/7 attacks he fled the UK for Lebanon and was subsequently banned from returning to Britain. His former supporters created successor groups to AM called 'Al-Gurabaa' and the 'Saved Sect', which were also later banned by the British government in 2006. One of Bakri's star pupils, Anjum Choudary, took his place as the face of AM and managed its various reincarnations until his imprisonment in 2016 for inviting support for ISIS.

Many young people were exposed to these ideas and some joined Abu Hamza and Omar Bakri's groups; not all of them went on to perform acts of violence. The influence of these extremist preachers declined as they left the country, and from the early 2000s recruitment to these types of groups was enabled by the availability of online material which bypassed the need for personal exposure to ideologues and participation in organisations. Instead, figures such as Omar Bakri and Abdullah el-Faisal communicated with their followers through online chat groups and YouTube.

None of the three preachers mentioned here would have been able to attract people to their cause without a wider socio-political ecology. Those drawn to radical messaging were rendered more susceptible by the convergence of various global and local factors. These 'glocal' factors were a mix of individual, national and international conditions that shaped the journeys of individuals that were drawn to radical movements. The personal biographies of radicalised British Muslims in the 1990s were more often than not marked by experiences of social alienation and racism. They were usually religious novices whose understanding and practice of Islam was mediated through their peers.

The extremist preachers were able to engage three dimensions of young Muslims' life experience. They were able to address their desire for a strong internal identity, spoke to their external social circumstances and provided a connection to an idealised past with promises of future greatness. Furthermore, they were able to offer compelling explanations for the socio-political problems facing Muslim societies and provided an attractive ideological alternative to the stifling inward-looking politics of their parents' generation.

Generation jihad

The pattern of international crisis events beginning in the 1990s – specifically, the first Gulf War in 1991, the US invasion of Somalia in 1992, ethnic cleansing of Muslims in Bosnia in the mid-1990s, the persecution of Muslims in Chechnya (1994–5) and Kosovo (1998–9) and the American-led wars after 9/11 – all reinforced the perception of many Muslims that there was a 'War on Islam'. This heightened awareness of the persecution of Muslims and a corresponding need to 'defend Islam'. The military interventions of the American and British governments, particularly after 9/11, were considered by many experts and state intelligence agencies to have the potential effect of increasing Muslim radicalisation and recruitment to violent militant groups.[23] All of these factors accumulated to shape a social change within British Muslim communities that would become manifest decades later.

Declassified documents later released in the publication of the Chilcot Report showed that in 2003, one month before the invasion of Iraq, the British government was briefed on the potential of 'Blowback', that is, of revenge attacks. These documents reveal how members of the Joint Intelligence Committee warned Tony Blair that invading Iraq would 'increase significantly' the threat of terrorist attacks in the UK. A secret report leaked to the media appears to concede the anger and disillusionment generated among many British Muslims as a result of British and Western foreign policy. It acknowledged that 'perceived Western bias in Israel's favour over the Israel/Palestinian conflict' represented a 'long-term grievance of the international Muslim community' which 'might contribute to a sense of helplessness with regard to the situation of Muslims in the world, with a lack of any tangible "pressure valves", in order to vent frustrations, anger or dissent'.[24]

A few weeks before the 7/7 attacks the Joint Terrorism Analysis Centre issued another warning to the government noting that occupation of Iraq was 'continuing to act as motivation and a focus of a range of terrorist-related activity in the UK'.[25] The impact of British foreign policy on youth radicalisation was also belatedly acknowledged in 2011 by former head of MI5 Eliza Manningham-Buller when she stated that 'our involvement in Iraq spurred some young British Muslims to turn to terror'.[26] For some this anger over British and US foreign policy hardened into the need to exact revenge.

This groundswell of resentment was not fully appreciated within communities as they failed to constructively channel these frustrations. As one researcher observes 'local imams and mosques failed to provide guidance on specific concerns of British Muslims, as a result they were more amenable to experimentation outside the mainstream'.[27] For those who could not bear to remain mere vocal critics or humanitarian workers, physical participation in jihad became an obligation. Most of those who travelled to theatres of conflict in the late 1980s and 1990s were idealistic and adhered to the normative teachings of Islam in relation to warfare. Travellers to these jihadscapes were motivated by an altruistic goal of defending persecuted fellow Muslims and fulfilling a pious religious duty rather than the nihilistic jihadism that would emerge in later years among a new generation of British Muslims.

The social realities for young Muslims growing up post 9/11 and 7/7 became extremely challenging after the introduction of new counter-terrorism legislation, intrusive forms of policing and a general rise in Islamophobia in society. The imam and youth worker that we met in Chapter 1, Alyas Karmani, writing in *The Independent* newspaper, passionately summarises the psychology of those attracted to the likes of ISIS:

> If we really want to understand the process of radicalisation then we have to strive to understand the lived reality of the 'War on Terror' generation. We need to accept the deeply traumatising effect of the last 13 years – the daily vilification

and demonisation of Muslims through a conveyor belt of stories depicting death, destruction, pornographic violence and hopelessness. Imagine these are your formative years and as you grapple with the challenges of being young and growing up in society you're having to deal with this daily barrage.

The young Muslims I work with are often deeply troubled by this reality and most of them have to negotiate the challenges of identity, integration and inclusion on their own. Just take some time and try to really imagine and understand this lived reality. Imagine your frustration that no one is listening to you and giving you a voice; that your parents don't understand; the mosque doesn't understand; and the Imam definitely doesn't understand.

Imagine that no matter how hard you try to fit into society you are always seen as the other; that you're always 'Muslimed' even though you want people to see you are more than this. Imagine a 300 per cent increase in stop-and-searches of people like you, anti-terror laws designed to entrap you, and the resurrection of 300 year old treason laws just to charge people like you.

Imagine seeing your co-religionists portrayed routinely as murderers, psychos, paedos, crackpots and shouting 'that does not reflect me,' and yet no one listens. Imagine a daily diet of death and destruction in the countries that your family and friends live in and come from. Imagine becoming desensitised to extreme pornographic violence, beheadings and martyrdom missions.[28]

The combined effect of these dynamics appeared to have pushed a minority to become disembedded from their family and friends, have no interest in existing community institutions and become as alienated from Muslim communities as they are from British society. They sought to find their place and identity among like-minded people offering a narrative that explained their condition. For a tiny minority the answer was to adopt the jihadist narratives and set up a network of terrorist cells to finance, incite and carry out various attacks on civilian, commercial and military targets in the years before and after 7/7. A number of attempted attacks were thwarted and the UK did not suffer any major incidents until the killing of Lee Rigby in 2013, which seemed to foreshadow events that occurred in the following year when militants who had broken away from Al-Qaeda in Iraq and Syria seized territory and claimed to have re-established a caliphate.

Welcome to the Islamic State

Anger and alienation are not the only factors that shaped the current generation of jihadists. Those drawn to ISIS were not only interested in fighting for religious ideals but were equally attracted by promises of material advancement and increased social status. The idea of 'jihadi cool', first coined by American terrorism expert Marc Sageman to describe the online influence of Al-Qaeda, could be seen in their glossy *Inspire* magazine which was intended to persuade British and American Muslim audiences to join their fight. This youth subculture was taken to another level in the literature and media productions of ISIS which produced carefully tailored Hollywood movie trailer-style propaganda videos.

Perversely mixing religious devotion with indirect references to violent videogames and rap music particularly appeals to jihadi wannabes from gang backgrounds familiar with the symbols of rebellion and confrontation – or in street parlance 'gangbanging badasses'. This blending of toxic masculinity, Islam and aggression was aptly described by one commentator as 'TNT' (Testosterone, Narrative and Theatre).[29] One British Muslim calling himself Abu Sumayyah Al-Britani, for example, could barely contain his glee upon arriving in Syria by tweeting 'It's actually quite fun. It's really, really fun. It's better than that game Call of Duty. It's like that but it's in 3D where everything is happening in front of you.'[30]

Life in territories controlled by ISIS promised the idea of a 'five-star jihad', with the allure of potential celebrity, living in luxury among deserted villas equipped with laptops, gaming systems and home comforts. The Twitter and Tumblr social media accounts of these youthful warriors are loaded with 'selfies' atop tanks and swimming pools or with their pet cats. British jihadi Abu Abdullah al-Britani is seen expressing 'his passion for Krispy Kreme doughnuts on Twitter while another . . . posted a photo of himself drinking Red Bull'.[31] If all this machismo, food and excitement were not enough to lure young men to the caliphate, potential recruits were informed that 'there are plenty of women here waiting to be married; waiting to bear the off-spring of the army of Imam Mehdi by the will of Allah'.[32] One young women writes:

> You may wear your veils without being harassed, no woman is harmed here and if she is, there is a harsh penalty as the woman's honour is not tampered with whatsoever, there are plenty of mujahedeen desiring to get married who have some of the most loving and softest characters I have ever witnessed even though they are lions in the battlefield, there are orphans here waiting for mothers to love them the way their parents would have. Come to the land of honour. You are needed here.[33]

This call to women – with promises of a better life and the contribution they could make as nurses and mothers to a new generation of virtuous carers and wives – worked. A number of British Muslims travelled to Syria. A notable example of someone who responded to this invitation is the Scottish Pakistani Aqsa Mahmood who later became a high profile recruiter for ISIS via various social media platforms, including Twitter and Tumblr. Dubbed the 'bedroom radical,' Aqsa came from a middle-class family in Glasgow, went to a private school and was apparently a fan of the *Harry Potter* books and the band Coldplay. According to her family, she became more religious in 2011 at the beginning of the Syrian civil war and dropped out of university and left for Syria in 2013.[34]

The case of Amira Abase, Shamima Begum and Khadiza Sultana – the trio of teenage girls from East London – was also particularly disturbing. There were no obvious signs of radicalisation as the three appeared to be normal, hardworking students at Bethnal Green Academy School in Tower Hamlets. It is speculated that Aqsa Mahmood may have influenced them;

others suggest it was a schoolmate, Sharmeena Begum, who had travelled to join ISIS herself in December 2014.

A third instance of young British Muslim women joining the jihad in Syria is the 'Terror Twins' Salma and Zahra Halane from Chorlton, Manchester. Of Somali descent, like other females migrants to the ISIS caliphate, they had a prior 'offline' introduction to ISIS ideology through their elder brother Ahmed Ibrahim Mohammed Halane, who allegedly left for Syria in 2013.[35] Zahra was another active recruiter and published photos on Twitter appearing to show female migrants being trained in self-defence – wearing Nike Air trainers and shooting rifles at targets which she described as a 'fun day training . . . with humble sisters'.[36] These stories and the fact that hundreds of British Muslims have left the country of their birth to join a terrorist group that claimed to have established a religious utopia after nearly ten years of counter-terrorism strategies leads us to consider the efficacy of the government's policies.

The problems with Prevent

Following the 7/7 attacks, the Labour government initiated a number of legislative, security and social policies that have had profound repercussions upon British Muslim communities over the last decade. Some built upon the Community Cohesion strategies that were installed in the years after the 2001 'Northern Riots' while others were focused on counter-terrorism interventions. Among the first responses was the creation of a 'Preventing Extremism Together' task force which was launched in August 2005. This comprised seven 'working groups' of 'experts' that were chosen to meet and generate suggestions to tackle violent radicalisation.[37] This 'community-policing' approach was intended to engage young people and Muslim women, to support local and regional community projects that addressed community safety, and to provide training for imams and mosques.

As we noted in the last chapter, following the shock of 7/7 the government was keen to engage a broader range of Muslim voices. In the beginning these groups met regularly for two months and offered a set of recommendations to the Home Office. The task force recommendations appear to have been too ambitious as the majority were inexplicably shelved and drew sharp criticism from many Muslim organisations. Of the sixty-four recommendations produced by members of the task force, only the 'scholars roadshow' and Mosques and Imams National Advisory Board (MINAB) were implemented.

The rationale behind the roadshow was to expose young British Muslims to 'a group of international and national mainstream scholars ... with credibility and influence ... to disseminate effective intellectual and theological counter-arguments against extremist interpretations of Islam'.[38] This eventually ran out of steam having been considered to be preaching to the converted as most attendees of the roadshows would have gone to see their favourite scholars anyway.

Two additional attempts were made to engage groups targeted by the government: youth and women. This took shape in the development of two advisory groups – the National Muslim Women's Advisory Group (NMWAG) launched in 2007 and the Young Muslim Advisory Group (YMAG) set up in 2008. These two attempts also came to an embarrassing end as members of YMAG felt that the group lacked any real influence and the co-ordinator of the NMWAG, Shaista Ghoir whom we met earlier, accused the government of creating an advisory board that was being used as a 'political pawn'.[39]

This 'collaborative partnership' approach of attempting to build trust between communities and authorities had mixed results as they were difficult to disentangle from the government's new 'Prevent' counter-terrorism policy. The 'CONTEST' strategy went live in 2007 and had four strands which were intended to '*Pursue*: to stop terrorist attacks, *Prevent*: to stop people from becoming terrorists or supporting terrorism, *Protect*: to strengthen our protection against terrorist attack and *Prepare*: where an attack cannot be stopped, to mitigate its impact.'[40]

The Prevent dimension of the policy has proved to be the most controversial for its conceptualisation of the idea of extremism and its delivery. Despite nearly a decade of implementing Prevent – and the expenditure of millions of pounds of public money – there is very little evidence to suggest that it has succeeded in its

intended outcomes.[41] As many critics have pointed out, the policy
has been fundamentally flawed in its conceptualisation and undermined in its delivery. If it was designed to make Britain safe from
terrorism, it has failed and has arguably increased the threat. Had
the intention been to reduce the number of young British Muslims becoming radicalised and travelling to places like Syria, it has
been unsuccessful. If it was to stop British citizens from becoming
terrorists, it did not work. If it was meant to create meaningful
partnerships between the state and Muslim civil society, it has also
faltered by not being able to develop trust.

For critics, the core problem with the Prevent strategy is its
theorisation of the concepts of radicalisation and extremism. Radicalisation as a term is deeply contested among specialists due to
its lack of clarity as a catch-all term. Some scholars distinguish
between 'cognitive radicalisation' – the support for ideas, beliefs,
ideologies, values and principles, and 'behavioural radicalisation' –
actual physical participation in acts of violence.[42] For the government, preventing radicalisation can only be achieved by 'winning
hearts and minds' of potential sympathisers who may be recruited
by extremist Islamic ideologies. This approach is reminiscent of
the counter-insurgency strategies used during the Cold War and
reflects the intellectual trace of thinkers from that period.

Following 9/11, many neoconservative US policymakers within
the Bush administration were inclined to the 'Clash of Civiliza-
tions' hypothesis. The phrase was popularised by the book of the
same name written by the late American academic Samuel Huntington, who asserted that cultural and religious identities would be
the primary source of future conflicts in the post-Cold War world
and that Muslim extremism would pose the biggest threat to world
peace. The cause of terrorism perpetrated by Muslims was said to
be a product of Islamic culture.

Huntington built upon the work of well-known British Orientalist Bernard Lewis, an advisor to the US government on the
Middle East, who argued that Islam had a cultural propensity to
a totalitarian rejection of modernity. This analysis, according to
Dr Arun Kundnani, author of *The Muslims are Coming! Islamophobia, Extremism, and the Domestic War on Terror*, 'has underpinned
counter-terrorism policy-making in the UK since 2006 and led

to viewing certain forms of religious ideology as an early warning sign of potential terrorism'.[43] Thus Prevent as a counter-terrorism strategy is intended to counter militant versions of Islam that are said to either provide the inspiration or empathy for acts of terrorism. But as many specialists have pointed out, the empirical evidence base for the efficacy of this model is far from conclusive and cannot explain why, given similar conditions, one person turns to violence and another one does not.

Successive British governments have rigidly held on to explanatory paradigms that reduce the causes of terrorism to an 'evil ideology' or versions of Islam such as Salafism or Islamism. The problem with such labelling is that it fails to distinguish the multiple varieties of both religious trends – Salafism has some extremely socially conservative and theologically intolerant tendencies but most of them are politically passive and non-violent and do not necessarily lead to jihadism. Similarly, Islamism is a broad mosque of various currents that range from moderate to revolutionary and cannot be reduced to a single phenomenon. The problem of course is variants of these religious trends converge to advocate terrorism as a path to achieving their goals.

Acts of violence carried out by Muslims cannot be fully understood outside of the broader historical and socio-political contexts in which they emerge. Supporters of a generic process of radicalisation hold onto the idea of an escalator theory or 'conveyor belt' that explains how individuals at risk seamlessly move along an imagined continuum from religious conservatism to adoption of oppositional political ideas, and from there to activism and finally engagement in acts of terror. Other models are more nuanced and will acknowledge other psycho-social factors such as moral outrage or trauma, but essentially argue that embracing a religious ideology can be the turning point towards terrorism. There are a number of problems with this approach. A leaked 2008 MI5 'Briefing note' entitled *Understanding Radicalisation and Extremism in the UK* was based upon detailed case studies of those known to have been involved with extremist activity. It conceded that there is not a single pathway to radicalisation and that most of those involved were religious novices who were not committed to practising their faith.[44]

Dr Marc Sageman, in his studies on Muslim terrorist networks, found a similar lack of religious literacy and argues instead
that the vast majority of those who have gone on to theatres of
conflict in the Muslim world had social bonds predating ideological commitment, social networks that inspired alienated young
Muslims to join the jihad. Those involved in attacks on targets
in Western countries tend to follow what he calls the 'Bunch of
Guys' model: small, self-organising networks that execute terrorist attacks.[45] This amateurism and lack of religious literacy were
comically illustrated by two young men from Birmingham, Yusuf
Sarwar and Mohammed Ahmed, when they purchased *Islam for
Dummies* and the *Koran for Dummies* before attempting to leave
for Syria in 2014. It also resembles the black comedy *Four Lions*
'which satirised the incompetence and sheer banality of British
Muslim jihadists'.[46]

The other problems with the Prevent policy are the ways in
which it has been implemented and the lack of accountability,
which have resulted in accusations of spying on Muslim communities, coercion and abuse of power.[47] Controversial intel-
ligence-gathering measures have included various instances of
the surveillance of individuals and entire communities such
as the case of CCTV cameras being installed in an area of
Birmingham with a large Muslim population.[48] Other cases
include reports of community and youth workers being pressured to provide to the police or local authority information
about the individuals with whom they worked.[49] *The Independent* reported that MI5 attempted to blackmail young Muslim
men from London and threatened one of them with the ultimatum 'if you do not work for us we will tell any foreign
country you try to travel to that you are a suspected terrorist'.[50]
Other cases detail how individuals have been approached by
the security services and intimidated into recruitment.[51]

These allegations have been strenuously denied by the government; nevertheless, these tactics have severely eroded trust between
the communities, police services and the state.[52] The journalist
Robert Verkaik, in his book *Jihadi John: The Making of a Terrorist*,
writes at length about the damaging effect of these surveillance
and recruitment methods in the most high profile of these kinds

of incidents.[53] It appears that Mohammed Emwazi's encounters with the security services traumatised him and influenced his decision to join ISIS.

Another problematic aspect of the Prevent policy is its potential to curb freedom of speech by enforcing an opaque definition of extremism. This has not only resulted in self-censoring but also in absurdities such as a three-year-old being accused of radicalisation and a Staffordshire University postgraduate student of counter-terrorism being suspected of terrorism.[54] Even former Cabinet Minister Sayeeda Warsi, in her memoir *The Enemy Within: A Tale of Muslim Britain*, warned that the continued delivery of Prevent risked creating a 'Cold War' with British Muslim communities and needed a radical overhaul.[55] Other critics have compared it to an Orwellian nightmare that threatens the possibility of committing 'thought crimes' by those holding certain types of beliefs without actually breaking the law – and resulting arrest or imprisonment.[56] While extremist ideologies need to be challenged, the government's polices potentially perpetuate the sources of grievance that vindicate extremist narratives.

As we have already indicated, in the last decade and a half, the British government has struggled to respond to the issue of Muslim involvement in terrorism. With the limited success of existing strategies, policymakers have been searching for new ways of preventing violent radicalisation. However, there appears to be a self-limiting process taking place in solving this conundrum. The French academic Olivier Roy, in his recent book *Jihad and Death: The Global Appeal of Islamic State*, argued there has been not so much as a 'radicalisation of Islam' as an 'Islamization of radicalism'. This novel interpretation rejects the culturalist explanation for radicalisation, that is, an appeal to specific verses of the Quran. This is not to say that Islam has no link to the cognitive rationalisation of violence, nor acts as an emotional vehicle and framework for thought to mobilise people into action by the use of sacred concepts and symbols. Instead, Roy argues that young (mainly) men attracted to jihad today in Western countries are not primarily motivated by religion or necessarily even by a politicised impulse to defend fellow Muslims from persecution but rather this is actually mainly about rebellion.

This rebellion is triggered by social disengagement from both Western society and their parental cultural heritage. It manifests itself in involvement in petty crime, music fashion tastes and partaking in a culture of violence that has greater affinity with those drawn to Mexican drugs gangs than with classical Islamic conceptions of sacred warfare. This sense of alienation and rebellion is not of course limited to young Muslim men and occurs in all subversive youth subcultures. These disaffected youth are often unable to identify with their ethnic ancestry and are excluded from the dominant culture in which they live so have little stake. British intellectual Kenan Malik opines that:

> At a certain point, the accumulation of such estrangements resulted in anger. Disengagement is, of course, not simply a Muslim issue. There is today widespread disenchantment with the political process, a sense of being politically voiceless, a despair that neither mainstream political parties nor social institutions seem to comprehend their concerns and needs, a rejection of conventional ideals and norms that seem detached from their experiences ... [i]n the past, disaffection with the mainstream may have led people to join movements for political change, from far-left groups to labour movement organizations to anti-racist campaigns. Such organizations helped both give idealism and social grievance a political form, and a mechanism for turning disaffection into the fuel of social change.[57]

Therefore, the challenge remains to address the difficult and complex realities of why some Muslims in Britain feel disenfranchised and are drawn to expressing their frustrations with sympathy for and involvement in terrorism. This is difficult given government policies aimed at tackling terrorism within Muslim communities seem to alienate and discriminate the very people whose co-operation is required. Durham University researchers Tufyal Choudhury and Helen Fenwick evaluated the impact of the counter-terrorism strategy and found that its implementation 'may breach human rights and equality laws. They also run the risk of undermining trust and confidence in the police and security services'.[58] The

British government's experience of dealing with terrorism from Northern Ireland serves as a reminder of how counter-terrorism measures have the potential to fuel resentment and even increase support for terrorism.

Current impasse (1): government

Post 7/7, British Muslims have received an unprecedented level of political and media scrutiny. This led to a 'two-fold approach to "managing" Muslims – with a focus on securitisation and migration control at the borders, and, internally, on issues of integration, cohesion and citizenship'.[59] Securitisation has become the dominant paradigm by which the government has come to relate to British Muslim communities. Understandable fears about the 'home-grown terrorism' and battle-hardened foreign fighters returning to the UK potentially engaging in acts of violence, as well as the three separate acts of terrorism experienced in London and Manchester between March and June 2017, underlined a very real threat to public safety.

The public mood after the Westminster Bridge attack and bombing of the pop concert in the Manchester Arena resembled the atmosphere after the 7/7 attacks in 2005. This is in addition to the estimated 800 British Muslims who travelled to join ISIS in Syria. Twelve years on from the devastating London bombings and despite hundreds of millions of pounds spent on counter-terrorism policies, several changes in legislation, an expansion of the powers of the police and security services and academic research, the threat of violent radicalisation appears not to have diminished and in fact has increased.

Furthermore, there have been unprecedented levels of anti-Muslim hate crimes as a result of these terrorist attacks which produce a mutually reinforcing vicious circle. Many Muslims complain that the rising levels of Right-wing extremism, such as the murder of British MP Jo Cox, have not been given the same attention and resources. This sad state of affairs begs a set of questions about what Prevent has succeeded in preventing and why the problem of violent extremism has not gone away. One wonders what lessons counter-terrorism policymakers have learnt in order to address its shortcomings. Similarly, Muslim organisations which emerged during this period claiming to tackle extremism and de-radicalise youth also need to be held accountable.

Perhaps the answers lie in the fundamental assumptions about contemporary Muslim theo-political violence. Many experts have pointed out that the fundamental premises that underpin UK government counter-terrorism policy have not changed since they were introduced by the Blair administration in 2006.[60] The official narratives on the relationship between British Muslims and terrorism have remained intact. This in essence boils down to the idea that ideology causes radicalisation. Edinburgh-based academic Dr Khadijah Elshayyal points out in her book *Muslim Identity Politics: Islam, Activism and Equality in Britain Since 7/7* that there has been a

> dogged refusal of government to acknowledge any role that its foreign policy decisions have played in increasing radicalisation among young Muslims, and thus threatening the nation's security ... despite the government's declared intention to tackle the factors behind the appeal of violent extremism amongst young British Muslims, critics were quick and persistent in pointing out an almost pathological blindness to any sort of recognition that foreign policy might have played a role in this regard ... For the Blair government, admission that foreign policy played a role in increasing the terror threat was dismissed as giving in to the terrorists, or 'making excuses' for their horrific acts and thereby granting them the hope of some legitimacy, no matter how minimal.[61]

The constant recurring theme in the speeches and testimonies of those who have carried out or attempted to perpetrate acts of terrorism cite foreign policy as their main reason.[62] Perpetrators of terrorism have consistently claimed they were motivated by Western military interventions in Muslim-majority countries, but these have been continuously ignored or dismissed as 'false grievances'. Successive governments have evaded this fact. To do otherwise would mean acknowledging that their actions were the primary cause for creating and sustaining this problem. Instead, successive governments have reformulated the Prevent programme which has gone through several versions after its initial creation in the aftermath of 7/7.

It was first revamped in 2011, then in 2013 and again in 2015, when it was made into statutory duty under the Counter-Terrorism and Security Act for public sector employees such as teachers, lecturers, youth workers and NHS staff to share information on 'at risk' Muslims to police counter-terrorism units. This has in effect transformed counter-terrorism policy into a counter-ideological project that has become a legal duty to teach public sector workers how to spot the 'signs of radicalisation'. This in practice means that they must not only function as surveillance operatives but also promote 'fundamental British values' and challenge 'extremist views'. As sociologist, Professor Tahir Abbas observed:

> 'Prevent' training is delivered by trainers often with limited understanding or appreciation of the nuances of the religion, the communities associated with it or the problems of violent extremism and terrorism *per se*. Police officers can confuse what are legitimate religious practices with ideas that these are violent tendencies on their own.[63]

This has led to disturbing cases such the arrest of Green Party MP Caroline Lucas at an anti-fracking demonstration being used as a case study for teachers in a police Prevent duty session.[64] Civil disobedience now can be interpreted as a sign of extremism, despite historically playing a crucial role in securing women's suffrage, racial equality and employment rights. The latest iteration of Prevent in 2015 reasserts the claim that violent extremism is enabled by an 'ideology that distorts Islam'.

The mistaken premise of a radicalisation contamination model in which people are infected by exposure to extremist messages simply has no empirical evidence and forgoes the personal psychosocial circumstances that might edge an individual towards violent extremism. The enforcement of Prevent generated a huge backlash not only from Muslim communities but also from a wide variety of civil society organisations, student organisations, teachers unions and academics. One of Britain's most senior ex-police officers has labelled Prevent a 'toxic brand'. The policy continues to be resisted and in July 2017 the government was forced to amend its guidance following a successful legal challenge by an Islamic activist whom they had named as a 'non-violent extremist'.[65]

Current impasse (2): communities

The present status of debate within communities on the issue of counter-terrorism policy is one of deadlock and exhaustion. *Some British Muslims fully support it while many are vehemently against the Prevent programme.* Pro-Prevent and anti-Prevent positions have sharply divided opinion within communities and further reinforced existing fault-lines within British Islam. This situation has occurred gradually over the last decade through the high profile interventions of numerous individuals who have tried to position themselves as representative voices from within the communities and receive state funding for their projects.[66] It has also taken place at a local level with small local projects accessing Prevent money, purportedly to do de-radicalisation work, but actually using it to fund their own projects.

As the Prevent policy became increasingly discredited, recipients avoided mentioning that their schemes were partially or fully funded due to the negative connotations that the policy carried.[67] Other organisations have been publically enthusiastic supporters of Prevent to the extent that they have launched attacks on other groups that disagree. Prominent among these are the Quilliam Foundation (QF) and Inspire. They have been at the forefront of Muslim organisations that have defended the Prevent counter-terrorism policy and echoed government narratives about the causes of radicalisation. In contrast, the Muslim Council of Britain (MCB), an umbrella body of over 500 affiliated mosques and Islamic organisations, has been critical of Prevent and noted that the vast majority of those identified at risk of radicalisation were misidentified. Figures demonstrate that '80% of referrals between 2006 and 2013 were rejected by Channel panels, demonstrating that children are being viewed through the lens of security, and practitioners are finding threats where none exist in many cases'.[68]

Many other groups and agencies have been critical of Prevent on the basis of the flaws discussed earlier – one of the most prominent is the advocacy group CAGE, which has produced numerous reports challenging the effectiveness of Prevent. While supporting the principle of preventing terrorism, they argue that this responsibility falls predominately upon the police services and security services through the *Prepare, Pursue* and *Protect* strands of the CONTEST strategy and that Prevent as a counter-radicalisation programme has failed and is inadvertently radicalising some young people. This lack of confidence in state agencies was vividly demonstrated recently after it was discovered that Salman Abedi, the man responsible for the Manchester Arena bombing, was known to UK intelligence and had been reported to the police on numerous occasions.

It is difficult to understate how polarising this issue has become between factions of the communities, which has been dramatically dubbed a 'Battle for British Islam' but in reality is nothing more than a noisy public contestation for representational power, government patronage and access to resources.[69] Some of the antagonists within this competition are attempting to address what they see as a pressing matter, while others are making the most of their media profiles, financial gain and the settling of scores.

Individuals from both sides of the argument bitterly contest the validity of each other's position and refuse to acknowledge one another, talk past each other, and prefer to engage interested liberal non-Muslim audiences.[70] This intra-community division is hardly unique to Muslims and is inevitable since they comprise a multiplicity of religious tendencies, as well as racial, class and political interests. The fallout has produced the problematic spectacle of the instruments of state, police and media arbitrating on matters of Islamic theology as Salafi and Islamist readings of the faith are judged to be a 'distortion' and efforts continue to support moderate, Liberal Muslims who are deemed secular, progressive and government-friendly. Some critics have argued that the only version of the religion that is acceptable to the establishment is a depoliticised Islam. Others have suggested that the best Muslim is the ex-Muslim.

There remains a lingering feeling that the government has unfairly targeted Muslim communities with a counter-terrorism policy that results in excessive stop and search tactics, high profile dawn raids, pre-charge detentions, stripping certain Muslims of their citizenship and arbitrarily banning speakers from entering the UK. There have been numerous instances of arrests and detentions of individuals that are publicised in the media – sometimes making front-page news. Their later release without charge does not receive the same coverage. This ranks among the greatest grievances within the British Muslim community who often complain about the sheer volume of stories that relate to radicalisation, extremism, terrorism or hostile commentaries on Islam in Britain.[71]

As noted earlier, this has not only alienated some young people but also contributed to increasingly hostile social attitudes towards Islam and anti-Muslim hate crimes.[72] Indeed, a large number of British Muslims are extremely anxious about their future as incidents of hate crime have spiked in recent years and in particular after terrorist attacks such as in London and Manchester. Again, this does not generate much in the way of media coverage. The police have recorded a doubling of racist abuse, acts of vandalism and bomb threats against mosques between 2016 and 2017.[73] A particularly alarming instance occurred when Muslims leaving Ramadan night prayers in June 2017 at Finsbury Park Mosque were attacked in a similar fashion to those on Westminster Bridge earlier in March, but there was a reluctance to call it a terrorist attack.

This perception of a double standard has been verified by various studies that demonstrate that not only are Muslims represented according to a cluster of narratives that cast them as either potential radicals, extremists or terrorists, but that these representations fuel prejudice and Islamophobia.[74] The government has also been blamed for failing to tackle growing anti-Muslim sentiment seriously and underestimating the risk posed by far-right extremists. Well-known journalist and broadcaster Mehdi Hasan, in an excoriating assessment of Theresa May's tenure as Home Secretary wrote:

May served as Home Secretary for six years, across two parliaments, in charge of both the police and the security services, yet during that period she made only the odd, passing reference to the 'hundreds' of anti-Muslim attacks in the UK each year while obsessing over the threat from 'Islamist extremism'. Why did she not take seriously the claim made by one of her own Home Office officials to the BBC in 2014 that the government's emphasis on the 'global jihadist agenda' risked ignoring the growing domestic terror threat from the far-right? ... Why, as Home Secretary, did she refuse to fully engage, or even formally meet, with the Cross-Government Anti-Muslim Hatred Working Group? ... Plenty of leading Conservatives have not just ignored Islamophobia but become keen and active purveyors of it.[75]

A sense of exhaustion pervades many Muslim communities who feel pressure to constantly disassociate themselves from violent extremists and publicly condemn those that commit acts of terrorism. The Independent Reviewer of Terrorism Legislation, Max Hill QC, stated in a report in the aftermath of the London and Manchester attacks:

Many in the Muslim communities are already doing a great deal and if they could be doing 'more', no one appears to have made clear what that means ... Failure to do so can lead to further alienation, frustration and perhaps even withdrawal for many in spheres where we all need to protect and preserve meaningful engagement.[76]

This also manifests itself in how mosques and religious institutions conduct their work, with many people saying that there is a climate of fear in place. The complex phenomenon of violent religious radicalisation cannot be wholly reduced to a mono-causal driver. There are multiple dynamics that converge to offer vulnerable young people a reason to reject or attack their country. Drugs, gangs, unemployment and anti-Muslim violence have been identified as posing more real pressing concerns within communities.

The combination of state counter policies, imbalanced media reporting, discrimination and increase in anti-Muslim hate crimes and a general hostile societal climate which stigmatises Muslims, provides jihadist recruiters with evidence that there is a 'War against Islam' and that Muslims are not welcome in the UK. These vulnerabilities are magnified among young men who are struggling with a broader crisis of masculinity, racism and Islamophobia and a wider social milieu which gives kudos to violence, materialism, narcissism and celebrity culture.

The problem of jihadist violence could very likely increase in Europe in the next decade if certain macro-trends continue, particularly 'the expected growth in the number of economically underperforming Muslim youth, expected growth in the number of available jihadi entrepreneurs, persistent conflict in the Muslim world, and continued operational freedom for clandestine actors on the Internet'.[77] Furthermore, some Muslims will rebel if the British government continues supporting authoritarian regimes in the Middle East, maintains its military interventions in Muslim states and covertly manipulates non-state actors and religious groups.[78]

Domestically, continuing discredited counter-terrorism policies, pre-charge detentions and unnecessary and intrusive surveillance and stifling dissent is not going to prevent young Muslims being drawn to extremism, rather it will only serve to alienate communities and generate further resentment among Muslim youth and push some to seek refuge in religious utopianism.

The problem of extremist radicalisation will not move towards resolution until all the stakeholders – governmental and community – begin a self-critical dialogue, develop a consensus and start to work across ideological and social divides that are currently preventing them from effectively dealing with this issue. An effective approach to this highly complex problem requires a holistic, comprehensive evidence-based approach in consultation with the diversity of groups within Muslim communities including those organisations that are critical of Prevent.

Universities, schools, colleges and mosques need to maintain safe spaces to debate, critique and challenge the arguments being presented by violent extremists and only clear cases of incitement to violence should be reported to the police. The lack of safe spaces for Muslim young people to vent their frustrations and be engaged in critical debate forecloses a necessary safety valve to release understandable grievance. Here the work of people like Hamid Mahmood, Dr Abdullah Sahin and Alyas Karmani provide useful resources and models of good practice that should be explored further.

Notes

1. London Bomber text in full, http://news.bbc.co.uk/1/hi/uk/4206800.stm.
2. 'Woolwich attack: the terrorist's rant', *The Telegraph*, 23 May 2013, http://www.telegraph.co.uk/news/uknews/terrorism-in-the-uk/10075488/Woolwich-attack-the-terrorists-rant.html. Michael Adebowale received a prison sentence of a minimum of forty-five years for the murder of Drummer Lee Rigby.
3. Jihadists use violence in the name of Islam to enact socio-political change and include a spectrum of movements inspired by al Qaeda and ISIS. For more a detailed discussion, see Jarret Brachman, *Global Jihadism: Theory and Practice* (London: Routledge, 2008), p. 4.
4. According to Ahmed al-Dawoody's *The Islamic Law of War: Justifications and Regulations* (London, Palgrave Macmillan, 2011), seventeen derivatives of jihad occur altogether, forty-one times in eleven Meccan texts and thirty Medinan ones, with the following five meanings: striving because of religious belief (twenty-one); war (twelve); non-Muslim parents exerting pressure, that is, jihad, to make their children abandon Islam (two); solemn oaths (five); and physical strength.
5. El Sayed M. A. Amin, *Reclaiming Jihad: A Quranic Critique of Terrorism* (Leicester: Islamic Foundation, 2014). Also, see Muhammad Abdel Haleem, *Exploring the Qur'an: Context and Impact* (London: I. B. Tauris, 2017).
6. Asma Afsaruddin, *Striving in the Path of God: Jihad and Martyrdom in Islamic Thought* (Oxford: Oxford University Press, 2013).
7. Richard Bonney, *Jihad: From the Quran to Bin Laden* (London: Palgrave Macmillan, 2004), p. 16.
8. Philip Jenkins, *'Is The Bible More Violent than The Quran?'*, National Public Radio, 18 March 2010. For interpretation of such difficult verses, see Paul Copan, *Is God a Moral Monster? Making Sense of the Old Testament God* (Ada: Baker Books, 2011).

9. Shadi Hamid, *Islamic Exceptionalism: How the Struggle over Islam is Reshaping the World* (New York: St Martin's Press, 2016), pp. 234–5.

10. Hugh Kennedy, *The Great Arab Conquests: How the Spread of Islam Changed the World we Live in* (London: Weidenfeld & Nicolson, 2010).

11. Muhammad Qasim Zaman, *Modern Islamic Thought in a Radical Age: Religious Authority and Internal Criticism* (Cambridge: Cambridge University Press, 2012), p. 285.

12. Scott Atran, 'Who becomes a terrorist', *Perspectives on Terrorism*, 2: 5 (2008), http://www.terrorismanalysts.com/pt/index.php/pot/article/view/35/html.

13. Titles of the three fatwas and the declarations such as a Common Word, Mardin and Marrakesh. For informative summaries of the perspectives of a number of well-known mainstream scholars, see Afsaruddin, *Striving in The Path of God* and Zaman, *Modern Islamic Thought in a Radical Age*.

14. Mark Curtis, *Secret Affairs: Britain's Collusion with Radical Islam* (London: Serpent's Tail, 2012), p. xvi.

15. Christopher Davidson, *Shadow Wars: The Secret Struggle for the Middle East* (London: Oneworld, 2016).

16. Jeevan Deol and Zaheer Kazmi (eds), *Contextualising Jihadi Thought* (London: Hurst & Co., 2012), p. 4.

17. Mark Curtis and Nafeez Ahmed, 'The Manchester bombing as blowback: the latest evidence', Mark Curtis' webpage, 3 June 2017, http://markcurtis.info/2017/06/03/the-manchester-bombing-as-blowback-the-latest-evidence/.

18. Abu Qatada who is Palestinian-Jordanian (b. 1960), real name Omar Othman, was always recognised as the senior of the two and commanded respect among Algerian and Egyptian jihadi both in the UK and in the Middle East. Originally an asylum seeker arriving on a forged passport, he became noted as a scholarly reference point for a range of armed North African Islamic groups in the mid-1990s and had links with the Groupe Islamique Armé (GIA), and at one point in time edited their magazine *al-Ansaar*. His influence was so great that one of his fatwas in 1995 – which concluded that it was Islamically acceptable to kill the wives and children of Muslim apostates –was applied by jihadist groups in Algeria to attack civilians who did not support them. In 1997, Qatada gave religious legitimacy to kill the wives and children of Egyptian police and army officers and in 2001 he issued rulings that justified suicide attacks. He was linked to one of the 9/11 attackers, Mohammed Atta, as his sermons were found at his flat

in Germany and has described the attacks as part of religious war between Islam and Christianity. However, he disassociated himself from al-Qaeda after his arrest in 2001 and surprised the authorities by appealing for the release of peace activist Norma Kember in 2005 and BBC journalist Alan Johnston in 2007. As such, the authorities have struggled to find concrete evidence to convict him of terrorism. Questioned and held in detention intermittently numerous times between 2005 and 2008, he was released under a control order and then was subsequently returned to custody and eventually deported back to Jordan in 2013.

19. Yahya Birt, 'The radical Nineties', in M. Al-Rasheed and M. Shertin (eds), *Dying for Faith: Religiously Motivated Violence in the Contemporary World* (London: Hurst & Co., 2009), pp. 105–10.

20. Philip Sherwell, 'Abu Hamza "secretly worked for MI5" to "keep streets of London safe"', *The Telegraph*, 7 May 2014, http://www.telegraph.co.uk/news/worldnews/northamerica/usa/10814816/Abu-Hamza-secretly-worked-for-MI5-to-keep-streets-of-London-safe.html. For more background, see Raffaello Pantucci, *We Love Death as You Love Life: Britain's Suburban Terrorists* (London: Hurst & Co., 2015).

21. *Judgment in Appeal of Crown v. El-Faisal, Supreme Court of Judicature, Court of Appeal, 4 March 2004,* https://web.archive.org/web/20120519051947/http://nefafoundation.org/miscellaneous/FeaturedDocs/RoyalCourtsofJustice_AlFaisal.pdf.

22. History records a far more complex story – where the concept of *khilafah* held multiple meanings and whose reality was manifested in many great achievements as well as dark episodes. For an authoritative account, see Hugh Kennedy, *The Caliphate* (London: Pelican Books, 2016).

23. *International Terrorism: War with Iraq,* http://www.iraqinquiry.org.uk/media/230918/2003-02-10-jic-assessment-international-terrorism-war-with-iraq.pdf.

24. http://www.globalsecurity.org/security/library/report/2004/muslimext-uk.htm.

25. James Sturcke, 'Intelligence warns of "Iraq Terror Link"', *The Guardian*, 19 July 2005, https://www.theguardian.com/uk/2005/jul/19/july7.uksecurity4.

26. http://downloads.bbc.co.uk/rmhttp/radio4/transcripts/2011_reith3.pdf.

27. Quintan Wiktorowicz, *Radical Islam Rising* (New York: Rowan & Littlefield, 2005), p. 100.

28. Alyas Karmani, 'Isis in the UK: how the "War on Terror" radicalised a generation', *The Independent*, 23 October 2014, http://www.independent.co.uk/voices/comment/isis-in-the-uk-how-the-war-on-terror-radicalised-a-generation-9813362.html.

29. Caroline Joan S. Picart, '"Jihad Cool/Jihad Chic": the roles of the internet and imagined relations in the self-radicalization of Colleen LaRose (Jihad Jane)', *Societies*, 5: 2 (2015), pp. 354–83.

30. Jytte Klausen, 'Tweeting the Jihad: social media networks of Western foreign fighters in Syria and Iraq', *Studies in Conflict & Terrorism*, 38: 1 (2015), pp. 1–22; 4.

31. Ibid. p. 4.

32. Ibid. p. 4.

33. Picart, 'Jihad Cool/Jihad Chic', pp. 354–83.

34. For a detailed profile, see https://www.counterextremism.com/extremists/aqsa-mahmood.

35. E. Saltman and M. Smith, *Till Martyrdom Do Us Part: ISIS and the Gender Phenomenon* (London: Institute for Strategic Dialogue, 2015), p. 20.

36. Ibid. p. 26.

37. S. Warraich and I. Nawaz (eds), *'Preventing Extremism Together' Working Groups* (London: Home Office, 2005), pp. 12–14.

38. Ibid. p. 14.

39. Ibid. Also, see Shaista Gohir, 'Muslim women are not political pawns', *The Guardian*, Comment is Free, 9 April 2009, http://www.guardian.co.uk/commentisfree/2010/apr/09/government-failed-muslim-women?INTCMP=ILCNETTXT3487.

40. *The Counter-terrorism Strategy*, http://www.homeoffice.gov.uk/counter-terrorism/uk-counter-terrorism-strat/.

41. Between 2008 and 2011, combined Prevent funding from the Home Office, Department for Communities and Local Government and Foreign and Commonwealth Office came to £186,760 million: see T. O'Toole *et al.*, 'Governing through Prevent? Regulation and contested practice in State-Muslim engagement', *Sociology*, 50: 1 (2016), pp. 160–77, http://soc.sagepub.com/content/early/2015/02/19/0038038514564437.full.

42. Alain Gabon, *The Twin Myths of the Western 'Jihadist Threat' and 'Islamic Radicalisation'* [*Cordoba Papers*, 4: 1 (February 2016)] (London: Cordoba Foundation, 2016), p. 18.

43. Arun Kundnani, *A Decade Lost: Rethinking Radicalisation and Extremism* (London: Claystone Institute, 2015), pp. 9–13.

44. 'MI5 report challenges views on terrorism in Britain', *The Guardian*, 20 August 2008, https://www.theguardian.com/uk/2008/aug/20/uksecurity.terrorism1.

45. See his *Understanding Terror Networks* (2004) and *Leaderless Jihad* (2008), both published by University of Pennsylvania Press, Philadelphia.

46. Mehdi Hassan, 'What the Jihadists who bought 'Islam For Dummies' on Amazon tell us about radicalisation', *Huffington Post*, http://www.huffingtonpost.co.uk/mehdi-hasan/jihadist-radicalisation-islam-for-dummies_b_5697160.html.

47. Various agencies have documented the problematic delivery of the Prevent policy. For a representative example, see *Failing our Communities: A Case Study Approach to Understanding Prevent* (London: CAGE, 2015), https://cage.ngo/publication/failing-our-communities-case-study-approach-understanding-prevent/.

48. Vikram Dodd, 'MPs investigate anti-extremism programme after spying claims', *The Guardian*, 18 October 2009.

49. Arun Kundnani, *Spooked: How Not to Prevent Violent Extremism* (London: Institute of Race Relations, 2009), p. 28.

50. Robert Verkaik, 'Exclusive: How the MI5 blackmails British Muslims', *The Independent*, 21 May 2009. One of these men has since been identified as Mahdi Hashi, a British Somali who claims to have been regularly harassed when travelling. He was deported from Somalia on the instructions of the British authorities, and is reported to have later been transferred to a US military base in Djibouti with the acquiescence of the British authorities. In 2012, his family was informed that he had been stripped of his British citizenship on the grounds of alleged extremism, making him one of only a handful of Britons to have had his citizenship revoked in modern times. Hashi has since been held in solitary confinement in the US, and was finally tried in 2015 where he pleaded guilty (arguably under coercion) to the charge of providing support to the Somalia terrorist group, Al Shabaab.

51. Robert Verkaik, 'MI5 "still using threats to recruit Muslim spies"', *The Independent*, 5 January 2010, http://www.independent.co.uk/news/uk/home-news/mi5-still-using-threats-to-recruit-muslim-spies-1857750.html.

52. Stephen Rimmer, 'Allegations made in the *Panorama* programme "Muslim First – British Second" on Monday 16 February', statement from the Office for Security and Counter Terrorism, 17 February 2009. In response to *The Guardian* investigation of

October 2009, a Home Office spokesman said: 'Any suggestion that Prevent is about spying is simply wrong. Prevent is about working with communities to protect vulnerable individuals and address the root causes of radicalisation', quoted in Andrew Hough, 'Anti-extremism scheme "spying on Muslims"', *The Daily Telegraph*, 17 October 2009.

53. Robert Verkaik, *Jihadi John: The Making of a Terrorist* (London: Oneworld, 2016). Michael *Adebolajo,* the murderer of Drummer Lee Rigby, also claimed to have been harassed by MI5 who had pressured him to become an informant and that he was tortured in Kenya with the full knowledge of British security services: Verkaik, 'MI5 "still using threats to recruit Muslim spies"'.

54. Chris Allen, 'The curious incident of the Muslim student in the university library who was reading a book (which clearly meant he was a terrorist)', *Huffington Post*, 25 September 2015, http://www.huffingtonpost.co.uk/dr-chris-allen/staffordshire-university-muslim-student_b_8192362.html.

55. Sayeeda Warsi, *The Enemy Within: A Tale of Muslim Britain* (London: Penguin, 2016).

56. 'PREVENT will have a chilling effect on open debate, free speech and political dissent', *The Independent*, 10 July 2015, http://www.independent.co.uk/voices/letters/prevent-will-have-a-chilling-effect-on-open-debate-free-speech-and-political-dissent-10381491.html.

57. Kenan Malik, 'The challenge of the jihadi state of mind', *Pandaemonium*, https://kenanmalik.wordpress.com/2017/05/11/the-challenge-of-the-jihadi-frame-of-mind/.

58. Tufyal Choudhury and Helen Fenwick, *'The Impact of Counter-terrorism Measures on Muslim Communities'*: *Project Report* (Manchester: Equality and Human Rights Commission, 2011), p. x.

59. Claire Alexander, Victoria Redclift and Ajmal Hussain, 'Introduction: The New Muslims', in C. Alexander (ed.), *The Muslim Question(s): Reflections from a Race and Ethnic Studies Perspective* (London: Runnymede Trust, 2013), p. 3.

60. Kundnani, *A Decade Lost*, pp. 9–13.

61. Khadijah El-Shayyal, *Muslim Identity Politics: Islam, Activism and Equality in Britain, since 7/7* (London: I. B. Tauris, forthcoming), pp. 158–9.

62. Mohammed Siddique Khan's 'martyrdom' video, *Aljazeera*, 2005; *Press TV* interview with Abu Izzadeen on his release from prison, 28 October 2010.

63. Tahir Abbas, 'Preventing spinning plates from falling', *Tahir Abbas*, 26 May 2017, http://tahirabbas.co.uk/index.php/preventing-spinning-plates-falling/.

64. Adi Bloom, 'Police tell teachers to beware of green activists in counter-terrorism talk', *TES*, 4 September 2015, https://www.tes.com/news/school-news/breaking-news/police-tell-teachers-beware-green-activists-counter-terrorism-talk.

65. Salman Butt, 'Judgement released: judicial review into Prevent', *Islam21c*, https://www.islam21c.com/politics/judgement-released-judicial-review-into-prevent/?sharex_.

66. The most well-known among those to have impacted outside of Muslim communities is the highly controversial Quilliam Foundation, which was set up in 2007 by two former members of radical-Islamist movement Hizb ut-Tahrir – 'Ed' Hussain Maajid Nawaz and Rashad Ali. For a representative selection of critical articles on the counter-radicalisation work of the QF and its CEO, see Nafeez Ahmed and Max Blumenthal, *Alternet*, 6 February 2016, http://www.alternet.org/grayzone-project/self-invention-maajid-nawaz-fact-and-fiction-life-counter-terror-celebrity; Jonny Spooner and Jonny Stubbings, 'Maajid Nawaz and Quilliam: the money trail behind the propaganda', *Loon Watch*, http://www.loonwatch.com/2017/03/maajid-nawaz-and-quilliam-the-money-trail-behind-the-propaganda/.

67. Kundnani, *Spooked*, p. 17; Therese O'Toole, Stephen H. Jones and Daniel Nilsson Dehanas, 'The new Prevent: Will it work? Can it work?', *Arches Quarterly*, 5: 9 (Spring 2012), pp. 56–62.

68. See, for example, Miqdaad Versi, *Meeting Between David Anderson QC and the MCB: Concerns on Prevent* (London: Muslim Council of Britain, 2015); Frances Webber, *Prevent and the Children's Rights Convention* (London: Institute of Race Relations, 2016).

69. Sarah Khan, co-founder and CEO of Inspire, has written a book with the very same title. She has been accused of having close links with the government and of promoting Prevent; see, for example, Simon Hooper, 'Top anti-extremism campaigner linked to UK "covert propaganda" firm', *Middle East Eye*, 3 May 2016, http://www.middleeasteye.net/news/feted-counter-extremism-campaigner-linked-covert-propaganda-company-746667480. Her perspective on Prevent can be found in: Sarah Khan, 'The anti-Prevent lobby are dominating the discourse, not all Muslims oppose Prevent', *London School of Economics Religion and the Public Sphere*, http://blogs.lse.

ac.uk/religionpublicsphere/2016/10/the-anti-prevent-lobby-are-dominating-the-discourse-not-all-muslims-oppose-prevent/.

70. 'Sara Khan blames CAGE, MEND and 5Pillars for trying to make PREVENT toxic', *5 Pillars*, 19 November 2015, http://5pillarsuk. com/2015/11/19/sara-khan-blames-cage-mend-and-5pillars-for-trying-to-make-prevent-toxic/.

71. There are a large number of studies that examine how Islam and Muslims are represented in the British media. A representative summary is presented in Chris Allen, *A review of the evidence relating to the representation of Muslims and Islam in the British media .Written evidence submitted to the All Party Parliamentary Group on Islamophobia* (Birmingham: University of Birmingham, 2012).

72. Tell MAMA, *The Geography of anti-Muslim Hatred in 2015:Tell MAMA Annual Report*, https://tellmamauk.org/geography-anti-muslim-hatred-2015-tell-mama-annual-report/.

73. Rachel Roberts, 'Hate crime targeting UK mosques more than doubled in past year, figures show', *The Independent*, 9 October 2017, http:// www.independent.co.uk/news/uk/home-news/hate-crime-muslims-mosques-islamist-extremism-terrorism-terror-attacks-a7989746. html.

74. See, for example, Christopher Mathias, 'How the British media helps radicalize people against Islam', *Huffington Post*, 21 June 2017, http://www.huffingtonpost.com/entry/darren-osborne-islamophobia-in-uk-media_us_594982bee4b00cdb99cb01b9. For a scholarly analysis, see Julian Petly and Robin Richardson, *Pointing the Finger: Islam and Muslims in the British Media* (London: Oneworld, 2011).

75. Mehdi Hasan, 'Theresa May wants to fight Islamophobia: you must be joking', *The Intercept*, 20 June 2017, https://theintercept. com/2017/06/20/theresa-may-wants-to-fight-islamophobia-in-the-uk-you-must-be-joking/.

76. *UK 'Building Bridges' Programme. Community Roundtables:A report on the aftermath of the terrorist attacks in London and Manchester* (London: Forward Thinking, 2017), http://www.forward-thinking.org/wordpress/wp-content/uploads/2017/07/UK-Building-Bridges-Programme_-Community-Roundtables_-A-report-on-the-aftermath-of-the-terrorist-attacks-in-London-and-Mancehster_July-2017-.pdf.

77. Thomas Hegghammer, 'The future of jihadism in Europe: a pessimistic view', *Perspectives on Terrorism*, 10: 6 (2016). It is also important to point out that terrorism carried out by Muslims is disproportionately reported. Sociologist Charles Kurzman has shown

in *The Missing Martyrs: Why There Are So Few Muslim Terrorists* that since 9-11, Muslim-American domestic terrorism has killed only a very small number of people and, according to Interpol statistics, Muslims were responsible for only 0.7 per cent of terror attacks in Europe between 2006 and 2013. The majority were committed by either ethno-nationalist separatist movements or Right- and Left-wing groups; see for example, Adrian Cousins, 'Graphic: Islamist terror accounts for only 0.7% of attacks in Europe', *Counter Fire*, 9 January 2015, http://www.counterfire.org/news/17599-graphic-islamist-terror-accounts-for-only-0-7-of-attacks-in-europe.

78. The Home Secretary Amber Rudd in July 2017 decided not to publish a report into the funding and support of extremist groups. The decision appeared intended to bury any criticism of Saudi Arabia. See Peter Walker, 'Rudd's refusal to publish full report into extremist funding "unacceptable"', *The Guardian*, 12 July 2017, https://www.theguardian.com/uk-news/2017/jul/12/uk-terror-funding-report-will-not-be-published-for-national-security-reasons?CMP=share_btn_tw.

5

Creating Culture: Emergence of the New 'Muslim Cool'

In mid-September 2017, the Muslims in Britain Research Network (MBRN) organised a conference exploring 'Contemporary Muslim Art, Culture and Heritage in Britain'. Events such as these disrupt narratives about the lack of Muslim integration and demonstrate that they are 'at home' in Britain and their presence and artistic impact on the UK can be traced back for decades. This unique MBRN event gathered academics, artists and researchers to examine the theme of British Muslim cultural production and how it relates the exploration of questions of identity, belonging and social change through art, culture and heritage. Panels critically discussed various topics such as what contemporary 'Muslim' and 'Islamic' art means, how Muslim arts in Britain are developing and whether the cultural industries are responding to the emergence of British Muslim artists. These questions also indicate the strains within Muslim communities around the nature of artist expression and the difficulties in gaining recognition in the mainstream art world.

The arts communicate emotions and stories, and manifest human creativity and technical skill. British Muslims have quietly been making various forms of art for decades. These forms of cultural production are often but not always informed by their faith and are acts of imaginative expression and exploration. In the last decade, a talented new generation of artists that include musicians, photographers, poets, novelists, visual artists, comedians, film makers and entrepreneurs are not only expressing themselves through art but are also challenging stereotypes and raising political consciousness. These artists and cultural producers explore difficult issues and help bridge the divides between communities. This development creates exciting opportunities but also uneasy tensions within communities as some forms of visual and performing arts are considered religiously problematic.

In this chapter we trace the emergence of cultural producers and change-makers, largely invisible to most outsiders: second- and third-generation (often) female artists and activists.[1] This group is crafting new Muslim subcultures in the arts, music, media and fashion by synthesising their religious values with a British flavour. This is another example of a work in progress that has not occurred without controversy and one which is challenged by critical voices within the communities. We examine several case studies that are reflective of these tensions, illustrate new thinking and point to more hopeful future developments. The formation of indigenised British Muslim arts and culture demonstrates the rootedness of Muslims in Britain, as the majority are now born here and do not think of themselves as immigrants or members of a diaspora like their parents or grandparents did. However, not everything that is being produced in the name of arts and culture is accepted by all elements of Britain's Muslim community. The contestations, as usual, are informed by religious, racial and political intra-Muslim differences and continue to produce lively debates about religious authenticity and orthodoxy.

Islamic authenticity and cultural fusion

The creation of new Islamic cultures in minority contexts is not a new process. One of the main reasons for the successful historical spread of the faith was its ability to remain a 'mobile idea' that was easily understood everywhere and was flexible enough to merge 'in intriguing ways to produce unanticipated new configurations'.[2] American Muslim scholar Dr Umar Farooq Abdullah, in an influential paper *Islam and the Cultural Imperative*, observed that:

> In history, Islam showed itself to be culturally friendly and, in that regard, has been likened to a crystal-clear river. Its waters (Islam) are pure, sweet, and life-giving but – having no color of their own – reflect the bedrock (indigenous culture) over which they flow. In China, Islam looked Chinese;

in Mali, it looked African. Sustained cultural relevance to distinct peoples, diverse places, and different times underlay Islam's long success as a global civilization.[3]

This dynamic cultural hybridisation has of course been occurring throughout much of human history and clearly is continuing within societies with significant minority communities today. For early Muslims, it occurred partly because seeking knowledge and intellectual enquiry were considered as religious obligations. Dr Abdullah Sahin writes that

> educational curiosity motivated early Muslims to deepen their understanding of Islam and the world around them. Naturally, this triggered the emergence of a dynamic and holistic Islamic epistemology, facilitating the advent of classical Muslim sciences and a creativity which generated new knowledge, insights and meanings. Early Muslims' educational openness, which was a key catalyst in the initial rapid expansion of Islam, enabled them to have the confidence to accommodate the creativity of the new Muslims who brought with them diverse sets of cultural and intellectual insights which enriched Muslim civilization.[4]

In the past, this outlook helped generate the great achievements of Islamic civilisation and moved the geographic centrality of the faith away from its origins in Arabia in all directions. Encounters with other faiths and civilisational traditions from Persia, Mesopotamia, Africa, India and China enabled intellectual exchange, synthesis and cultivation in all branches of learning – science, technology, arts – in addition to the formation of new cultural habits, traditions, customs and social relations. Historian of Islam, Marshall G. Hodgson, in his classical work *The Venture of Islam*, described the growth of these phenomena as 'Islamicate', that is to say, the organic creation of cultures which are the products of regions in which Muslims were culturally dominant. These civilisational artefacts 'would refer not directly to the religion, Islam, itself, but to the social and cultural complex historically associated with Islam and the Muslims, both among Muslims themselves and even when found among non-Muslims'.[5]

Another distinguished Professor of History, Richard Bulliet, in his book *Islam: The View from the Edge*, distinguishes between what he called the territorial centre and edge of Islamic civilisation and noted that 'the impetus for change in Islam has more often come from the bottom than from the top, from the edge than from the centre'.[6] He argues that some of the most innovative cultural production took place at the geographical and ideological periphery of lands of Islam and arose from Muslims integrating their faith values with new cultural contexts.

Today this cultural exchange and fusion has accelerated massively through the realities of a globalised world, instant communication and continuous flows of people, goods and services. The idea of an edge of an Islamic civilisation is more difficult to place but could be used to describe the conditions in which Western Muslims find themselves. Converts and second- and third-generation Muslims in Britain and America are at the forefront of a process of adaptation and reinterpretation of Islam which seeks to reconcile their faith with secular Western cultures and is resulting in critical new thinking and cultural bricolage.

We have seen in earlier chapters how this reinterpretation and adaptation is taking place in Britain in the areas of Islamic religious authority and political participation, and the debates in the cultural realm are equally fluid if not more exciting! Faith continues to inspire the creation of art and popular culture among British Muslims but in varying degrees. Traditional scholars from the Muslim world exercise a certain amount of influence but as there is no centralisation of religious authority in the UK, past hierarchical debates around what is or is not Islamic are far more democratic and contentious. Some conservative, religiously committed, young Muslims may consult their local imam or well-known religious leaders but Google tends to be the first port of call on matters that pertain to Islam. Today, online shaykhs, tele-evangelists and even Muslim chat-show hosts are more likely to be approached than a local imam to help decide if something is sufficiently Islamic.

This individualised approach to religion is also occurring among believers of other faiths, but among many contemporary

British Muslims, an interesting distinction between the spirit and the letter of Islamic law is taking place. This could be understood simply as two broad approaches that differ on the importance attached to following the 'rules' as opposed the 'values' of Islam. The 'rules based' approach insists on the maintenance of sharia-oriented legalistic paradigms that are defined by reference to past and present traditional Islamic scholarship and place an emphasis on permissibility and impermissibility of human actions. The 'values based' *maqasid* approach, while respecting classical consensus, displays greater flexibility and emphasises the ethics and intended public good of Islamic teachings.[7] This has resulted in a wide spectrum of opinion of what constitutes as Islamic and how certain phenomena may not be religiously mandated but nevertheless can be sufficiently recognised as being Muslim in substance.

For many Muslims, Islam is not only private faith and the practice of rituals but is a 'complete way of life'. Those aspects of their public lives that are at variance with their beliefs are filtered and responded to through the theological and spiritual guidance found in the Quran and the example of the Prophet. Some commentators have interpreted the overall effect as an attempt at the 'Islamisation of Modernity', while others have labelled these efforts as 'Modernising Islam'. This could alternatively be described as socio-cultural Islamisation of the public sphere, where religiously minded Muslims strive for autonomy by shaping alternative spaces in which aspects of secular modernity are re-constituted. This creative re-reading of religion produces faith-inspired forms of material culture, consumption, debate and social engagement, enabled by the intimate knowledge of Western culture, political literacy and access to global communication networks.

(Re)defining Muslim art, culture and citizenship

This reconstructive process blending religious ethics and cultural artefacts has provoked several internal debates about what constitutes 'Islamic Art' and how it may differ from 'art produced by Muslims'. This reflects the earlier point about older historical debates about authenticity and Islamicate and the fact that there has never been a uniform, static Islamic culture. Globally influential religious paradigms ensure that these debates remain live issues as conservative literalist groups such as the Salafis believe culture is inherently problematic, an 'un-Islamic' pollutant that must necessarily be purged, since Islam and culture are mutually exclusive. They foolishly or ahistorically regard localised Muslim culture – legacies such as the Taj Mahal, for example – to have been the chief cause of Muslim decline and fall in history.[8]

This mindset blames previous generations of Muslims for allowing newly converted peoples to retain local vernacular traditions that enabled syncretism and compromised doctrinal purity. As a result, Salafis seek a 'deculturation' of Islam as practised by the majority of Muslims by removing its folk customs and de-linking it from national and regional cultural additions, 'arguing that a strict constructionist interpretation of the Quran and Sunnah is sufficient to guide Muslims for all time and through all contingencies'.[9] They resist the formation of encultured identities because they believe that they have the potential to undermine the integrity of Islamic theology and religious practice. According to them, there is only one true Islamic Culture – that practised by the Prophet and his community in seventh-century Arabia. Needless to say, this ahistoricism perpetuates a pious fiction of an imagined past.

Islamists are generally more pragmatic when it comes to developing new cultural forms and display alternating levels of ambivalence towards modernity. So, for instance, while rejecting aspects of Western secularity and lifestyle choices they have no problem in appropriating its scientific material achievements. This is characterised by the view that technology is 'culturally' neutral and they fail to grasp the epistemic, political and social assumptions that lie behind the development of modern science. In the field of culture production, Islamists tend to view the performing arts and entertainment as immoral and 'unIslamic', unless Islamised to serve the promotion of piety.

In reality, cultural and aesthetic creativity in Islamic civilisation in the past was a product of the confluence of Quranic imperatives that celebrated the oneness of creation and encouraged the search for knowledge, achievement of virtue and cultivation of beauty. In fact, forms of art and architecture in Muslim cultures historically

placed a premium on the achievement of beauty and were seen
as the physical manifestation of theological axioms such as 'God is
beautiful and loves beauty'. In terms of aesthetics, Islamic architecture in particular needed to fulfil both its functional requirements
and display a purposeful sense of beauty.[10] These signature features
can be identified across all types of material arts, crafts and cultural
expression and are illustrated in vastly diverse contexts across the
Muslim world.

Today, Muslims in Britain attempt to re-enact the process of
cultural hybridisation that their ancestors initiated as they encountered societies with very different religions and traditions. Whereas
their forbearers benefitted from the translation of the knowledge
systems that they initially interacted with, those born and bred
in Britain have engaged educational and cultural socialisation
directly and have no need for epistemic translators. However,
crafting authentic British Muslim culture has proved to be more
challenging, not only in terms of producing something that genu-
inely incorporates the best of the Western and Muslim cultures,
but also in a way that it is recognisably 'Islamic'.

For instance, for more religiously demanding Muslims, merely
Islamising the content of musical lyrics or labelling food products
'Halal' does not sufficiently create an authentically Islamic final
product. For some Muslims, this is not only about maintaining
religious authenticity but also reflects an unresolved attraction/
repulsion relationship with the non-Muslim societies in which
they live. This affects their sense of identity and how they position themselves within Britain even though most would comfortably describe themselves as British or may hyphenate their
self-descriptors.

Debates about the use of the phrase 'British Islam' illustrate this
point. Today some Muslims reject the idea on political grounds
because they believe that it is capitulation to state attempts to engi-
neer a 'Moderate Islam'. While there is indeed an ongoing government policy to favour more politically compliant forms of religiosity
in the post 7/7 era, most people who make this objection are either
ignorant of or ignore the fact that the phrase 'British Islam' was in
limited use in the late 1980s and early 1990s through the attempts
of reformist Islamist groups such as Young Muslims UK, the Islamic

Society of Britain and Sufi 'Traditional Islam' adherents associated with Q-News. The attempt to enculture the faith was a necessary adaptation given the vastly different social realities of the UK and the nations from which Muslims had emigrated. It was also required because it was felt the core Islamic values needed to be separated from problematic ethnic cultural practices, which would allow Islam to be integrated within the cultural norms and idioms of British culture.

Producing an indigenised Islam became an identity project to demonstrate that the faith was not a foreign religion but one which is embodied and communicated within the cultural environment in which Muslims choose to live. Islam and the West are shown to have an overlapping history and shared future, containing interlocking narratives that have coexisted and learned from one another and whose interests lie in continuing to do so. This narrative also frames Islam as having the creative potential to adapt to different cultural contexts and cites the historical establishment of various Muslim communities in Europe.

This argument is evidenced by the fact that many prominent nineteenth-century English converts such as the 'Shaykh of the British Isles' Abdullah Quilliam, Lady Evelyn Cobbold, Lord Stanley of Alderley and the famous translator of the Quran, Marmaduke Pickthall, were all actively involved in the creation of an early twentieth-century British Muslim culture. This reclamation of early British Muslimness through these individuals, especially the figure of Abdullah Quilliam, has produced a growing interest in Britain's early Muslim communities among younger British Muslims. He is seen as source of inspiration and case study for those seeking to discover what lessons can be applied from the recent past to help guide Muslim Britons in the present.[11] A binding thread in all these efforts is the use of the English language. Dr Aminul Hoque, author of *British Islamic Identity: Third Generation Bangladeshis from East London*, found that:

> Many third-generation Bangladeshis have reclaimed their religious identity and rediscovered and redefined Islam as a modern and progressive form of British Islam. British Islam,

therefore, can be considered as a publicly expressed *new* identity and form of ethnicity. This religiously based identity has been accelerated by the ability of the third generation to read and speak English, allowing them to research via textbooks, conferences and the internet in the dominant language.[12]

English has become the preferred language of communication for educated Muslims across the world and is arguably becoming an 'Islamic language'. This is no surprise given that it is the *lingua franca* for international commerce, science, academia and the internet. Creating British forms of Islamic arts and culture through the medium of English was the inevitable outcome of those born and raised here and signalled the intent to reconcile, celebrate and educate others about their faith in a predominately secular, non-Muslim society.

Creating the 'Muslim Cool': art and activism

The idea of a 'Muslim Cool' was first coined by Algerian French researcher Amel Boubekuer in a 2005 article entitled 'Cool and Competitive Muslim Culture in the West'.[13] She uses the concept to refer to a growing urban Muslim phenomenon – an 'ethislamic', an ethics inspired by the stylish fusion of faith and Western popular youth culture which shapes concepts, conversations, fashion and activism. This 'new Islamic culture presents itself as cool and fashionable (i.e. modern), along with being competitive' in relation to the West's political, economic and cultural dominance.[14]

The term gained wider traction after the release of the 2009 documentary film *New Muslim Cool*, which explored the growth of a distinct Islamic subculture in the United States.[15] Based on the experiences of Puerto Rican American Rap artist Hamza Perez, it follows his journey after converting to Islam as he tries to establish a new life and share his faith through the medium of hip hop, in post 9/11 America, to resist discrimination and communicate positive messages to young people. Muslim American sociologist Dr Hisham Aidi, in his illuminating book *Race, Empire and the New Muslim Youth Culture*, demonstrates that international links between Islam, music and political activism among different generations of Muslim youth have existed for many decades before the more recent developments. Dr Aidi shows how Islam influenced many of the early pioneers of jazz and rap music and that some of the most famous rap stars were either Muslims or utilised Islamic imagery and references in their lyrics.

Similarly, African American Studies scholar Suhail Daulatzai, in *Black Star, Crescent Moon*, writes about the shared history between Black Muslims and radical activists; the Muslims who forged global connections and political alliances that led to a vibrant exchange of musical influences in different Muslim communities in the US, Europe and Latin America. African-American Muslim anthropologist Su'ad Abdul Khabeer brings this history up to date in her engaging study entitled *Muslim Cool: Race, Religion, and Hip Hop in the United States*. Dr Abdul Khabeer argues that hip hop culture resonates with poor and working-class black and Latinos, because it addresses issues of self-determination, self-knowledge and political consciousness. These themes that transcend the experiences of American minority communities found receptive audiences everywhere among marginalised groups interested in the socially transformative power of music and have clearly found a home in the UK.

British Muslim music: the sounds of a new generation

In a recent volume on British Muslim youth cultures, sociologist of religion Dr Carl Morris traces the formation and progression of various religious musical styles among communities in Britain.[16] He provides a fascinating account of how sonic traditions such as qawwali, na'ats and nasheeds, travelled with first-generation South Asian and Arab Muslims in the early 1960s and how new musical genres appeared and evolved over the following decades. Qawwali is a diverse spiritual genre of devotional music that is popular in Pakistan and India. Most often recited in Urdu, Punjabi or Persian, they consist of various forms that praise and express love for God, his Prophet and the pious deceased.[17] Na'ats are religious melodies that are normally performed at mosques and religious celebrations.

Nasheeds are poetic chants which express pious themes, sung in a capella style or with the accompaniment of instruments. All three traditional forms have been adopted and adapted by younger generations who have shaped today's British Muslim musical scene.

Experiences of racism influenced second-generation expressions of Muslim music that emerged in the 1980s and 1990s, through experimentation with alternative styles of vocal and instrumental sound. Perhaps the most well-known during that period was the band 'Fun-Da-Mental', who blended a mixture of qawwali, heavy rock and rap. Even though they interlaced some of their lyrics with verses of the Quran, they were 'perhaps less concerned with expressing their Islamic identity than they were with belonging to a broad anti-imperialist movement, within which "Islamic" motifs often slotted quite comfortably – such as Malcolm X or the Palestinian struggle'.[18] However, this particular genre was never really embraced by the mainstream of Muslim communities and remained somewhat of a niche musical taste, later subsumed within the category of 'Asian Music,' which has several of its own vibrant subgenres.

In the latter part of the 1990s the two styles that became the most popular were rap and nasheeds, and these continue to exercise influence on contemporary Muslim musical culture. The desire to produce Islamic popular music paralleled patterns in Europe and North America, where the emerging appetite of young Muslims to listen to music reflected their experiences and aspirations of growing up in non-Muslim societies. Amateur groups such as Native Deen and professionals such as Yasin Bey (aka Mos Def) produced forms of Islamic rap and hip hop which were emulated by British Muslim artists. This second style gained popularity partly due to the increasing numbers of converts from African-Caribbean backgrounds. The *Malcolm X* movie produced by Spike Lee in the mid-1990s helped 'a new generation of Black Britons to connect Afrocentric ideologies to Islamic belief and Muslim identity'.[19] Muslim rap music in its diverse forms is a creative act of faith, a vehicle of self-expression and social commentary. Much like their peers in America, for many young British Muslims rap music is the soundtrack to their lives and reflects particular social, political and cultural concerns of a multicultural, urban youth population.[20] This could be seen as part of a formation of a distinctively modern, cultural-political space that is not specifically American or British, but is, rather, a hybrid of the two which has produced a form of 'Islamic-Atlantic' – akin to the concept of 'The Black Atlantic' developed by British cultural theorist Paul Gilroy. The trans-Atlantic exchange of ideas, experiences and travel and family connections between American and British Muslims over the last two decades has influenced tastes in music and many other areas.[21]

The group Mecca2Medina, fronted by Rakin Fetuga and Ismael Lea South, were the first British Muslims to gain prominence for their Islamised rap music. Considered as pioneers, they are also known for their active community work. Fetuga is a teacher, South has a background in youth work and is founder of the 'Salam Project' which works with disaffected young people in the inner cities. They have also helped to promote younger acts such as Mohammed Yahya, Poetic Pilgrimage and Pearls of Islam.

Sukina Abdul Noor and Muneera Rashid, dubbed the 'Hip-hop Hijabis', formed Poetic Pilgrimage in 2002 and have been at the cutting edge of spoken word poetry. Both women are converts of Jamaican heritage and were influenced by a variety of musical traditions that include Afrobeat, soul, jazz and reggae. They see themselves as a bridge between Muslim communities and the wider hop-hop culture and cite the influence of American socially conscious hip hop musicians Mos Def, Common and Nas. Their lyrics confound stereotypes and are infused with a mix of Islamic spirituality, racial pride and a sense of Britishness. Their performances used to upset more conservative audiences who questioned women singing in public but are now generally welcomed due to their established profiles and message, which has garnered mainstream media attention and received widespread praise.[22]

Both are also known for their social activism – Muneera mentors young people and is an expert in video production. Sukina is the editor of *Muslim Hip Hop* magazine and hosts a lifestyle show on the Islam Channel. She is also married to the Mozambican-born hip hop artist Mohammed Yahya. Mohammed is known for his spoken word poetry, is one of the founders of Rebel Muzik Arts foundation and, along with Daniel Silverstein, established the first Muslim-Jewish hip hop collective in the UK. He is also the president of Speech for Peace, 'an organisation that aims to create a positive movement that will inspire all communities to work together towards constructive engagement between one another exemplifying understanding and compassion in the work for social justice and human dignity'.[23]

Two other female Muslim artists who have become well known for their spoken word poetry are the Pearls of Islam. The children of Afro-Caribbean converts, Rabiah and Sakinah are two sisters who write and perform a range of styles that includes rap, folk, soul and nasheed songs, accompanied by the guitar and djembe and darbouka drums. Their music gravitates to softer, spiritual themes which reflect the influence of their teacher – the late Sufi Shaykh Nazim (d. 2013). Dr Carl Morris writes that their lyrics

> attempt to translate their Islamic beliefs into a universal lan-
> guage of spirituality and morality, with the aim of achieving
> a wider resonance beyond the boundaries of the traditional
> Muslim collectivity. Their music correspondingly tends to
> focus on personal and spiritual journeying – a delicate and
> at times beautiful evocation of faith, belief and optimism in
> modern Britain.[24]

Nasheeds have a hymn-like form and are often sung in Arabic and Turkish, though most are written and performed in English with lyrics addressing religious concerns. Second-generation Muslims, such as members of the Young Muslims UK, started to experiment with English lyrics and released a number of audio-cassette albums in the early 1990s, but nasheed as a style was given its biggest boost by Yusuf Islam (aka Cat Stevens) – an iconic figure for many British Muslim musicians. After he returned to making music in the mid-1990s, his creative output channelled through his company Mountain of Light, set the standard for production quality. This was emulated by new companies such as Awakening Records who emerged to profit from the increasing demand for professionally produced material and helped launch the singing careers of many of today's Muslim nasheed artists such as Mesut Kurtis, Hamza Namira, Raeef, Harris J, Sami Yusuf and

Maher Zain. The latter two became globally successful and have sold tens of millions of albums.

Sami Yusuf is the biggest British Muslim popstar since Yusuf Islam. He achieved fame after the release of his first album in 2003 and went on to develop a career that transcended the nasheed genre. His successful career is a case study in how contemporary Muslims have made Western musical models their own, both in terms of content and presentation. His early work reworked traditional nasheed styles and was sung in English and Arabic with some tracks also performed in Turkish and Urdu – this demonstrated a shrewd marketing decision given that he is not a speaker of either language. Awakening Records invested a significant amount of money into producing the second album, with one of the song's accompanying video being filmed in India, Egypt, Turkey and the UK. The formula proved to be successful as it was able to tap into youth consumer markets in each country and became a commercial success around the world. Sami Yusuf's style of music, aura of Islamicity, image, marketing and timing enabled him to become a household name that took nasheed music to a new level of professionalism and spurred many imitators.

Fifteen years on from the rise of Sami Yusuf, dozens of artist populate the nasheed music scene and have a following of several million young, often female, fans ready to buy their latest offerings. One of the most recent and popular is Harris J, a young British Muslim artist with Indian and Irish heritage. Harris J's current output and image bears a resemblance to the early phase of young Canadian pop star Justin Bieber's career. His boyish good looks and catchy lyrics have triggered tens of millions of YouTube views. Harris's road to fame came after he entered a social media talent contest in 2013 organised by Awakening Records.

These artists and the English nasheeds are shaping a younger-generation conception of religiously inspired music and are shaping millennial British Muslim identities – and becoming celebrities in the process. This colourful, innovative music subculture in both its nasheed and rap variants also reflects a bigger shift in tastes and interests resulting from the global dominance of Western popular culture and the generational changes taking place across Muslim communities in majority and minority contexts. This is worth noting, as people aged 25 and below make up more than 50 per cent of many Muslim nations. However, these changes in youth culture have not been unanimously welcomed and have triggered a backlash from both conservative Muslims who question the Islamicity of its forms and others who have questioned the content and raised issues of representation.

Unhappy with 'Happy Muslims'

On 16 April 2014, an anonymous group calling themselves 'Honesty Policy' released a video on YouTube of some British Muslims, some of whom were public figures, singing and dancing through the streets to the American singer Pharrell Williams' international hit 'Happy'. The 'Happy British Muslims!' video became an overnight sensation, received over a million views within a few days and inspired a number of copy-cat versions by Muslims in the US, Germany and Holland. It also created an equally passionate backlash from other British Muslims. This apparently innocent attempt at depicting Muslims letting their hair down is a revealing window into intra-British Muslim cultural politics.

The negative reactions ranged from mild to the outraged. Conservatives judged the video to be 'unIslamic', that it contravened religious prohibitions on the use of musical instruments, showed Muslim women dancing in public and promoted illicit Western music. Some argued that it was problematic due to the fact that the song was written and produced by an artist who had been well known for his misogynistic, hyper-sexualised material in the past. Other voices asked how Muslims could be happy when they were victims of social discrimination and persecution in various parts of the world. Another more ambivalent viewer felt that while the intent was correct, its content needed editing, and then went on to release a 'halal' version with all the women's appearances removed!

For one British Muslim academic, the video represented something more troubling. The subtext of the video screamed 'moderate Muslims' and was hence judged to be a politically driven production that craved acceptance. For Dr Raana Bokhari, it was undermined by a sense of insecurity:

The first emotion that gripped me in seeing this odd, bizarre, contrite performance of 'happiness' was how unnatural and staged the whole event is. You see, this is not simply about a group of people coming together to express joy: this is a specific agenda, by an elitist, affluent and political/media savvy middle-class group, who it seems that in yet another attempt at apologia, are offering a palatable, sanitised, acceptable, 'version' of both 'Muslimness' and 'happiness'.[25]

She goes on to ask rhetorically:

what is refreshing about a group of Muslims, who appear to be so reactive and apologetic for being Muslims, that they appear as if they are desperate to 'show' they are happy? How is happiness measured? If the Western media, governments and powers that be have decided that happiness is measured by dancing and singing, then should all groups, no matter what race, creed, faith or culture, be obliged to accept that definition of happiness? Is Western cultural hegemony the only way forward?[26]

Dr Bokhari claimed that the people in the video apparently did not reflect the diversity of theological leanings among British Muslims and the majority in the production were 'well known, middle class, professional Muslims essentially from the Sunni school, either involved in politics or the media'. For her it raised the question of whether 'privileged, reformist, non-traditional British Muslims have the right to speak on behalf of the majority "other"?'[27] There were no formal responses to these critiques by the Honesty Policy other than to say that 'the video is part of a process by which British Muslims work out their identity and that process may be unusually rancorous and painful'.

People who appreciated the video felt that the criticisms were a huge over reaction and unnecessary politicisation of a harmless expression of joy. The video was intended to normalise British Muslims and challenge stereotypes – particularly the negative imagery of Muslim women – but at no point attempts to 'represent the majority'. To read it as anything other than an attempt to buy into a song that resonated in popular culture actually vindicates the perception that Muslims are one-dimensional people that do not appreciate music. The restrictive conservatism advocated by some religious figures, who spent hours delivering YouTube responses, over looked well-established principles in the Islamic ethics of legal disagreement. This event is also demonstrative of the deep underlying divisions within Muslim communities and the fictive nature of community unity. There has never been one homogenous British community – but there is a collective faith entity of diverse peoples, living together and sharing the basics of one faith that might agree on issues that affect them as members of a religious group such as the damaging effects of British and American foreign policy, rising Islamophobia, negative effects of anti-terror legislation and counter-terrorism policy.

It also indicates a failure of the critics to understand the organic nature of culture or how to contribute to its development. Using an idea and appropriating it from one person is not necessarily validating other uses and is a specious argument that would disable Muslims from drawing upon anything from non-Islamic references. The outrage over the happy video resembles the reaction to the release of a similar production by American Muslims in late 2013. The 'Mipsterz' (Muslim Hipsters) video entitled 'Somewhere in America' shows a number of trendy young hijab-wearing women having fun listening to music, posing, laughing, biking, skateboarding and fencing, set to a soundtrack of the rapper Jay Z. The video provoked a heated social media debate, with some praising it for its empowering, stereotype-defying presentation of Muslim women, yet other Muslims criticised it for capitulating to Western standards of normality and for trying too hard to appear hip. American Muslim journalist Sana Saeed expressed her unease with the video, argued it 'was produced, created and directed primarily by Muslim men. Yes, it's cool, she says – but that's about it.' She writes:

> In the name of fighting stereotypes, it seems we're keen to adopt ... tools and images that objectify us (either as sexualized or desexualized; as depoliticized or politicized)

rather than support us where we need that support. We're so incredibly obsessed with appearing 'normal' or 'American' or 'Western' by way of what we do and what we wear that we undercut the actual abnormality of our communities and push essentialist definitions of 'normal', 'American' and 'Western'.[28]

The gross over-reactions to these attempts at reflecting hybrid expressions of faith have a stultifying effect on future Muslim creativity for fear of the backlash and close down an important route to engaging young people. For some, the negativity indicates a lack of a sense of humour or the perception that 'Muslims can't take a joke'. This stereotype, like most, is wide off the mark. Attempts by Muslims to humanise themselves through music at a time of widespread fear and anxiety can also be seen in other areas of cultural production. One of the most interesting and entertaining is humour.

'Islamic comedy' from YouTube to the BBC

The use of comedy to educate and make fun of social attitudes has a long pedigree among minorities in majority cultures and there are well-known Jewish and African-Caribbean performers. The 'Islamic Atlantic', alluded to earlier, has allowed American Muslim comics to influence upcoming British Muslim artists cited here. In particular, Azhar Usman, Bryant 'Preacher' Moss and Mo Amer – the trio who made up the 'Allah Made Me Funny' collective has been performing around the world since 2004. But what makes their shows distinctly Islamic? Intent and content. The stated aim of the routines is to provide a place for Muslims to let off steam and laugh at themselves in a light-hearted manner by puncturing stereotypes and challenges of being a Muslim in the West. The jokes are delivered within the parameters of Muslim decorum, which means no profanity, sexual references or backbiting. As they are frequently invited to appear at non-Muslim venues they request that comedy clubs do not serve alcohol or pork, or allow smoking during performances. The content remains the same and allows them to challenge any misunderstandings that the audience may have about Islam and Muslims.

Former Birmingham Science teacher Shazia Mirza was the first British Muslim woman to have developed a stand-up comedy career. She came to public attention in the months after 9/11 with her satire routine that would begin with the deadpan remark, 'My name is Shazia Mirza. At least, that's what it says on my pilot's licence.' Another Brummie ex-school teacher who has pursued stand-up comedy as a profession is Gulam Khan, better known by his stage name 'Guzzy Bear'. Using observational humour, his many YouTube videos have gone viral. In June 2015, Khan made a short film *Roadman Ramadan* as part of the British Muslim Comedy series, five short films by Muslim comedians commissioned by the BBC. The sketches follow Khan's character, Mobeen, help his English convert friend, Trev, navigate his first Ramadan.

Humza Arshad similarly developed a large following on You-Tube with his 'Diaries of a Bad Man' videos which have been viewed by tens of millions of people. Playing a fictional version of himself, they chronicle his adventures as a self-styled 'badman with seriously good looks', a caricature of the streetwise Asian young male stereotype found in urban Muslim communities. His web-cam monologues and skits provide satirical takes on the challenges of racism, his relationship with his parents and frivolous antics with his friends, and finish with short moral messages. Arshad's success has led to him being asked by the police to front an anti-extremism tour of high schools and he has since produced an online comedy for BBC Three.

The latter two projects represent the successful transition from amateur, home-made YouTube productions targeting niche Muslim audiences to the mainstream. Their artistic and commercial success no doubt motivates the increasing number of social media performers trying to gain fame. Within this scene are several types of people who have tried to emulate the popular style of YouTube broadcasts – these include vloggers, pranksters, hijab tutorialists and filmmakers that have global audiences and opportunities to monetise their content.[29] This underlines the influence and appetite of a new generation of young Muslims who are seeking creative, well-made online content that resonates with their faith values. It also indicates the lack of public role models that inspire them. The rise of the Muslim telegenic YouTube figure has not been welcomed wholesale as it is enmeshed in a shallow, narcissistic, celebrity culture that engages in consumerism and condones behaviours at odds with Islamic values. British Muslim journalist Omar Shahid argues that many Muslim YouTubers who have gained large followings

> start off quite innocent, their videos fairly innocuous, and their intentions (God knows best) probably just to have some fun and express their thoughts and lifestyles. But as the 'likes' increase, the views shoot up and the fame takes over, they all, one by one, lose sense of who they were, their values become secondary and maintaining their fame seems to be more important than anything else.[30]

This sentiment is also expressed by other observers who are alarmed at the way social media has mutated the intentions of many of the people who originally set up their channels to educate non-Muslims about Islam. Amarah Fahimuddin, who blogs at the *Muslimah Diaries* website for instance, writes:

> YouTubers are no longer clarifying misconceptions about Islam, but instead are taking measures in order to gain the approval of a wider audience. For example, some Muslim YouTubers are now using derogatory and even sexual connotations as titles for their videos as a form of 'click bait', which of course means more money and fame for them. We now see that the more popular Muslim YouTubers are those who are known for putting out more scandalous content. But why should we care? They're not causing any harm, right? Well, let's consider the bigger picture. The major problem with the actions that some, not all, of these social media stars is the influence they have over young impressionable viewers. They have become role models whether they intended to or not.[31]

She further argues that many of these Muslim YouTube 'celebrities' have become hugely influential but have not exercised the responsibility that comes with that status and instead are more interested in gaining more followers and have paradoxically normalised values and behaviour that are at odds with Islamic teachings. After reaching a certain point, after being validated by their eager fans, some stop including religious references in their videos and are more interested in increasing their audience. This has in some case led to individuals acquiring pseudo-scholarly profiles and pronouncing on religious issues that they have no qualifications to speak about. These tensions will no doubt continue as religious authority structures become more fragmented and struggle to compete with self-styled preachers, 'YouTube scholars' or the individualised approach to seeking information from the internet by 'Sheikh Google' and 'Wiki Islam'.

Efforts are being made, however: in addition to some of the younger generation of scholars highlighted in Chapter 2, other attempts are being made to provide co-ordinated responses in the age of digital Islam. One such attempt that stands out is the Imams Online initiative lead by social entrepreneur Shaukat Warraich. As the Chief Executive of Faith Associates, he has authored some path-breaking documents such as the *Mosque Management Toolkit*, the *Madrassah Management Guide*, a Madrassah Quality Standards Framework (MQSF) and, significantly, worked with a number of female Muslim scholars, academics and activists to produce the *Muslim Women's Guide to Mosque Governance, Management and Service Delivery*.

Extensive collaboration with mosques across the UK and internationally, helped shape the development of the Imams Online portal. This virtual platform aims to provide a voice and point of information and inspiration for British imams, women religious scholars and Islamic leaders interested in interfaith work and civic responsibility. It has over 200,000 Facebook 'likes' and thousands of subscribers to the YouTube channel. It has held digital literacy conferences for imams and, in 2017, launched a YouTube series on 'What British Muslims Really Do' and a 'Campaign for Imams Fair Wage Campaign', which aims to

> spark a much needed conversation in the Muslim community around the role of a 21st Century British Imam and the establishment of defined duties and viable remuneration

that will help legitimize the role, support and reward Imams for their hard work and enthuse young seminary graduates in pursuing it as a career.[32]

Some of the imams associated with this initiative, such as Qari Asim, have gone on to develop prominent public profiles, are very tech savvy and are active in public debates about Islam in the UK, frequently appearing on television and radio.

British Muslims have been active in broadcast media since the technology was made available and have developed numerous religious satellite channels. The three most watched of the English language broadcasters are the Islam Channel, Peace TV and British Muslim TV. The London-based Islam Channel has numerous programmes such as Women's AM, IslamiQA, City Sisters, Education Matters and the Health Show.[33] Most of the content focuses on teaching matters of faith and worship with some current affairs and documentaries. Peace TV is broadcast from Dubai and was set up by Indian preacher Dr Zakir Naik; it hosts various shows that discuss aspects of Muslim belief and practice.[34] The third of the free–to-view channels – British Muslim TV – pitches itself as a channel which aims to 'make British Muslims feel confidently Muslim and comfortably British'.[35] Located in Wakefield, Yorkshire, the intent of the channel is more overtly integrationist compared to the other two which are more Salafi oriented. British Muslim TV is more eclectic in its intellectual influences and tends to invite Muslims from a greater diversity of backgrounds to discuss aspects of being Muslim in Britain and has a wider variety of shows.

Other Muslims have taken a more direct route to engaging the public by training in the mainstream media sector and have become accomplished filmmakers, journalists and presenters. Mishal Hussain is a familiar face and voice on the BBC; hijab-wearing newsreader Fatima Manji is on Channel Four News; and, similarly, Sabbyiah Pervez is a reporter for BBC North. This is an important sign of inclusivity from mainstream broadcasters and inspiration for Muslim women everywhere. However, this development has not been welcomed by all sections of British society and this was demonstrated when visibly Muslim Fatima Manji was criticised by the former editor of *The Sun* newspaper after the terrorist attacks in Nice in July 2016. He questioned whether she was an appropriate choice to present the news given that she shared the same faith as the attackers and likened it to an Orthodox Jew reporting on the Israel–Palestine conflict. This prejudice, like much current anti-Muslim sentiment, is not purely a matter of opinion as it often translates into street-level harassment and violence – Manji was subjected to verbal abuse a few weeks later.

Writing Muslims

An increasing number of talented Muslim newspaper journalists and freelance writers are writing for the most prominent publications – many of them women. Nersine Malik is a sharp commentator who writes for *The Guardian* and *Independent* and in her articles regularly punctures myths about Muslims, migrants and race. Similarly, Remona Aly, as well as writing for *The Guardian*, is a thoughtful contributor on BBC Radio 2 for the *Chris Evans Breakfast Show*, presenter for Radio 4's *Something Understood* and a host for the 'Things Unseen' podcast which explores issues of morality, spirituality and ethics. One of the most recognisable of this new wave, the convert Dr Myriam François, has carved out a career in broadcast journalism from writing about Muslim issues in the *New Statesman*, *Huffington Post* and *Emel* magazine. She appears regularly as commentator on television programmes such as the BBC's *Big Questions* and *Newsnight*, and *Sky News* and has produced a number of informative documentaries. This increased representation within the media and journalism is a welcome way in which Muslims are creating a positive visible presence within mainstream culture. They are also impacting arts and creative industries in the fields of literature, poetry, visual arts and photography and heritage sectors.

Each of these areas is incredibly rich and diverse, so only a small selection from each is highlighted here. British Muslim writers have been producing notable works of fiction for many years and have gained the recognition of critics and prize-giving boards, and best-seller status. Dr Claire Chambers, in her book on *British Muslim Fictions*, quotes an amusing passage from the 1993 novel

East of Wimbledon by Nigel Williams, to demonstrate the difficulties of defining Islamic English literature. In this scene, Robert, the main protagonist, tries to pass as a Muslim to get a job at the Islamic Boys School:

> He [the School's headmaster, Mr Malik] spread his hands generously. 'You, of course, among your other duties, will be teaching Islamic English Literature.'
>
> Robert nodded keenly. His floppy, blond hair fell forward over his eyes, and he raked it back with what he hoped was boyish eagerness. ... 'In that context,' he said, 'do you see Islamic English literature as being literature by English, or Welsh or Scottish Muslims?'
>
> They both looked at each other in consternation. Perhaps, like him, Mr Malik was unable to think of a single Muslim writer who fitted that description.
>
> 'Or,' went on Robert, struggling somewhat, 'do you see it as work that has a Muslim dimension? Such as ... *Paradise Lost*.' What was the Muslim dimension in *Paradise Lost*? Robert became aware that the room had suddenly become very hot.
>
> 'Or,' he went on swiftly, 'simply English literature viewed from a Muslim perspective?' 'You will view English from a Muslim perspective,' said Malik with a broad, affable grin, 'because you are a Muslim!'[36]

This imaginary dialogue illustrates the challenge of appropriate definition when trying to interpret this genre and the internal debate among Muslims about what makes a piece of art Islamic or Muslim? It also exposes the lazy assumption that by being a Muslim, one automatically holds a religious worldview or a static, universal identity. As we have noted throughout this book, Muslims come in all shapes and sizes and degrees of religiosity – while some are highly committed to their faith, others can be passionately secular and relate to their faith as a cultural inheritance. Dr Chambers opts to use the phrase 'writers of Muslim heritage' to describe the diverse perspectives of writers she interviewed for her volume, which included atheists and secular Muslims such as Tariq Ali, Hanif Kureshi, Nadeem Aslam, Tahmina Alam and Mohsin Hamid. The quotation from William's novel also has aged – twenty-five years on, there is no longer a dearth of Muslim writers from all parts of the British Isles who have made significant contributions to fiction, memoirs, novellas and biographies.

Mahfouz Sabrina's *The Things I Would Tell You: British Muslim Women Write* is a lively recent anthology of short stories and poetry that covers serious themes such as love, politics and patriarchy, to more light-hearted portraits such as a disenchanted imam who becomes a TV chat-show host. The contributors to this collection include established writers such as Kamila Shamsie and Ahdaf Soueif, as well as emerging voices like Aisha Mirza, Hibaq Oman and Selma Dabbagh. Two of these short stories by Dabbagh, *Take Me There* and *Last Assignment to Jenin*, explore love and relationships in besieged locations and point to the increasing trend of Muslims writing about love; Ayisha Malik's Sofia Khan romantic comedy novels have been described as the 'Muslim Bridget Jones', Na'ima B. Robert has written an engaging series of fiction stories aimed at young adults and how they navigate the complexities of growing up in multicultural Britain with titles such as *From Somalia with Love* and *Boy vs Girl*. In *Dear Infidel*, Tamim Sadikali recreates the tensions and tragedies of family life of young Pakistani Muslim men in post-9/11 Britain. Written in a gritty, realistic prose it engages the themes of religion, love, hate, longing and sexual dysfunction.

Among the increasing autobiographical accounts of Muslims in Britain, Bengali science teacher Alom Shaha's *The Young Atheist Handbook* is worth reading. Part painful memoir, part polemic against Islam, it opens a window into the increasing phenomena of British Muslim apostasy. The author, Suma Din, is among the few British Muslim biographers having written a book on the founder of the world's biggest Muslim charity – Islamic Relief. In addition to books on Islam for educationalists, her book *Muslim Mothers and their Children's Schooling* offers an important commentary on parent–school relations from the perspective of women from different backgrounds and should be read by teachers, parents and policymakers.

Artists, poets and photographers: retrieving Muslim heritage

Mukhtar Sanders is the founder of Inspiral Design Ltd which synthesises British design, Islamic art and language, in print and digital forms. Son of the renowned photographer and English convert Peter Sanders, he has established himself as an expert in typography and Arabic calligraphy. He and his wife Soraya co-founded Nutqa, which is a user-generated mobile museum of Islamic calligraphy.[37] Zarah Hussain describes herself as a visual mathematician and an award-winning artist of Islamic geometry. Her stunning three-dimensional 'Numina' light installation won the Lumen prize and is an example of tradition meeting modernity.[38] One of the most interesting and influential visual artists and designers is Ruh al-Alam, who has created a distinct style that combines classical Islamic with the contemporary. He was a featured artist in the BBC documentary *The Hidden Art of Islam* and has developed his own company – the Islamic Design House – which began in the mid-2000s by selling modest wear and has expanded to a number of products such as home décor and a novel re-imagining of the traditional prayer mat.[39]

A number of other British Muslim poets have been at work across communities in the UK. In May 2017, twenty-two-year-old Suhaiymah Manzoor-Khan delivered a powerful performance at the Roundhouse Poetry Slam that went viral. Addressing media stereotypes about Muslims she argued counter intuitively that Muslims should not be valued on how relatable or recognisable they are, and denounced the public pressure to be a 'Good Muslim' in her 'This is not a Humanising Poem':

I refuse to have to prove my humanity to you by cracking a smile, and saying how 'I also cry at the end of Toy Story 3'. I won't try to tell you about 'the complex inner worlds of Sumeahs and Aishas . . .' No, this will not be a 'Muslims are like us' poem. I refuse to be respectable . . . Because if you need me to prove my humanity, I'm not the one that's not human . . . Instead, love us when we are lazy. Love us when we are poor . . . Love us high as kites, unemployed, joy

riding, time wasting, failing at school, love us filthy. Without the right color passports, without the right sounding
English.[40]

Another ground-breaking creative is the photographer Mahtab
Hussain. His work *You Get Me?* examines issues of masculinity
and isolation among young working-class Pakistani men and the
emotional impacts of sweeping media generalisations. His exhibition and accompanying book helps to explain how they struggle
with the transition to adulthood and the lack of social mobility
compared to their more aspirational peers. Mahtab explains:

> It's about urban culture and the types of messages these
> young men have had over the years about how to hold
> themselves. I think men in some communities are going
> through a period of male redundancy, as women become
> more educated, want careers and no longer want to get
> married and so on. These guys are performing a type
> of masculinity that is dying. The book is questioning
> that mind-set, but also celebrating it, allowing men to
> be powerful, and I think that is something that men are
> struggling with.[41]

These conditions correlate with what we touched upon in the
previous chapter about alienation, disengagement and the sense
of powerlessness that many young men feel, which in turn affects
their sense of self-esteem, mental health and need to 'get respect'.
In this case, it has not provided the conditions in which violent
radicalisation has taken root but instead has created a distinct
working-class male subculture that is often permeated with a toxic
masculinity that is misogynistic and insular.

Representation continues to be among the most frequently
raised issues within British Muslim communities. The over
dominance of South Asian Muslims in discussions about British
Muslims is a particular grievance of Muslims from African-
Caribbean backgrounds. Many Black Muslims feel that not only
are they not fully represented in British history but are also
absent from the debates about Islam in Britain. According to

the Muslim Council of Britain report, which we cited in the Chapter 1, about 10 per cent of British Muslims are of African descent. Converts often experience a 'double marginality' by having to deal with discrimination from both society as well as from 'born-Muslims' who claim a more authentic piety.[42] This is felt most acutely by Muslims of African-Caribbean ancestry and is rarely discussed in public by the wider British Muslim communities. Moments in the BBC documentary *Muslims Like Us* illustrated these tensions and highlighted the difficult conversations taking place about anti-Black prejudice within Muslim communities.[43]

This sensitive subject is being discussed more frequently. One of the most high profile attempts to address the issue took place in March 2017, in a symposium held in East London. Organised by the 'Everyday Muslim' team, this event aimed to explore constructions of Black Muslim identity and heritage in the UK and showcase the stories of Black British Muslims working in academia, heritage, arts and media.[44] The event brought together some of the most talented and influential artists, academics and activists from Britain's Black Muslim communities. There were fascinating presentations, such as the 'Invisible Muslimah' by young academic Hannah Abdule; Cambridge-based academic Shaykh Michael Mumisa; Habeeb Akande, author of *Illuminating the Darkness: Blacks and North Africans in Islam*; and filmmaker Sheila Na'ima Nortley, among others. Issues of visibility and cultural erasure are now explored frankly in productions such as *Black and Muslim in Britain*. Saraiya Bah, a cofounder of the initiative which worked with the Everyday Muslim team to produce this series, argues that 'it is vital for the Black Muslim narrative to be documented for themselves, by themselves' and she wanted to document the 'thoughts, experiences, and the rich cultural diversity of Black British Muslims in its rawest form'.[45]

The Everyday Muslim project is another example of an exciting Muslim women-led initiative that is innovative and important. The project is almost entirely staffed by women and seeks to create a centralised archive of Muslim lives, arts, education and cultures from across the UK, with the long-term objective of collating and documenting an unmediated portrayal of Muslim life in Britain.[46]

Three other individuals have recently made names for themselves in the area of British Muslim heritage. Mobeen Butt is a social entrepreneur and activist who created the British Muslim Museum Initiative. The first virtual resource of its kind, it offers an online history of Islam in Britain and information points for those interested in Muslim arts and culture.

Abdulmaalik Tailor is a convert from Hinduism of more than twenty years and is the first professionally qualified Muslim Tour Guide in London. He has set up Muslim History Tours to offer Muslim tours of Britain, and specialises in the Muslim heritage present at some of the top UK tourist spots: Trafalgar Square, Westminster Abbey, St Paul's Cathedral.[47] Tharik Hussain is a British Bangladeshi-born travel writer who works as a journalist, travel writer, photographer and broadcaster – his radio documentary on 'America's Mosques: a Story of Integration' for the BBC World Service, won the award of Best Religious Program at the New York Festivals World's Best Radio Programs Awards. He writes about the Muslim religious heritage of places as diverse as Albania, Macedonia, Dublin and Vietnam.[48]

Performing piety: faith and fashion

Is it possible to look both fashionable and Islamic? Most British Muslim women would say yes, according to Professor Emma Tarlo, author of the important book *Visibly Muslim: Fashion, Politics, Faith*. Her fascinating study details how Muslim women have redefined the sartorial boundaries of their faith and shaped the global trend in 'modest fashion'. As she explains:

> For some 'Islamic fashion' means wearing fashionable clothes 'Islamically' by which they mean in conformity with covering restrictions based on interpretations of Islamic texts. For others it means selecting from a new range of clothes designed and marketed specifically as 'Islamic fashion'. For many, it means a mixture of both.[49]

The idea that Muslim women's clothing could be 'cool' might surprise those who associate the female dress with restrictions imposed by men. While that is true in a handful of societies such as Saudi Arabia, Iran and Afghanistan, Islamic clothing is worn in a multitude of ways that range from trendy, loose-fitting head wraps to designer *niqabs* and *abayas* (long, cloak-like garment). Many British Muslim fashion designers developed their styles because they were 'self-confessed lovers of fashion and it was their desire to reconcile their love of fashion with their desire to express their faith'.[50] The result was the development of labels and clothing lines that combined traditional styles with British fashion trends to eventually produce a highly creative look that acts as a bridge to the mainstream and has caught the interest of high street chains such as H&M and Dolce & Gabbana, and now is a multi-billion-dollar global industry.

British styles are given an Islamic inflection to enable Muslim women to feel comfortable and stylish as they distance themselves from parental or grandparental imported, ethnic styles, while experimenting with adapting and adopting British norms. The 'Cool Hijabi' image is now also marketed by Nike, who launched their own sports hijab two days before International Women's Day 2017. The Nike Pro hijab was accompanied by a series of advertisements targeting Muslim women, using known Muslim hijabi athletes including Parkour trainer Amal Mourad, boxer Arifa Bseiso, singer Balqees Fathi and boxer Arifa Bseiso for the ads.[51] The 'Burkini' modest swimming outfit has even been donned by the likes of celebrity chef Nigella Lawson.

One of the reasons for the rise in Islamic fashion is the increasing number of women offering tutorials and styling tips on YouTube. One of the most famous is Leicester-based entrepreneur Amena Khan, aka 'Amenakin', who has nearly 400,000 subscribers to her channel, runs a successful business and models L'Oreal make-up products.[52] Her online hijab tutorials and lifestyle videos 'blend different affects and aesthetic styles, so Amena can imitate the affects and styles of the mainstream lifestyle videos on YouTube while incorporating a particular Islamic sense of piety'.[53] British-Egyptian hijab blogger Dina Torkia is another popular figure among fashion-conscious hijab wearers and has nearly 700,000 subscribers to her YouTube channel.[54] She was invited to the World Muslimah beauty pageant in Indonesia and was the subject of a BBC3 documentary that followed her experience of the event. These two individuals have helped shape the way young Muslim women present themselves online and have influenced other aspiring Muslim make-up tutorialists.

Given that they focus on enhancing appearance, there is an awkward contradiction in the videos of these hijabi tutorialists as their attempt to present images of female modesty run counter to traditional Islamic teachings which discourage women displaying their beauty in the public sphere. There is now something of an anti-Islamic fashion backlash among other Muslim women who express ethical and aesthetic concerns that Islamic values and priorities may become diluted, distorted or lost given the direction of the industry and its co-option by big business.

This can be seen when hijab-wearing Muslim women perform at catwalk presentations in the gaze of male and female audiences. Increasingly, female voices are pointing out that the style in which Islamic fashion shows are staged and the suggestive ways in which the models are photographed, appear no different from the mainstream and miss the point of female modesty. Aisha Hasan, who also writes for the *Muslimah Diaries*, points out that the presentation of female Muslim bodies often resembles the depictions in Orientalist art:

> In the post 9/11 era, the Muslim woman is once again presented as an object of intrigue; and increasingly so in the West, she is not shown as an example of backward conservatism, but instead as an exotic modern fusion. As the Muslim millennial culture converges with that of modern secular norms, Muslim women seem to have 'halal' equivalent for every imported 'progressive' standard by which women are judged. It is easy to see simply from the huge industry that modest fashion has become; from hijabi catwalks and models, to Muslim designers and makeup artists, that the depiction of Muslim women as mysterious yet beautiful has returned, albeit in a more modern context.[55]

It is possible to see the irony here as the idea of hijab was meant to protect women from being sexually objectified by society.

Reversing these developments will be difficult given the cultural shift that has taken place among the second and third generation of British Muslims and the very large commercial investments made by both Muslims and non-Muslims. Being a 'Cool Muslim' costs money and there is a growing middle class of Muslims who have that purchasing power to consume faith-inspired fashion, goods and services.

Muslim consumerism and 'Generation M'

The American Muslim scholar Vali Nasr argues in his book *Mecca-nomics* that 'The great battle for the soul of the Muslim world will be fought not over religion but over market capitalism.'[56] This is being fuelled globally by an upwardly mobile middle class of Muslims entrepreneurs, investors, professionals and consumers searching for halal-certified products. According to estimates in *The State of Global Islamic Economy* report of 2016/17, Muslims spent over 1.9 trillion dollars in 2015. In Britain, Muslims contributed an estimated 31 billion pounds to the economy in 2013.[57] There are also around 10,000 Muslim millionaires.[58] This rise of a prosperous middle class converges with the rise of the 'Muslim Cool' phenomenon and has implications for the way in which Islam is interpreted and accommodated in minority contexts such as the UK. The increased demand for sharia-compliant finance products and availability of halal products in British high street retail outlets such as Tesco, Sainsbury's, Asda and Marks & Spencer, confirms the power of the 'Muslim Pound', but has also reignited debates about religious slaughter methods, the labelling of products and wider economic and political influence of Muslims in British society.

For critics, it represents the creeping Islamising of institutions and political capitulation, for others it provides evidence that Muslims are fully integrating and contributing to the UK. Other Muslims are ambivalent. While they welcome a greater recognition of their religion in public life, they are wary of the way in which commercialisation is taking place in the name of Islam. They point to the compromising of their faith's moral frameworks which emphasises ethics, personal restraint, economic justice, discouragement of waste and respect for the environment. These are not values that are associated with modern industrialised production or the global economy.

In her book *Brand Islam: The Marketing and Commodification of Piety*, Dr Faegheh Shirazi examines this growing industry and questions the extent to which the products, goods and services in the global halal industry are really halal. For instance, she considers how the Barbie doll is rendered 'Islamic' by dressing it in a hijab or whether it is necessary to transmute even the most mundane products, such as water, into Islamic commodities to convert pious concerns into profit. This is clearly evident in the proliferating number of events that host exhibitions, such as the annual Muslim Lifestyle Expo, which partner the halal business sector and non-Muslim companies keen to cash in on this growing market.[59] There are even consultancy firms that offer a 'how to sell to Muslims' service. London-based writer and advertising professional Shelina JanMohamed, Vice-President of Ogilvy-Noor, whom we have cited before, is an industry insider who reveals how:

> Demonstrate that you are aware of the needs of Muslim consumers. Second, invest what could be just a small amount to verify your products are halal. Next, ensure that the halal status is clearly communicated. What worries some brands is whether to shout about this or not. You don't need to. Simple, clear and well-documented verification of halal status is the key step.[60]

In her informative book, *Generation M: Young Muslims Changing the World*, she highlights and celebrates the achievements of the types of religiously committed young Muslims that we have highlighted in this chapter. Some parts, however, read like a marketing guide on how to sell products to young Muslims and uncritically endorse consumerist culture. A less than generous review of the book takes issue with this sentiment, as journalist Angela Saini questions Shelina JanMohamed's argument:

> 'Generation M love brands,' . . . By creating an enormous parallel economy of halal products, she argues that Generation M is making it possible for people to replicate a

modern lifestyle without breaking the rules … It's difficult to get a handle on just what role feminism plays for this particular generation. She is insistent that Generation M is feminists like herself, but she also rejects mainstream feminism.[61]

Nevertheless, these trends are here to stay and may perhaps influence wider cultural attitudes, religion and economics.

The emergence of this new generation of British Muslim cultural producers, artists and change-makers reflects patterns across the globe in which a growing, young, educated middle class is shaping the cultural tastes and consumption patterns for Muslims who aspire to be successful, influential and cool. In many ways they are an elite layer of their societies but are role models and thought leaders in their communities. British Muslim broadcaster Navid Akhtar, CEO of *Alchemiya* – the Muslim version of Netflix, has described these creatives as Global Urban Muslims or 'Gummies'. One hopes that the optimistic outlook of these faith-inspired social entrepreneurs translates into broader positive changes within their communities.

Notes

1. They represent part of a growing international elite of Muslims who are excelling in a wide variety of fields that encompass arts, business, creative industries, religious scholarship, media, journalism and sports. For an introduction to some of these individuals, see the *Creative Ummah* website hosted by Australian convert Peter Gould, http://creativeummah.com/change-makers/.
2. Umar F. Abdullah, *Innovation and Creativity in Islam* (Chicago: An Nawawi Foundation, 2006), p. 1, citing Noah Feldman, *After Jihad: America and the Struggle for Islamic Democracy* (New York: Farrar, Straus and Giroux, 2003), pp. 11–12.
3. Umar F. Abdullah, *Islam and the Cultural Imperative* (Chicago: An Nawawi Foundation, 2012), p. 1. Available at http://www.nawawi.org/wp-content/uploads/2013/01/Article3.pdf.
4. Abdullah Sahin, 'Dignity of difference and recognition of interdependence: reimagining Islamic social ethics within the context of European Muslim diaspora', *Crucible, the Journal of Christian Social*

Ethics, Muslim Ethics and Islam in Britain Issue (October 2017), pp. 39–54.

5. Marshall G. Hodgson, *Venture of Islam*, vol. 1 (Chicago: University of Chicago Press, 1974), p. 59.

6. Richard Bulliet, *Islam: The View from the Edge* (New York: Columbia University Press, 1994), p. 195.

7. For notable examples, see Tariq Ramadan, *Radical Reform: Islamic Ethics and Liberation* (Oxford: Oxford University Press, 2009); Jasser Auda, *Maqasid Al-Shariah as Philosophy of Islamic Law: A Systems Approach* (London: International Institute of Islamic Thought, 2016); Khaled Abou El Fadl, *Reasoning with God: Reclaiming Shari'ah in the Modern Age* (Lanham: Rowman & Littlefield, 2017).

8. Abdullah, *Islam and the Cultural Imperative*, p. 11.

9. Sadek Hamid, *Sufis, Salafis and Islamists: The Contested Ground of British Islamic Activism* (London: I. B. Tauris, 2016), p. 71.

10. An accessible introduction to this subject can be found in Kathleen Kuiper's *Islamic Art, Literature and Culture* (New York: Britannica Educational Publishing, 2010).

11. See Ron Geaves, *Islam in Victorian Britain: The Life and Times of Abdullah Quilliam* (Markfield: Kube Publishing, 2010).

12. Aminul Hoque, *British Islamic Identity: Third Generation Bangladeshis from East London* (London: Trentham Books, 2015).

13. Amel Boubekeur, 'Cool and Competitive Muslim Culture in the West', *ISIM Review*, 16 (Autumn 2005).

14. Ibid.

15. Ginia Bellafante, 'Islam, Hope and Charity Inspire Dealer Turned Rapper', *New York Times*, Review, 22 June 2009, http://www.nytimes.com/2009/06/23/arts/television/23view.html?_r=0.

16. Carl Morris, 'Finding a voice: young Muslims, music and religious change in Britain', in Sadek Hamid (ed.), *Young British Muslims: Between Rhetoric and Realities* (London: Routledge, 2017), pp. 78–95.

17. The late Nusrat Fateh Ali Khan (d. 1997) is largely responsible for helping qawwali music to gain popularity among international audiences through his collaborations with Peter Gabriel for the soundtrack to the film *The Last Temptation of Christ*; experimental vocals were integrated into the work by other artists such as Alanis Morissette after his death.

18. Morris, 'Finding a voice'.

19. Morris, 'Finding a voice'.

20. Muslim rap has generally escaped the more controversial forms associated with the mainstream such as 'Gangsta Rap' but has been

used by groups that are jihadi sympathisers. Among the most well-known are two British Muslims calling themselves 'Sheikh Terra' and the 'Soul Salah,' who produced a song called 'Dirty Kuffar' which hit the mainstream media headlines after it was released in 2004.

21. Paul Gilroy, *The Black Atlantic – Modernity and Double Consciousness* (London: Verso, 1993).

22. For example, see the *Al-Jazeera* documentary 'Hip-Hop Hijabis': http://www.aljazeera.com/programmes/witness/2015/03/hip-hop-hijabis-150305091541022.html.

23. Cited on Muslim Rap.Net: http://www.muslimrap.net/mohamme-dyahya/.

24. Morris, 'Finding a voice'.

25. Raana Bokhari, 'To Be #Happy Muslim Or Not To Be – #Anthroislam', *Allegra Lab*, 8 May 2014, http://allegralaboratory.net/to-be-happy-muslim-or-not-to-be-anthroislam/.

26. Ibid.

27. Ibid.

28. Cited in Callie Beusman, '"Muslim Hipsters" music video ignites debate', *Jezebel.com*, 12 March 2013, https://jezebel.com/muslim-hipsters-music-video-ignites-debate-1475885148.

29. 'YouTubers You Need to Checkout!', *Creative Ummah.com*, http://creativeummah.com/muslim-youtubers-you-need-to-check-out/.

30. Omar Shahid, 'The rise of fame-hungry Muslim YouTubers', 2 April 2016, https://omarshahid.co.uk/2016/04/02/the-rise-of-fame-hun-gry-muslim-youtubers/.

31. Amarah Fahimuddin, 'Muslim sensationalism sells', *The Muslimah Diaries*, 12 May 2017, https://themuslimahdiaries.com/2017/05/12/muslim-youtubers-sensationalism-sells/comment-page-1/.

32. http://imamsonline.com/imams-fair-wage-campaign/.

33. In the past the channel has run into problems with the regulator Ofcom, who have fined it for breaching the broadcasting code on the grounds of political impartiality in 2007 and in 2009 in rela-tion to a discussion on the Arab–Israeli conflict, and again in 2014 because it gave the Tower Hamlets politician Luthfur Rahman an unchallenged platform.

34. Dr Naik, while popular with many Muslim audiences, is considered by others to be a controversial polemicist whose forays into com-parative religion are often nothing more than crude polemics that promote Islamic supremacist ideas; he has also been taken to task for his views on terrorism, women's rights, evolution and apostasy. For a

review of his work, see Mohammed Wajihuddin, 'The controversial Preacher', *The Times of India*, 27 June 2010.

35. http://www.britishmuslim.tv/about.html.
36. Claire Chambers. *British Muslim Fictions* (London: Palgrave Macmillan, 2011), pp. 4–5.
37. Can be viewed at https://www.nuqta.com/.
38. See her work online at http://zarahhussain.co.uk/#ad-image-0.
39. See http://www.ruhalalam.com/.
40. Watch https://www.youtube.com/watch?v=G9Sz2BQdMF8.
41. Bruno Bayley, 'The problems facing Britain's working class Muslim men', *Vice.com*, 21 August 2017, https://www.vice.com/en_uk/article/vbb7gy/powerful-portraits-of-the-uks-young-muslim-men?utm_campaign=global.
42. For further information, see Kate Zebri's *British Muslim Converts: Choosing Alternative Lives* (London: Oneworld, 2007).
43. Miqdaad Versi, Remona Aly and Alia Bano, 'Was *Muslims Like Us* a helpful portrayal of Islam in the UK?', *The Guardian*, 14 December 2016, https://www.theguardian.com/commentisfree/2016/dec/14/panel-muslims-like-us-islam.
44. Event schedule viewable at https://www.richmix.org.uk/events/spoken-word/everyday-muslim-symposium-exploration-black-muslims-british-history-and-heritage.
45. Aisha Ghani, 'These young black British Muslims were so fed up with being erased they made their own web series and it's lit', *BuzzFeed.com*, https://www.buzzfeed.com/aishagani/black-and-muslim-in-britain?utm_term=.mi1Za07PgD#.trWxLgd951.
46. Everyday Muslim website, http://www.everydaymuslim.org/.
47. More information is available on the Muslim History Tours website, http://www.muslimhistorytours.com/en_GB/about.
48. Further background available on his personal website, https://www.tharikhussain.co.uk/about.
49. Emma Tarlo, 'Re-fashioning the Islamic young visible Muslim', in S. Hamid (ed.), *Young British Muslims: Between Rhetoric and Realities* (London: Routledge, 2017), p. 161.
50. Ibid. p. 178.
51. https://www.youtube.com/watch?v=F-UO9vMS7AI.
52. See Amena Kha's YouTube channel, https://www.youtube.com/user/Amenakin.
53. Kristin Peterson, 'Performing piety and perfection: the affective labor of hijabi fashion videos', *CyberOrient*, 10: 1 (2016).
54. See Dina Torkia's YouTube channel, https://www.youtube.com/user/dinatokio.

55. Aisha Hasan, 'We need to talk about the sexualisation of Muslim women', *The Muslimah Diaries*, https://themuslimahdiaries.com/2017/07/27/we-need-to-talk-about-the-sexualisation-of-muslim-women/. For a scholarly discussion of these matters, see Emma Tarlo and Annelies Moors, *Islamic Fashion and Anti-Fashion: New Perspectives from Europe and North America* (London: Bloomsbury Academic, 2013).

56. Nasr Vali, *Meccanomics: the March of the New Muslim Middle Class* (Oxford: Oneworld, 2010).

57. 'The Muslim Pound: celebrating the Muslim contribution to the UK economy', *The Muslim Council of Britain at the 9th World Islamic Economic Forum 2013* (London: Muslim Council of Britain, 2013).

58. 'Modesty sells: British Muslims are a growing market', *The Economist*, 2 June 2016, https://www.economist.com/news/britain/21699971-british-muslims-are-growing-market-modesty-sells.

59. http://muslimlifestyleexpo.co.uk/.

60. Shelina Janmohamed, 'The Muslim consumer: building your brand for a fast-growing segment', *The Financial Times*, 5 January 2012, https://www.ft.com/content/55ff3a61-5ded-3ae5-9946-954125804e62.

61. Angela Saini, 'The New Cool: a review of *Generation M: Young Muslims Changing the World* by Shelina Janmohamed', *Feminist Dissent*, 2 (2017), pp. 209–13.

Conclusion

Moving forward

For over half a millennium, before the colonisation of much of the Muslim world from the Balkans to Bengal, Persian along with Arabic were the linguistic vehicles for an Islamic civilisation in which meaning was not confined to Islamic law, but sought through philosophy, Sufism and literature.[1] For a new global generation of Muslims, English is *the* language for communication and knowledge transmission – or, arguably, the new Persian. This study has illustrated such new thinking, creativity and activism whereby British Muslims are integrating insights drawn from the social sciences and humanities to generate new expressions of Islam and Muslim culture. Through English, they can access the best thinking and practice generated by Muslims in Britain, America and across the world, irrespective of ethnic background.

An illustrative case study of this creativity is the novel *Home Fire*, by the British Muslim author Kamila Shamsie, which has made the Man Booker longlist.[2] The novel features the intertwined lives of five characters from two, London-based, Muslim families caught between the convulsions of the wider Muslim world and growing anti-Muslim antagonism at home. The book opens with Isma, a young woman off to America to study for a PhD in sociology, being interrogated at Heathrow. We discover her late father was a jihadi and her younger brother, Parvaiz, had been radicalised in north London and had gone off to Raqqa to join the Islamic State.

We follow Isma to America where she falls in love with Eamonn, the son of an ambitious British Muslim politician about to be appointed Home Secretary, reviled for trading loyalty to Islam for high political office. Eamonn returns to Britain and ends up having an affair with Parvaiz's twin sister, Aneeka, a law student. The book explores the inter-generational tensions within families between love, loyalty and belonging, not least as impacted by religion and state. This story explores many of the themes touched upon in this work. We are dealing with educated British Muslims whose mastery of English opens them up to a range of experiences, positive and negative. One opts for a future in America, another in the Middle East. A third character, from a humble northern background, indicates how ability and ambition can open the way to high political office, albeit at some considerable cost. A fourth character – 'Googling While Muslim' – explores the many different components of her identity. A fifth character, although radicalised, cannot cast off his education and socialisation in Britain, and soon becomes disillusioned with the Islamic State.

Kamila Shamsie has rendered such characters and dilemmas accessible, intelligible and compelling. Moreover, by subtle allusions to Sophocles' *Antigone*, she indicates many of these dilemmas are as old as recorded history. Her exploration of how love relativises competing commitments lends it universal appeal. Written in English, it is likely to enjoy the attention of the ever burgeoning, educated, English-speaking public, Muslims and non-Muslim alike, not least in the proliferating mega cities across the world. This is the kind of novel that would be found in the Bradford Literature Festival. Founded by two Muslim women, Irna Qureshi and Syima Aslam, in 2014, its last event attracted over 30,000 people, who attend 200 events over ten days. Along with providing the usual feast of contemporary writing, the festival organisers had deliberately provided a space to debate contentious issues. 'We welcome controversy: it's a good thing,' says Qureshi. 'We're all so afraid of offending each other. But those things that are controversial are the ones that need to be addressed and talked about.'[3] After the first such festival, Yasmin Alibhai-Brown tweeted: 'Bradford: from Book Burning to Literary Festival'.

This is the constituency to which Alchemiya also appeals. Alchemiya has just been successful in launching its online subscription-based video streaming services on Amazon Prime channels. Its founder, Navid Akhtar, explains that they are committed to 'sharing the very best films, documentaries and lifestyle content from across the world, and from Muslims who live as minorities in the West'.[4]Alchemiya unapologetically aims to promote and celebrate the cultural impact of Islam on the world. Akhtar is a journalist, film and TV producer with over twenty years' experience in mainstream media. Alchemiya is targeting '"Gummies" – professionals, the highly educated, English-speaking, digitally connected who buy cars and go on holidays ... [who] also practice and care about the image of Islam'.[5] The word Alchemiya – the Arabic word from which we derive the term chemistry – is about transformation:

> We want people watching our programmes to be stimulated in their thinking. Whatever we deliver has to be as good as the British mainstream with no place for the preachy style of Muslim TV channels. This particular demographic is proud of Islamic Spain and Islamic diversity. They want to be entertained, invited to think and are allergic to sectarian and ideological voices. In particular, there is a need for good Islamic history absent from most Muslim media outlets.[6]

Throughout this book, we have discussed the concerns of the new professional classes, part of an international, educated English-speaking elite across the world, especially active in the emerging mega cities, from London to Abu Dhabi, New York to Islamabad, Sydney to Kuala Lumpur. However, as this book has made clear, there is also a growing constituency of the left-behind in deprived, concentrated ethno-Muslim, quarters of the inner cities. Attempts are also being made to address their needs. This was clear in an important seminar on 'Islamic Charity Giving in the UK', organised in the spring of 2017 in Bradford by the Professional Muslim Institute (PMI) – mentioned in the Introduction. The seminar had invited a panel to discuss the issue: a Bradford MP, Naz Shah; the Leeds-based imam, Qari Asim; and Nazir Afzal, now the Chief

Executive of the Association of Police and Crime Commission-ers, after his retirement as the northern prosecutor for the Crown Prosecution Service.

Some sixty Muslim professionals from Bradford and across the north attended. Given the unrivalled generosity of British Muslims to Islamic charities, the seminar discussed whether a percentage of such contributions should be set aside to address the escalating problems within the Muslim communities in the UK.[7] One such problem was a crisis in leadership amongst Muslim organisations – not least the charities sector – which did not reflect the concerns of young people and women. The seminar did not shy away from naming some of the most wor-rying issues: prevention and support for victims of domestic abuse, sexual abuse and drugs; the growing menace of criminal-ity within communities and Muslims disproportionately over represented in prison; as well as the need to address such intrac-table problems as educational underachievement.

Participants welcomed the visible help offered by Muslims during the recent floods in Britain, indicative of Muslim concern with the needs of wider society.[8] However, they worried that resourcing such groups from Islamic charities was at best ad hoc and what was required was a shift to becoming more proactive with resources earmarked for such domestic needs. Unsurpris-ingly, it was the networks of younger professionals setting the agenda who recognise the need to work with Islamic charities and Muslim scholars. Islamic law has defined and delimited cat-egories of need which entitle people to benefit from charity – *sadaqa* and *zakat*. The participants wanted scholars to revisit these categories to see how far they could be stretched to meet the many new needs identified. One of the organisers, Ishtiaq Ahmed, a member of the Bradford Council for Mosques (BCM), mentioned that the report and recommendations of the seminar would be discussed by BCM and was being sent to other councils across the north of England.

It was evident from the introduction to this study that the Muslim Women's Council had sought to enable a continuing dialogue across the many fractures within Muslim communities, whether gender, sectarian, *ulama* versus Muslim academics or inter-generational. This remains one of the greatest challenges. Here Muslims could usefully learn from the experience of the Jewish communities. A previous Chief Rabbi, Lord Sacks, wrote that before Jews were allowed to access the European mainstream more than two centuries earlier, all were held together by Jewish laws. As they increasingly engaged European society, this idea collapsed: 'Jewish existence has become adjectival'.[9] Writing more recently, a Jewish sociologist points out that such intra-Jewish disagreements are now exacerbated by deeply held differences over the State of Israel. He urges dialogue and civility across such differences, otherwise conflicts in Britain, US and elsewhere will continue to grow and undermine the integrity of Jewish communities.[10] Dialogue marked by civility seems an urgent continuing priority for British Muslims. Such will require a multiplication of spaces where sensitive issues can be discussed.

Challenges ahead

While all these trends and achievements are very hopeful, they function in very trying circumstances. British Muslims are moving forward in many ways, but have to deal with various challenges not faced by other minority faith groups. Transnational, diasporic links to Muslim-majority nations maintained by travel and telecommunications sustains a sense of connection to the causes affecting their family and fellow believers. In an age of globalisation, these linkages mean most British Muslims empathise with what takes place in faraway lands. A generation of young people have grown up in the age of the 'War on Terror' in which hostility and fear of Muslims and their faith have become embedded in the public imagination. The intractable issue of violent radicalisation along with other negative narratives have forced some elements within these communities to feel besieged and reinforce certain isolationist tendencies. Furthermore, the regular highlighting of negative news stories about Muslims has also helped to increase the popularity of far-right organisations' Islamophobia, which translates into discrimination and street-level violence.

These negative attitudes are underpinned by a number of anti-Muslim narratives that have gained widespread currency and are often implicitly adopted at a policy level. The researcher Arzu

Merali argues that the most prevalent perceptions of British Muslims are that they constitute an unprecedented security threat, are failing to integrate, and are prone to misogyny and criminal perversion.[11] In this study we have attempted to contextualise some of these narratives and highlight voices from within communities that are addressing difficult issues. Various surveys and studies have demonstrated that the vast majority of Muslims feel fully at home in Britain, make major contributions and are loyal even though they may not share in all of its cultural norms and practices.[12] While residential clustering continues at ward level in cities such as Bradford, Birmingham, Blackburn and Burnley, this is often the legacy of immigration patterns, housing policies, 'White flight' and the natural human desire to live among people like themselves. At the same time, Muslims are increasingly moving out of those clusters into more mixed areas. Let us also not forget that other groups across the UK enact forms of social segregation based on race and economic class. Furthermore, the idea of integration is a two-way street – or perhaps a spaghetti junction – which requires Muslims and other minority groups, together with the majority white British population, to find ways of engaging and living well together across ethnic, cultural and faith differences.

While there is cause for concern about the association of young Muslim men with certain types of criminal activity, this should be discussed in a balanced and constructive manner. This is not currently taking place and is not helped by sensationalist media coverage of Muslim communities which increases misunderstanding and fear. This has been demonstrated in detail by Julian Petley and Robin Richardson in their book *Pointing the Finger: Islam and Muslims in the British Media*, which shows how most reportage of British Muslims after 9/11 and 7/7 relies on the assumption that 'Islamic' and 'British' values are essentially incompatible.[13] This 'Othering' of Muslims perpetuates a cultural hostility that was vividly displayed by the reaction to a lecture given by the Archbishop of Canterbury on 'Civil and religious law in England: a religious perspective', in 2008. Most opinion pieces in the papers seized on his comments on the practice of sharia law and implied his approval of a form of parallel jurisdiction to the civil law, when in

fact all that he said was that Muslims should have access to a sup-
plementary jurisdiction on certain, carefully demarcated issues.[14]
The resulting furore is indicative of the extent of anti-Muslim
sentiment in sections of the media.

This media bias predates the rise of the terrorist attacks of
2001. A study conducted by Cardiff University after analysing
nearly 1,000 press stories between 2000 and 2008, found that
three frames – 'Terrorism or the War on terror', 'Religious and
Cultural issues' and 'Muslim Extremism' – accounted for nearly 70
per cent of stories published on the faith and its followers.[15] This
obsessive focus helps to normalise prejudice and is so prevalent
that, in 2017, the former political editor of *The Sun* newspaper,
Trevor Kavanagh, could write about 'The Muslim Problem' in
Britain and without realising the Nazi undertones of this phrase.[16]
A perverse irony to this perpetuation and condoning of bigotry is
that it indirectly discourages the full participation of Muslims in
public and civic life and vindicates extremist narratives that por-
tray the UK as inimical to Islam.

In addition to the issue of public representation, many British Muslims, as we have discussed earlier, struggle with the day
to day realities that accompany socio-economic disadvantage. A
recent government report has acknowledged that 'Muslims suffer the greatest economic disadvantages of any group in society
. . . [due to a mix of] discrimination and Islamophobia, stereotyp-
ing, pressure from traditional families, a lack of tailored advice
around higher education choices, and insufficient role models
across education and employment.'[17] Another study by the Social
Mobility Commission noted that Muslims are 'more likely than
non-Muslims to experience neighbourhood deprivation, housing, educational and health disadvantage, and unemployment.'[18]
These factors mostly impact women and young people with
many feeling that they have 'to work "ten times harder" than
their counterparts due to cultural differences and discrimination'
and deal with 'teachers who have either stereotypical or overly
low expectations of young Muslims' and worryingly that 'young
Muslims feel a real challenge in maintaining their identity while
seeking to succeed in Britain'.[19] The latest research also indicates
evidence of a 'Muslim penalty' in the area of employment which

disadvantages them by their religion and ethnicity. Professors
Tariq Modood and Nabil Khattab found that:

> If you are a Muslim in the United Kingdom, you are likely
> to face a penalty regardless of your colour or geography. If
> you are a Christian in the United Kingdom, you are not
> likely to face any penalties unless you are black. If you are
> white you will also be protected unless you are a Muslim or
> to a lesser extent atheist . . . The penalty will peak if you are
> a Muslim and black.[20]

Other studies have found many British Muslims have been turned
down for a job, or been denied promotion or training opportunities for ethno-religious reasons.[21] All of these factors present
challenges and will of course require major changes both in how
central and local governments address these issues as well as in
how Muslims deal with the difficult matters that are currently
inhibiting the realisation of their full potential. The Citizen's UK
The Missing Muslims report, cited earlier, has provided a detailed set
of recommendations that should be taken seriously by the government, media, business sector, civil society and Muslim communities. Applying this type of holistic approach has the potential to
achieve greater social equality for British Muslims and signal that
they are integral members of British society.[22]

   We have discussed some of the many efforts taking place within
British Muslim communities to tackle the difficult issues and
empower women and young people. However, there is a growing
consensus that much more needs to be done. As already pointed
out, more mosques need to make institutional space for women,
especially at leadership level. A second and third generation have
grown impatient with existing religious institutions that are perceived as dominated by patriarchal, older men and are responding
by creating innovative alternatives. Encouragingly, British born
imams, trained in British universities are slowly having an impact
on mosque governance structures. Leading institutions such as
the East London Mosque, in addition to being a place of worship,
offers dozens of services and works with non-Muslim agencies
to help local communities. However, these institutions are few

in number and greater efforts need to be made in developing accessible infrastructures that respond to community needs, support female religious scholarship and replace stagnant forms of conservatism with the contextualised approaches to Islam described earlier.

The scarcity of this kind of scholarship manifests at the local level with most mosques being ill equipped or indifferent to the need for relevant, accessible religious teaching for young people. Meanwhile, some turn to the internet and follow celebrity shaykhs and popular preachers or Islamic organisations to learn about their faith. In contrast, others have joined the increasing number of younger Muslims who are struggling to remain believers and eventually become atheists. This phenomenon has been skilfully analysed by Simon Cottee in his book *The Apostates: When Muslims Leave Islam*.[23] Based upon interviews with former Muslims from Britain and Canada, it provides an exploration of how Muslims become irreligious and examines the consequences for ex-Muslims. In addition to the questions of doubt, are the problems of evil, human suffering and Islamic conceptions of salvation; another reason why people leave the faith is because of the normative Islamic position on homosexuality. Some former Muslims have not been able to reconcile their sexual identity with their faith and felt that they had to choose the former over the latter. Others have remained within the faith and formed Muslim LGBQT support groups such as the London-based organisation Imaan.[24] These topics remain largely taboo within communities and will need to be addressed sensitively.

How we collectively respond to these challenges in the next decade will define how Islam is perceived and accommodated within British culture in the foreseeable future. The socio-economic disadvantage experienced by Muslims and ethnic minorities must be tackled by the state in addition to combating discrimination on the basis of race and religion. Islamophobia in the media needs to be held to account as does the increasing instance of anti-Muslim hate crime. British Muslims should be credited with the many societal contributions that they make across a wide range of professions in the public, private and charity sectors, and also supported in areas where they require assistance. While there is no doubt that there are many complex, immediate and long-term challenges that need to be addressed, by highlighting a few of the positive developments that are taking place within communities, we hope to draw attention to a more hopeful narrative of creative co-existence. These efforts may take another generation to come to fruition – but change is on its way.

Notes

1. This is the burden of the provocative and stunning work of scholarship by the late Shahab Ahmed, *What is Islam? The Importance of Being Islamic* (Princeton: Princeton University Press, 2016).
2. We have described Kamila Shamsie as Muslim since she appeared in a discussion at the Bradford Literary Festival entitled 'The things I would tell you: British Muslim women write' based on an anthology in which one of her short stories appears (1 July 2017). This leaves open whether the identifier 'Muslim' is primarily understood as religious or cultural.
3. Josh Glancy, 'Heathcliff, hijabs and chutzpah: the Bradford you've never seen', *Sunday Times*, 15 May 2016.
4. See their website, www.alchemiya.com.
5. See Shelina Janmohamed, *Generation M: Young Muslims Changing the World* (London: I. B. Tauris, 2016), p. 181.
6. From a conversation with Navid Akhtar, 5 October 2016.
7. The Muslim communities, for example, in 2015 raised £200 million for the five biggest Islamic charities. Muslims, of all communities, give the most per head to charity, £371, compared to the next most generous donors, Jews, who give £270, with the non-religious giving least at £116 – according to figures given at the presentation. We are grateful to Mr Ishtiaq Ahmed of the Bradford Council for Mosques for allowing us to see a copy of the report of the seminar he produced from which the information is drawn. The seminar took place on 18 May 2017.
8. For example, The Al-Imdaad Foundation were among the first to respond to the floods that affected people in Cumbria and delivered £10,000 in donations to victims. Muslims raised £38,000 to purchase new life-saving equipment for the Royal Preston Hospital; volunteers from Sunni Muslim Youth, 'Bite-Size Maddrasah' of Oldham, Greengate Trust and the Drive4Justice Team from Blackburn raised thousands of pounds and drove to help refugees in Calais. For

more examples, see '35 Great things British Muslims did in 2015', *Asian Image*, 30 December 2015, http://www.asianimage.co.uk/news/14173869.IN_PICTURES__35_great_things_British_Muslims_did_in_2015/.

9. See Jonathan Sacks, *One People? Tradition, Modernity, and Jewish Unity* (London: The Litman Library of Jewish Civilization, 1993). Sacks lists the fragmentation of the Jewish community: 'There are Orthodox, Reform, Conservative, Liberal, Reconstructionist and secular Jews. There are Israeli and diaspora Jews, Zionists and non-Zionists. Each label is further subdivided. Zionists are religious or secular. Religious Zionists are messianic or pragmatic. And so on' (p. 21).

10. See Keith Kahn-Harris, *Uncivil War: The Israel Conflict in the Jewish Community* (London: David Paul, 2104).

11. Arzu Merali, 'The wrong side of Britishness: anti-Muslim narratives in the UK', *University of Leeds Counter-Islamophobia Kit*, 21 September 2017, https://cik.leeds.ac.uk/2017/09/21/the-wrong-side-of-britishness-anti-muslim-narratives-in-the-uk/.

12. See for example, Alan Manning and Sanchari Roy, 'Culture Clash or Culture Club? The identity and attitudes of immigrants in Britain', CEP Discussion Paper no. 790, http://cep.lse.ac.uk/pubs/download/dp0790.pdf.

13. Julian Petley and Robin Richardson, *Pointing the Finger: Islam and Muslims in the British Media* (London: Oneworld Publications, 2011). Also, see Paul Baker, Costas Gabrielatos and Tony McEnery, *Discourse, Analysis and Media Attitudes: the Representation of Islam in the British Press* (Cambridge: Cambridge University Press, 2013).

14. Ibid. p. 208.

15. Kerry Moore, Paul Mason and Justin Lewis, *Images of Islam in the UK: The Representation of British Muslims in the National Print News Media 2000–2008* (Cardiff: Cardiff University School of Journalism, Media and Cultural Studies, 2008).

16. Richard Wilson, 'Tabloid hate is damaging our society. *The Sun*'s advertisers must help stop it', *The Guardian*, 15 August 2017, https://www.theguardian.com/commentisfree/2017/aug/15/tabloid-hate-sun-advertisers-trevor-kavanagh.

17. House of Commons, *Women and Equalities Committee Employment Opportunities for Muslims in the UK Second Report of Session 2016–17*, 12 July 2016.

18. Jacqueline Stevenson *et al.*, *The Social Mobility Challenges Faced by Young Muslims* (London: The Social Mobility Commission, 2017).

19. Ibid. pp. 2–4.

20. N. Khattab and T. Modood, 'Both ethnic and religious: explaining employment penalties across 14 ethno-religious groups in the United Kingdom', *Journal for the Scientific Study of Religion*, 54: 3 (2015), pp. 501–22; 520.

21. A. Heath and Y. Li, *Review of the relationship between religion and poverty – an analysis for the Joseph Rowntree Foundation*, CSI Working Paper 2015-01, available at http://csi.nuff.ox.ac.uk/wp-content/uploads/2015/03/religion-and-poverty-working-paper.pdf.

22. Citizens UK, *The Missing Muslims: Unlocking British Muslim Potential for the Benefit of All* (London: Citizens UK, 2017).

23. Simon Cottee, *The Apostates: When Muslims Leave Islam* (London: Hurst & Co., 2015).

24. See the organisation's website, https://imaanlondon.wordpress.com/about/.

An Annotated Bibliography

We have necessarily focused in this work on a number of key themes to make a particular argument. The study makes no claims to be a primer on Islam, past and present, or an adequate review of the ever expanding field of Islamic Studies. We identify here a few stimulating works which will add depth to some of the important debates to which we have alluded.

Afsaruddin, Asma, *Contemporary Issues in Islam* (Edinburgh: Edinburgh University Press, 2015). This is an exemplary treatment of hot-button issues – politics, war and peace, gender and inter-religious relations – rooted in her own research and framed by an excellent methodological chapter entitled 'Engaging the Sharia: rereading the Qur'an and hadith'.

Ahmed, Shahab, *What is Islam? The Importance of Being Islamic* (Princeton: Princeton University Press, 2016). A long work, not for the faint hearted! The most stimulating and provocative work on Islam to have appeared in the last couple of decades. The author retrieves a fascinating world, from the Balkans to Bengal, which existed for half a millennium before the impact of the West in the mid-nineteenth century. A world in which the elites, to make sense of their experience Islamically, were more likely to turn to poetry, Sufism and philosophy than Islamic law. The medium of this rich culture was Persian.

Ali, Kecia, *Sexual Ethics and Islam: Feminist Reflections on Qur'an, Hadith, and Jurisprudence*, 2nd edn (Oxford: Oneworld, 2016). A landmark work which does not shrink from tackling the most difficult issues for Muslim feminists wishing to re-engage the Islamic tradition. Its second edition provides an overview of how key debates have moved on in the intervening ten years. It is clear that female Muslim academics such as Ali are part of a vibrant new field of study now attracting a third generation of scholars.

Brooke, J., and R. Numbers (eds), *Science and Religion around the World* (Oxford: Oxford University Press, 2011). In the context of providing material across the world's religions, two chapters by leading Muslim scholars – Ahmad Dallal and Ekmeleddin Ihsanoglu – on early Islam and modern Islam provide a good way in to these important debates. It also includes excellent bibliographies.

Chambers, Claire, *Britain Through Muslim Eyes: Literary Representations, 1780–1988* (Basingstoke: Palgrave Macmillan, 2015). A delightful and well-written study drawing on memoirs, travel writing and short stories to illustrate Muslim travel accounts of Britain. Orientalism in reverse!

Cook, Michael, *Ancient Religions, Modern Politics: The Islamic Case in Comparative Perspective* (Princeton: Princeton University Press, 2014). If the late Shahab Ahmed lamented a fatal thinning of Islamic culture in the modern world to a narrow preoccupation with Islamic law, Cook explains the inner dynamics of this return to the past and why contemporary Muslims seem preoccupied with politics. This is worked out in comparison with Catholicism in Latin America and Hinduism in India to draw out the specificities of the Islamic experience.

Dressing, N., N. Jeldtoft, J. Nielsen and L. Woodhead (eds), *Everyday Lived Islam in Europe* (Farnham: Ashgate, 2013). A fine collection of essays foregrounding a theme which will become increasingly important as Islam is normalised within a European context. One especially stimulating essay has the intriguing title, 'Elastic Orthodoxy: the tactic of young Muslim identity in the East End of London'.

Haleem, M. A., *Exploring the Qur'an: Context and Impact* (London: I. B. Tauris, 2017). Professor Haleem, a specialist in Quranic studies who lectures at the School of African and Orientalist Studies, London University, sheds light on a range of controversial issues in Quranic interpretation. He is not afraid to contest interpretations which are embedded in the revered commentary and legal traditions, as well as disagreeing with non-Muslim scholars.

Hamid, S, *Young British Muslims: Between Rhetoric and Realities* (London: Routledge, 2017). A refreshing series of windows into the complex, lived reality of young Muslims today exploring a diverse set of topics ranging from Islamic fashion and online activism to music.

Hefner, Robert (ed.), *Shari'a, Law and Modern Muslim Ethics* (Bloomington: Indiana University Press, 2016). A sparkling series of essays covering Mali to Morocco, Egypt, Pakistan and Turkey examining the varied meanings and uses of Islamic law and the prospects for democratic, plural and gender-equitable Islamic ethics.

Khalidi, Tarif, *Images of Muhammad: Narratives of the Prophet Across the Centuries* (New York: Doubleday, 2009). A classic by one of the finest historians of Islam. In ten chapters he unpacks how the Prophet of Islam has been variously understood in Islam's many religious disciplines and traditions – Sunni, Shi'ite and Sufi – past and present. His chapters on modern biographies of the Prophet in the Arab world are especially illuminating.

Maher, Shiraz, *Salafi-Jihadism: The History of an Idea* (London: Penguin, 2017). This is a useful introduction to the violent strand of contemporary Salafi thinking, which gives a detailed account of how it differs from quietist strands of Salafism and provides context to violent extremist discourses.

Mahfouz, Sabrina, *The Things I Would Tell You: British Muslim Women Write* (London: Saqi Books, 2017). An excellent anthology of short stories and poetry capturing the creativity and variety of such writers who self-describe as British and Muslim, where the latter ranges from practising to those for whom Islam is an indispensable part of their culture.

Martin, Richard C., and Barzegar Abbas (eds), *Islamism: Contested Perspectives on Political Islam* (Stanford: Stanford University Press, 2009). This is one of the best volumes to interpret the highly charged concept of Islamism and offers diverse perspectives on the phenomena of politicised Islam.

Meijer, Roel (ed.), *Global Salafism: Islam's New Religious Movement* (London: Hurst & Co., 2009). This volume is the best introduction to the different varieties of this globally influential religious current. It has a range of country studies and explorations of how Salafi religious beliefs and practices are received in different contexts.

Moosa, Ebrahim, *What is a Madrasa?* (Edinburgh: Edinburgh University Press, 2015). An indispensable and readable insight into the world of South Asian traditional madrasa – scholars, texts, teaching methods and ethos – written by one of America's leading Islamic scholars. He revisits the madrasas he studied at more than thirty years earlier in India to critically evaluate their syllabi and the potential for change.

Nasr, Vali, *Meccanomics: the March of the New Muslim Middle Class* (Oxford: Oneworld, 2010). Nasr is a professor of International Relations who has advised President Obama on policy in Iran, Afghanistan and Pakistan. This hopeful work maps the emergence across the Muslim world of an upwardly mobile middle class of entrepreneurs, investors, professionals and consumers. Nasr is cautiously optimistic that, in the long term, their blend of Islam and capitalism will generate reform and defeat extremism.

Panjwani, F., L. Revel, R. Gholami and M. Diboll (eds), *Education and Extremisms: Rethinking Liberal Pedagogies in the Contemporary World* (Abingdon: Routledge, 2017). Important essays for educators of teachers, police and policymakers charged with addressing the increased incidence of extremism, political and religious. One of the key themes of the book is the importance of good history to undercut the appeal of ideological religion. The book is worth buying for one essay alone: 'Misplaced Utopia: education and extremism – the case of Pakistan'. This splendid essay could provide a cautionary tale for Britain.

Siddiqui, Mona, *My Way: A Muslim Woman's Journey* (London: I. B. Tauris, 2015). An engaging and beautifully crafted memoir by one of Britain's few Muslim public intellectuals, a professor of Islam and Interreligious Studies at Edinburgh University.

For some of the best contemporary writing on Islam and Muslim communities, the quarterly magazine, *Critical Muslim* – a sort of Islamic *Granta* – is excellent. Each issue is devoted to a particular theme.

Websites

These online platforms offer an entry point into some of the different expressions of Islam in Britain mentioned in this study.

For conservative Deobandi traditionalists, www.inter-islam.org; for those from a Deobandi background whom we would describe as critical traditionalists, see www.hamidmahmood.co.uk.

For the Barelwi tradition, The British Muslim Forum (BMF) provides a representative window into the political concerns and priorities of one of the two largest South Asian religious currents among Muslims, see http://www.britishmuslimforum.co.uk/.

The Muslim Council of Britain (MCB) is one of the largest umbrella bodies to represent British Muslim concerns and has many useful resources on its site, see http://www.mcb.org.uk/

The writer and academic Yahya Birt is a leading commentator on British Muslims and his two websites are a well-stocked source of

scholarly analysis and insightful journalistic commentary, https://
medium.com/@yahyabirt and https://yahyabirt1.wordpress.com/.

For liberal reformist Muslims, *New Horizons in British Islam* is an
important network which hosts an array of seminars and conferences which can be reviewed on their website www.pacata.org.

For a considered, Sufi 'Traditional Islam' inflected commentary,
see the online news source for British Muslims, www.muslimview.
co.uk.

For an innovative history resource identifying the links between
Britain and the Muslim world over 1400 years, www.muslimmu-
seum.org.uk, and for a celebration of Muslim heritage in the UK,
see www.everydaymuslim.org, an excellent archive and oral history committed to providing resources for schools, etc.

www.Muslim-science.com – informative about contemporary
developments and debates.

An excellent site which includes informative articles and debate
on Islam and Muslim issues in Britain, www.opendemocracy.net.

For those interested in inter-faith and inter-community relations:

The Christian Muslim Forum is a pioneering initiative begun in
2006. It has developed some excellent guidelines on a range of
sensitive topics including inter-faith marriages and runs a variety
of activities, www.christianmuslimforum.org.

For a Jewish-Muslim women's network, Nisa-Nashim, see www.
nisanashim.org, which has more than twenty groups across the
country.

For Near Neighbours, which encourage and support localised
relations and shared activities across two or more religious/ethnic
communities, see www.cuf.org.uk/near-neighbours.

The Ramadan Tent Project was begun by SOAS students in 2013 to enable social change by creating bridges between individuals and communities and fostering interfaith dialogue. Through its flagship project Open Iftar, it invites the homeless and the public at large, Muslim and non-Muslim, to break the fast together during the month of Ramadan each year – initially in London and now also in Manchester; see www.ramadantentproject.com.

Index